Soldiers' Lives through History
The Nineteenth Century

Soldiers' Lives through History
Dennis Showalter, Series Editor

The Ancient World
Richard A. Gabriel

The Middle Ages
Clifford J. Rogers

The Early Modern World
Dennis Showalter and William J. Astore

The Nineteenth Century
Michael S. Neiberg

The Twentieth Century
Robert T. Foley and Helen McCartney

Soldiers' Lives through History

THE NINETEENTH CENTURY

✯ ✯ ✯

Michael S. Neiberg

Soldiers' Lives through History
Dennis Showalter, Series Editor

GREENWOOD PRESS
Westport, Connecticut • London

Library of Congress Cataloging-in-Publication Data

Neiberg, Michael S.
  The nineteenth century / Michael S. Neiberg ; Dennis Showalter, Series Editor.
      p. cm. — (Soldiers' lives through history)
  Includes bibliographical references and index.
  ISBN 0–313–33269–X (alk. paper)
  1. Soldiers—History—19th century. 2. Sociology, Military—Europe—History—19th century. 3. Military art and science—Europe—History—19th century. 4. Soldiers—History—20th century. 5. Sociology, Military—Europe—History—20th century. 6. Military art and science—Europe—History—20th century. I. Title.
  U41.N45   2006
  355.0094'09034—dc22   2006029487

British Library Cataloguing in Publication Data is available.

Copyright © 2006 by Michael S. Neiberg

All rights reserved. No portion of this book may be reproduced, by any process or technique, without the express written consent of the publisher.

Library of Congress Catalog Card Number: 2006029487
ISBN: 0–313–33269–X

First published in 2006

Greenwood Press, 88 Post Road West, Westport, CT 06881
An imprint of Greenwood Publishing Group, Inc.
www.greenwood.com

Printed in the United States of America

The paper used in this book complies with the Permanent Paper Standard issued by the National Information Standards Organization (Z39.48–1984).

10 9 8 7 6 5 4 3 2 1

SERIES FOREWORD

The song "Universal Soldier" has been a staple of peace rallies since the 1960s. Written by Buffy Sainte-Marie and performed by Donovan Leitch in 1965, when it became popular, the song indicts the soldier as war's agent, unlike most other songs of its type, which cast the soldier as war's victim: "He knows he shouldn't kill / And he knows he always will...."

The killing, of course, goes on apace. Sometimes it will be by neighbors once thought of as friends, as in Rwanda during the 1990s. Sometimes it will be by bureaucratic utopians who see the path to the future obstructed by Jews in Hitler's Germany—or by class enemies in Stalin's Russia—or by people who wear glasses in Pol Pot's Cambodia. Sometimes it will be by zealots who expect to gain paradise by dying while killing others, like the Crusaders of the Middle Ages, or today's Jihadis.

Historians are currently engaged in a debate on the existence of a "Western way of war," which distinguishes the West from the rest of the world, and arguably defines Western civilization as well. Underlying that debate, and structuring it, is the question of whether there is a distinctively Western soldier. Victor Davis Hanson writes eloquently of free men voluntarily committing themselves to conquer or die in order that they might return to the homes they saved. Critics such as John A. Lynn in *Battle: A History of Combat and Culture* assert the cultural specificity of approaches to war in both Western and global contexts. The ancient Greeks, for example, sought quick decisions because of particular values emphasizing individual worth and independence. Nineteenth-century Europe's concept of the decisive battle was influenced heavily by a Romantic high culture as opposed to specific military factors, such as rapid-firing weapons and mass armies.

This series, Soldiers' Lives through History, is the first to address comprehensively the cutting-edge experiences of the Western soldier from his initial appearance at the beginning of history to his latest avatars in Vietnam and the Middle East. Richard Gabriel's volume on the soldiers of the ancient world notes that the first archaeological evidence of organized war is in present-day Iraq. Thousands of years later the wheel has turned a full circle. The authors of each volume, Richard A. Gabriel; Clifford J. Rogers; Dennis Showalter and William J. Astore; Michael S. Neiberg; and Robert T. Foley and Helen McCartney, address not only "the face of battle," but also its frameworks. The soldiers' civil origins, their emotional and intellectual makeup, their daily lives in peace and war, and above all their reactions to facing death and dealing it–these are the kinds of themes developed in all five volumes of the series. The authors' intentions are to facilitate understanding of one of history's fundamental questions: Why do humans fight wars? That question's continuing relevance is made plain everywhere, in television and in newspapers, on the Internet, in video games, and not least in the cemeteries where bugles still sound over those who gave all in war and to war. Did they do so as heroes, fools, perpetrators—or perhaps a little of all three, structured by individual factors defying collective analysis?

In this series, Greenwood Press takes a major step in providing substance to the issue of the soldier's identity and the soldier's place in Western civilization. One point that Hanson and his critics share is an agreement that war making in the West has evolved away from any class or caste restrictions on participation. War has been every man's business—and, increasingly, the business of women as well. Most men and women who will read these books have known someone who was a solider, have soldiers in their family trees, and have the potential to be soldiers themselves. In that sense, this series is about all of us: the heirs and successors of the Universal Soldier.

Dennis Showalter

ACKNOWLEDGMENTS

Acknowledgments are an opportunity to thank the people who helped an author put a work together. I have been fortunate in having a network of friends and colleagues upon whom I can call for such help. I would like to thank the series editor Dennis Showalter for offering me the opportunity to write this book. William J. Astore, who will have his own volume in this series, graciously read the manuscript and, as always, offered numerous helpful comments. Several Air Force Academy colleagues deserve mention. My department chair, Colonel Mark Wells, was an invaluable resource on Napoleonic warfare. Major Michael R. Terry (ret) helped me to shape the airpower portions of this book. Major David "Q" Schlortt and Captain Jonathan Klug, USA, shared their knowledge of small arms with me. Lt. Colonel John Abbatiello and Major Derek Varble served as important sounding boards for ideas. Professor Jeanne Heidler patiently answered my questions on aspects of the American Civil War and let me raid her library whenever I needed to do so.

Several colleagues from other institutions helped as well. Donald Mrozek, who came to USAFA as a visiting professor from Kansas State University, helped me to shape the concepts of the conclusion. The University of Calgary's Holger Herwig and the University of Exeter's Jeremy Black took time from their own busy research and teaching schedules to help me clear up finer points. I also wish to thank Heather Staines at Praeger for her support of this project. All translations are my own, except for the assistance I received from Richard Lemp on "Quand Madelon," and, of course, I take full responsibility for any errors that remain.

Thanks are also due to my wife Barbara, and my daughters Claire and Maya, for forgiving me for taking the time I needed to write this book. My in-laws, the Lockley family, have provided a wonderful support system for which I am eternally grateful. I am long overdue in dedicating a book to my parents, Larry and Phyllis Neiberg, and my sister, Elyssa Neiberg. They have been unwavering in their support of all I have tried to do. I hope they will pardon the tardiness of this dedication and accept it with my love and thanks.

✳ ✳ ✳

INTRODUCTION:
FROM CLASS TO WORLD

Frederic Manning's highly autobiographical work, *Her Privates We*, tells the story of a tightly knit battalion of British infantrymen during the Battle of the Somme in 1916. One of the finest books about the soldier of the modern age, *Her Privates We* vividly and realistically explores military service as the men at the front lived through it. The nature of a mass citizen army is arguably the book's most important recurring theme. Manning clearly understood that the military of the First World War bore scant resemblance to the militaries of years past. The old notions of honor that had sustained those armies, Manning wrote, "may have been very well so long as it had been possible to consider the army a class or a profession, but the war had made it a world."[1] Manning meant that the massive expansion of the British army from 1914 to 1918 (and the expansion during the same time period of other European armies as well) had destroyed much of the isolated and insulated character of prewar armies. Once the nearly exclusive preserve of men at the very top (the officer corps) and near-bottom (the "other ranks") rungs of society, military service during the course of the war became the responsibility of all British males. By the end of the First World War, the army had become an institution that represented a much wider portion of European society than had ever been the case before. For reasons that this book will explore, Britain's development of a representative citizen's army occurred well after that of most European nations, making it all the more painful for Britons.

The goal of this book is to trace European soldiering from the "class" phase Manning mentioned to the "world" it had become by 1918. The Jacobin governments of the period of the French Revolution brought to Europe the widespread concept of military service as the responsibility of all citizens. This belief depended upon the concept of individual connections with their larger society, a situation that the unrepresentative states of the pre-1789 period had no interest in fostering. The democratic and republican governments created and inspired by the French Revolution, however, ideally linked self-governing citizens (as opposed to obedient subjects) to their states in ways that formed linkages and identities unlike those that had come before. Military service therefore became a citizen's obligation and, to many men, an honor.

This system developed inconsistently throughout the nineteenth century. The authoritarian governments of the period of the Restoration (1815–1848) often had a difficult time enticing men to serve in the military, specifically because men failed to see any connections between their own lives and the aims of the state's ruling elite. Much of the motivation for the massive emigration from Europe in the same period stemmed from the desires of men to avoid compulsory military service in states they despised. The affirmative and enduring popular responses to calls for military service in 1914 and afterward, however, show a general pattern throughout this period of men becoming increasingly willing to risk their lives for the goals of their state. The development of nationalism and the growing presence of the state in the lives of individuals played a critical role in effecting this change of mentality.

SCOPE

Soldiers' Lives through History: The Nineteenth Century will examine how the military fit into the patterns of the development of nationalism and how soldiers experienced them firsthand. This book illuminates the experience of military service from the perspective of common soldiers like the ones Frederic Manning so vividly brought to life. It is not a history of warfare or campaigns in the nineteenth century nor does it cover in detail the lives and careers of the great captains of nineteenth-century warfare. Instead, the soldiers' experiences are front and center. Warfare forms an important part of this analysis, but discussions of the peacetime lives of soldiers receive significant treatment as well.

The focus here is predominantly on European soldiers and, somewhat less systematically, their Western counterparts in the United States, Canada, Australia, and New Zealand. Although these men sometimes did their best to kill one another, they nevertheless came from a culture with many shared traditions, belief systems, and notions of military organization. They therefore usually fought wars that were symmetrical; that is, their doctrine, weapons, and basic force structures were similar. I have limited my definition of "soldier" to that used in the period under study here: a uniformed practitioner of officially sanctioned, state-sponsored violence answerable to a state's code of discipline. In many cases, this definition blurred with guerrillas, police forces, and paramilitary organizations, all of which occasionally showed some of the same characteristics. Nevertheless, the professionals of European militaries drew sharp distinctions between themselves and the groups just mentioned.

ARRANGEMENT

The book is divided into two sections, with roughly parallel organizations. The break point is the Franco-Prussian War of 1870–1871. This organization allowed me to treat the two periods somewhat separately, although the reader will be able to find important points of continuity between the sections. While dividing the book as I did created a few areas of modest repetition, I believe that the two periods are sufficiently different to merit the separation. The first half of the book (chapters one through four) thus covers the period from the French Revolution of 1789 to the Franco-Prussian War, which I have called "the age of men." As the first four chapters will show, the wars of the French Revolution represent a major watershed in military history. The most important change involved the types of men who became soldiers and their motivations for doing so. Although there were some changes in weaponry (most notably the widespread adaptation of the rifle), new technology did not shape soldiers' lives in this period as deeply as did the development of the professional, national soldier.

The second half of the book (chapters five through eight) covers the period from the Franco-Prussian War to the end of First World War. This period, notable for the development of industrial methods for the manufacture of weapons, I have called "the age of machines." I do not, of course, mean to imply that developments in military technology made human beings irrelevant to warfare. Still, in this period the increase in the killing power of weaponry was so vast and so little planned for that it had tremendous impact on the daily lives of soldiers, and not just on the battlefield. In this era, the infantry weapon that killed the most soldiers went from being the rifle, which fired roughly six shots per minute in the hands of a trained soldier, to the machine gun, which could fire 600 rounds per minute. Developments in artillery, armor, aviation, gas, and mining all complete a picture of an age of warfare dominated by machines.

Each section's chapters follow a chronology roughly based on how a typical soldier might have experienced his time in the military. Each of the book's two sections begins with the process of recruitment, discussing why men volunteered for military service, how they entered military service, and, in many cases, how they avoided it. Next, the book examines the complex process of training men for military service. Military training programs aimed to remove as much of a man's civilian identity as possible and replace it with a new identity based on group loyalty and dedication to larger goals. The book next discusses the material conditions of life for soldiers, including their food, their uniforms, and their weapons. I have not attempted to present here a complete catalog of uniforms and weapons. Rather, I am interested in weaponry and uniforms to the extent that they reveal larger patterns of life in the armies of the nineteenth century. Finally, *Soldiers' Lives through History: The Nineteenth Century* describes battle as the soldiers of the period experienced it.

Other information in this book includes a timeline, following this introduction, which helps put some of the significant events and dates of this period in further perspective. A bibliography of recommended resources and a general index conclude the work.

THE HISTORY OF NINETEENTH-CENTURY SOLDIERS

The volumes in this series are not the first books to look at the lives of soldiers, nor is this book the first to do so for this period of history, but they offer fresh insights and information. In the 1970s, a new generation of military history made terrific strides in changing the study of warfare from an overemphasis as great commanders toward the men that they led. John Keegan's *The Face of Battle*, John Ellis's *Eye Deep in Hell*, and Dennis Winter's *Death's Men*, among many others, were major steps forward in creating this new means of understanding war.[2] Today few military historians would seriously contemplate researching their subject without undertaking a detailed study of the morale, background, motivations, and experiences of everyday soldiers.

By focusing on soldiers' daily lives, I do not intend to argue here that war can be studied without a careful analysis of commanders. Indeed, elsewhere I have written about senior military leadership and its importance in developing strategy, operations, and tactics.[3] It is critical for historians not to allow a focus on soldiers (appropriate though it surely is) to turn their eyes away from command. In this study, then, I am not suggesting that a study of soldiers can or should replace the study of high command. Rather, I am arguing that the two are synergistic; a complete picture of either is impossible without the other. The history of warfare depends on seeing the total picture both from top to bottom and from bottom to top.

When I first began studying military history, I presumed that the shift from a top-down approach to a bottom-up approach in the 1970s was largely a generational one. Older, more traditional military historians, I thought, were interested in command, technology, and grand strategy. A younger generation, influenced by the explosion of academic interest in new areas of inquiry that characterized academe in the 1960s, turned their eye to new subjects and gave us a new way to see warfare.

I do not doubt that part of that story is correct. But as I began to write this book, it became increasingly obvious to me that the major hindrance to a study of soldiers' lives is the general lack of sources. Even during the time period under study here many soldiers, especially in eastern Europe, were either completely or functionally illiterate. They therefore left few records about their experiences. Many of our sources about their lives either come from a small and unrepresentative group of literate soldiers, their equally unrepresentative (almost by definition) officers, or journalists. Painting an accurate and complete picture is therefore a difficult endeavor. For these reasons, the wars of eastern Europe will appear to be underrepresented, a slight I regret, but could do little to correct. In any case, it has not been my intention to cover all nations and all wars equally, but to draw on the experiences of all in order to paint a representative general picture.

Even when men did leave written records, these sources have not always survived. Great Britain's Imperial War Museum, created during the First World War to preserve such records, is unique. We will never know how many men's letters, diaries, and memoirs are still in attics or basements or how many have been destroyed or thrown away over the years. Most military and civilian governmental archives touch on soldiers' daily lives only sporadically and indirectly. The lack of a direct and sustained interest in soldiers' daily lives manifested in official paperwork is an indication in itself of the secondary role that the needs of daily life played in the minds of officers and governmental officials.

Writing about war has always been difficult for soldiers and veterans. Paul Fussell and others have argued that war is so different from everyday experience that language is often inadequate to express what men saw and felt.[4] In many cases, veterans intentionally held back in their written recollections in order to spare the feelings of their loved ones or to shield them from the horrors they had both witnessed and participated in. French scholars Stéphane Audoin-Rouzeau and Annette Becker remind us that soldiers are often more willing to talk about their victimization than they are about their own role as killers.[5] Death is often discussed as having been dispensed anonymously or from such a physical distance that soldiers can create a psychological distance from the act of killing.

Many of my conclusions are therefore based on evidence from the sources that have survived. These include the memoirs and diaries of soldiers who took the time to record their experiences during the war. They also include books and unpublished memoirs written by soldiers long after their experiences were over. Both of these types of sources present their own challenges. I have therefore also relied on the secondary work by historians who have turned their eyes toward the problem of understanding soldiers and their lives during this time period.

Observant readers will already have noticed that I have played a bit fast and loose with the term "nineteenth century." Historians have commonly used the term "long nineteenth century" to describe the period from 1789 to 1914. The obvious implication is that the period from the start of the French Revolution to the outbreak of the First World War constitutes one reasonably continuous period in European history. Nationalism, developing industrial economies, and the emergence of a more closely interwoven continent lend credence to such a periodization.

I have taken a further, and likely more controversial, liberty in extending the "nineteenth century" to 1918. In doing so I am not trying to argue that the Europe of 1918 resembled the Europe of 1789 more than, say, the Europe of 1939. Indeed, the inclusion of the First World War changes the periodization considerably from that traditionally advanced. Nevertheless, it seemed to me impossible to bring the story up to 1914 and then stop just before the most important military experience of European history up to that point. I am grateful to the series editor, Professor Dennis Showalter, for tolerating my argument and allowing me to include the First World War in my analysis.

Despite the book's explicit argument for the importance of the First World War in "nineteenth-century" warfare, I have tried as much as possible to avoid teleology. That is, I have written the first section of this book, covering the French Revolution to roughly 1870, without the presumption of the outbreak of the First World War. One of the difficulties in writing history is, of course, the retrospective knowledge that we have of events. Nevertheless, it is important to understand history as it occurred to the people who lived and made it. Thus, I have tried to understand the period of the French Revolution and the Napoleonic Wars for what they were, not as mere preludes to the events of 1914–1918.

The same task becomes more difficult in the second half of the book, covering 1870 to 1918. Some scholars have simplistically understood the First World War as a mere dress rehearsal for the Second World War thus the facile classroom quip that the Second World War was merely the First World War fought on wheels. But the men of 1914–1918 did not yet know that their war would soon be overshadowed by another. Indeed, most soldiers of that war fought with the deep and sincere hope that theirs might be the last large war of the modern age. That they and their sons would have to experience an equal horror scarcely one generation later did not become apparent until the late 1930s. Therefore, it seems to me that to understand the First World War one must forget as much as possible the Second, even if doing so amounts to ignoring the 1,000–pound elephant sitting in the corner. I therefore leave a discussion of soldiers' lives after 1918 in the eminently capable hands of Professors Robert Foley and Helen McCartney, whose own volume in this series will cover these years.

Because this book does not analyze the battles and wars of this period for their own merit, readers may want more background. I recommend the books that I have cited in the notes to the individual chapters as well as the bibliography that follows chapter eight. In particular, I especially recommend the following readable and solidly argued historical surveys on the subject of warfare from 1789 to 1918: Dennis Showalter, *The Wars of German Unification* (London: Edward Arnold, 2004); Geoffrey Wawro, *Warfare and Society in Europe, 1792–1914* (London: Routledge, 2000); Jeremy Black, *Western Warfare, 1775–1882* (Bloomington: Indiana University Press, 2001); Black, *Warfare in the Western World, 1882–1975* (Bloomington: Indiana University Press, 2002); Hew Strachan, *European Armies and the Conduct of War* (London: Routledge, 1983; 1993); and Strachan, *The First World War* (London: Viking, 2004). More specialized treatments of certain topics can be found in the essays in Manfred Boemke, Roger Chickering, and Stig Förster, eds. *Anticipating Total War: The German and American Experiences* (Cambridge: Cambridge University Press, 1999) and Chickering and Förster, eds. *Great War, Total War: Combat and Mobilization on the Western Front, 1914–1918* (Cambridge: Cambridge University Press, 2000).

NOTES

1. Frederic Manning, *Her Privates We* (London: Hogarth Press, 1986), p. 25. The book was originally published in 1929 under the title *The Middle Parts of Fortune*.

2. John Keegan, *The Face of Battle* (New York: Viking, 1976); John Ellis, *Eye Deep in Hell: Trench Warfare in World War I* (Baltimore: Johns Hopkins University Press, 1976); and Dennis Winter, *Death's Men: Soldiers of the Great War* (London: Allen Lane, 1978).

3. See my *Foch: Supreme Allied Commander in the Great War* (Dulles, VA: Brassey's Press, 2003) and *Fighting the Great War: A Global History* (Cambridge: Harvard University Press, 2005).

4. Paul Fussell, *The Great War and Modern Memory* (Oxford: Oxford University Press, 1975) and Fussell, *Wartime: Understanding and Behavior in the Second World War* (Oxford: Oxford University Press, 1989).

5. Stéphane Audoin-Rouzeau and Annette Becker, *14–18: Retrouver La Guerre* (Paris: Gallimard, 2000).

TIMELINE

1789	Start of the French Revolution removed many nobles from key appointments in the French army
1792–1798	War of the First Coalition between France and an alliance led by Austria, Prussia, and Great Britain
1792	Battle of Valmy marked the victory of French Revolutionary forces over Austrian and Prussian professionals
August 1793	Issuance of the *levée en Masse* by the French government. The document underscored the responsibility of all French citizens to assist in the war effort, regardless of age or gender
1794	French Service de Santé formed to oversee the health of French soldiers and veterans
1798–1800	War of the Second Coalition between France and an alliance led by Britain, Austria, and Russia
1798	Passage of the Jourdan Law represented the first large-scale attempt to introduce conscription to Europe
1800–1815	Napoleonic Wars between France and a series of coalitions involving most of the powers of Europe
1810	Process of canning meat invented, allowing soldiers to bring preserved food with them on campaign

1812–1815	War of 1812 between the United States and Great Britain
1813	Issuance of Frederick William's call to the Prussian People
1818	U.S. Army Medical Service formed
1848	Outbreak of Revolutions across Europe
1850s	General adaptation of the rifle vastly increased the range of infantry weapons and thus the killing power of the average infantryman
1854–1856	Crimean War witnessed the first large-scale use of many new technologies, including the telegraph and the rifle. The appalling health conditions of the war inspired widespread efforts to improve military medicine
1861–1865	American Civil War between the North and the South showed the devastating power of the rifle
1861	Abolition of Russian serfdom as a means of modernizing Russia in the aftermath of the humiliating loss of the Crimean War
1863	Red Cross formed in part to improve the medical conditions inside armies
1866	Austro-Prussian War between Austria and Prussia
1868	Cardwell reforms in England improved the conditions of British soldiers
1871	Purchase of commissions ended in England
	Franco-Prussian War led to the unification of Germany, as well as major improvements in military medicine
1884	Invention of the Maxim machine gun
1890s	Dreyfus scandal in France drastically reduced the image of the French army
1893–1897	Invention of hydrostatic recoilless artillery
1898	Spanish-American War between Spain and the United States led to American possession of Cuba, Puerto Rico, and the Philippines
1899–1902	Boer War against Dutch settlers in South Africa forced the British to recruit 500,000 men
1904–1905	Russo-Japanese War led to revolution in Russia
1907	Creation of the British Expeditionary Force
1908	Formation of the Boy Scouts in England
1913	Extension of mandatory military service to three years in France
1914–1918	First World War between the alliance led by France, Britain, Russia, Italy, and the Untied States and the alliance led by Germany, the Austro-Hungarian Empire, and the Ottoman Empire

1915	First large-scale use of poison gas at the Second Battle of Ypres
January 1916	British Military Service Act introduced conscription to Great Britain
September 1916	Introduction of tanks
1917	Bolshevik Revolution in Russia and the start of the Russian Civil War

PART I

✷ ✷ ✷

*The Age of Men: From the
French Revolution to German Unification*

One

✦ ✦ ✦

RECRUITMENT, EVASION, AND DESERTION

The citizen must have two suits of clothes, one for his trade and one as a soldier.
—*Diderot.*[1]

VALMY AND THE "NEW ERA IN THE HISTORY OF THE WORLD"

On September 20, 1792, the celebrated German poet Johann Wolfgang Goethe was near the eastern French town of Valmy to chronicle the expected victory of an army of 79,000 men led by one of Europe's most highly regarded commanders, Prussia's Duke of Brunswick. That army, part of what soon became known as the First Coalition, included Prussians, Austrians, and aristocratic French émigrés chased from their native land by the Revolution of 1789. The duke seemed to be an excellent choice to lead an army of reaction against what conservatives across Europe saw as a band of brigands and outlaws. He had served with distinction in the Prussian army during the Seven Years' War (1756–1763) and afterward had married a sister of England's King George III. He also had the complete trust of his own king, Prussia's Frederick William II, ruler of the most intensely militarized state in Europe. The continent's ruling classes placed their faith in the duke and counted on him to defeat a revolutionary army of just 36,000 Frenchmen under the command of General Charles Dumouriez, a twice-wounded veteran of thirty-four years' service.

The larger and more highly trained Allied force should have made quick work of the French. Most of them were not professional soldiers. Many of the men, even in the regular battalions, had only recently volunteered for military service in a fit of idealism and commitment to the revolution that had begun at the Bastille in Paris in July 1789. The French soldiers, largely urban and from the artisan class, had an élan and a belief in the importance of their cause that their conscripted peasant opponents clearly lacked. They were willing to lay down their lives, if necessary, in the interests of saving the gains the revolution had already made. Nevertheless, they were outnumbered by more than two to one, had little practical experience of warfare, and faced a highly trained and well-led opponent.

Despite these disadvantages, the battle quickly turned in France's favor. Brunswick, in hostile territory and afraid of partisan attacks on his lines of communication, kept almost half of his troops to the rear, significantly evening the odds for Dumouriez and his French soldiers. The remainder of Brunswick's army fared poorly in the face of accurate and heavy French artillery fire. Brunswick had never cared for the idea of fighting so far from home. He also did not relish the notion of attacking the French, who had selected excellent defensive positions and therefore held the tactical advantage. Brunswick judged his situation to be unfavorable and prepared to retire from the field. The leaders of the enthusiastic French army soon realized their advantage and attacked, accompanied by passionate shouts of "Vive la Nation!" and "Vive la République!" The French routed the Allies, and chased the Duke of Brunswick and his invaders all the way to the far bank of the Rhine River and out of French territory.

As Goethe watched the battle, he concluded that geography and superior French artillery alone had not caused the stunning French victory over the more skillful and experienced Allies. As Brunswick's army began a silent and stunned retreat from the battlefield, a Prussian survivor of the battle turned to Goethe and asked him for his thoughts. "At this place, on this day there has begun a new era in the history of the world," the poet replied, "and you can all claim to have been present at its birth." Goethe's words have survived as the most enduring epitaph of the battle and the most prescient synopsis of its larger meaning. A Prussian officer was more blunt, saying, "We have lost more than a battle."[2]

Valmy was not a particularly large battle for its time, nor was it decisive in ending what became known as the War of the First Coalition. Goethe had watched as French artillerists had expertly and decisively fired upon Allied soldiers, but he had not seen any radically new weapons, technological advances, or tactics. The French army had not shown any particular skill at the art of warfare and few of the battle's soldiers went on to prominent military careers. Yet Valmy had marked a new era in the history of soldiers' lives, in large part because of the composition of the victorious French army. That army was in many ways radically different from traditional European armies.

As Goethe and Brunswick both knew, the French army's poor tactical performance was partly a function of its severe lack of competent officers. This problem predated the revolution itself as the *ancien régime* (the term revolutionaries used to describe the social and political order of Europe they were replacing) tried to keep nobles in firm command of the military. The Ségur Ordinance of 1781 had required any Frenchman to be able to prove four generations of nobility in his family before he could be admitted into the officer corps. This system worked as designed on the social level, leaving the power of the aristocracy deeply entrenched, but, as its planners intended, it also deprived France of thousands of potential officers from the emerging middle class.

Because the nobles were so often targeted by the revolutionaries, they were often the first to leave France. More than one-third of French officers had left their homeland since the outbreak of the Revolution in 1789; many had joined Brunswick's army in the hope of crushing the revolution and restoring King Louis XVI to his throne. The artillery was one notable exception to the general pattern of noble dominance of the officer corps because artillery required a higher technical knowledge than nobles normally possessed. As a result, artillery officers tended to be more middle class in their social origins and, consequently, more often stayed with the army after the upheavals of 1789.

Given its lack of experienced professional leadership, therefore, the French army at Valmy had shown rather amateurish tactics. The artillerists, not the infantry, had won the battle for France. Like their officers, the men of the artillery branch were not new volunteers, but skilled veterans of the pre-revolutionary Royal Army who had made a conscious decision to remain in military service with the republic. A sober military analysis of the battle might well conclude that the revolutionaries had played little role. The specific credit for the victory lay in the traditional strength of the French army, its powerful artillery.

Goethe, therefore, had not seen technical or material superiority from the French army. He did, however, see an enthusiasm and an élan in the French volunteer forces that no other army in Europe possessed. He had witnessed the first deployment of a citizen army fighting not out of fear of its own officers, but for a commonly held belief in safeguarding its liberty and protecting the heritage of the revolution for future generations of Frenchmen. A force that for two years had concerned itself with the internal problems of protecting the French Revolution from hostile Frenchmen had "turned [its] bayonets outward" and prepared to deal with its external enemies as it had dealt with its domestic enemies.[3]

The men Goethe saw at Valmy were products of a call to defend the French Revolution against foreign reactionaries determined to destroy it. In August 1791, Emperor Leopold of Austria and King Frederick William of Prussia had issued the Declaration of Pillnitz, in which they pledged to use force to restore the monarchy in France and thereby destroy the republic that the Revolution of 1789 had ushered in. The two brothers of the French king Louis XVI had gone into exile to form and lead an army to convert the sentiments of Pillnitz into action. The rulers of Russia, Spain, and Britain all offered their support. Leopold's sister, France's unpopular Queen Marie Antoinette implored the monarchs of Europe to come to her aid, calling the First Coalition the French monarchy's "only source of help."[4] The Duke of Brunswick later issued his own declaration, holding the entire citizenry of Paris responsible for the safety of the king and queen, whom the republic had imprisoned after the royal couple's unsuccessful attempt to flee France in 1791.

Popular French fears of a foreign invasion and a restoration of the hated Bourbon monarchy led the republic to a rash declaration of war against Austria in April 1792. In July, the French government rallied its citizens with a cry of "La Patrie en danger" (The fatherland is in danger). Early indications did not favor France, because the new army, lacking leadership and experience, had performed poorly in the first military encounters. After pushing enemy forces away from the important manufacturing center of Lille in the northeast, the French advanced into the Habsburg-held province of Flanders in modern-day Belgium. There a numerically inferior Austrian army broke and chased the inexperienced French back to Lille. The raw French volunteers had panicked at the first sight of Austrian professionals and had not even fired a shot in their own defense. With French border fortresses in dismal shape, it seemed that the Austrians would be able to invade France and end the revolution quickly and without many battlefield casualties.

The republic's declaration of war, however, was met by an astonishing wave of enthusiasm throughout France that added 100,000 eager young men to the republican army in just two months. The passion and zeal with which Frenchmen volunteered to join the army stood in marked contrast to the typical system of military recruitment before the French Revolution. In the days of the monarchy, most French subjects looked upon soldiers as little better than criminals who pillaged even French towns and attracted an unsavory collection of camp followers that normally included prostitutes, drunkards, and thieves. One of Europe's most famous philosophers, Voltaire, denigrated soldiers as little better than assassins and wrote wistfully of a utopian society that would not have any need for them. The French custom of billeting troops in private homes and forcing the owners to feed and care for the men did little to encourage warm sentiments for the army.

Before the French Revolution, few men joined European armies out of patriotism or the desire to defend their nation against its enemies. The goals of war centered around dynastic aims with little or no connection to the daily lives of most Europeans. The localized worldview of most Europeans, moreover, mitigated against any abiding hatreds of neighboring nations later so useful in propelling men into military service. Most soldiers consequently entered the army through a combination of local coercion, poverty, and a need to escape from a disreputable past. Thousands of men enlisted only because the army offered them their last chance to escape abject poverty. Recruiters normally found their jobs easier to perform in times of bad harvests or downturns in the manufacturing sector.

Many men used the system against itself, signing up under assumed names, collecting their bounties, and moving to another district or another state to perform the trick again. The high rate of desertion underscored the social problems of the French army, as well as those of most European armies. The huge gulf in the French Royal Army between officers (nine in ten of whom were aristocrats), and enlisted men combined with intense discipline to create an army that was all too often an embarrassment to the very people it was designed to serve. Conditions in many regiments were so bad that the Royal Army depended heavily on foreign mercenaries.

The army that fought at Valmy, by contrast, saw itself as the ultimate expression of the ideal of the citizen-soldier. Almost all of the French soldiers at Valmy had freely volunteered for military service in order to preserve the revolution and the republic it had created as a birthright for their children and grandchildren. The army proudly envisioned itself as a mirror of the new, more egalitarian nation that the revolution had created. Discipline became less harsh and less capricious and the men attained the right to elect their own corporals and sergeants. The army and the republic soon adopted the maxim "tout citoyen doit être soldat, tout soldat citoyen" (every citizen a soldier, every soldier a citizen). In sharp contrast to the monarchical system, the men who volunteered in 1791 were politically active and openly discussed the issues of the day.

The end result was an army infused with the revolutionary call for "liberté, fraternité, égalité." The men of the new French volunteer army at Valmy, moreover, saw their cause as the "cause of all humanity."[5] After winning a victory at Jemappes in Belgium in November 1792, the French Republic somewhat rashly promised help to all European peoples who sought to rid themselves of their monarchs as France had done. To the soldiers of 1792, the French Revolution represented the universal values of liberty over tyranny, fraternity over privilege, and equality over discrimination. They believed that they spoke not only for themselves but for all of the people of Europe who suffered under reactionary regimes. The soldiers of the French army believed in their cause enough to leave their homes voluntarily and join the army, once one of the nation's most hated institutions, but, by 1792, one of its most prestigious. Victory on the field of battle, the men knew, meant the triumph of the will of the people; defeat meant the return of tyranny.

This army was the one that Goethe saw at Valmy. Instead of the cool, professional martinets that France had traditionally fielded, the volunteers of Valmy, called Carmagnoles after the sleeveless vests that were fashionable during the revolution, showed a passion and a bloodthirstiness that the French army had manifestly failed to show in Flanders earlier in the year. After Valmy, the Carmagnoles broke the Austrian siege of Lille, seized Brussels, and cleared the Scheldt Estuary of Austrian forces. At Jemappes and elsewhere, they had fought well, finishing battles with the bayonet and close hand-to-hand fighting, proving a military prowess that they had not needed to show at Valmy. The Carmagnoles interpreted their successes as definitive proof of the value of republican citizens in uniform, fighting for a cause in which they believed with their minds, their hearts, and their souls.

As Goethe must have realized, the indiscipline and crude tactics of the new French army hid its essential strengths. Once the French army learned to harness the soldiers' élan and trained such enthusiastic men in the rigors of modern warfare, it would have at its disposal a citizen force possessing a power not seen in Europe since the Roman Republic. As Valmy foreshadowed, the French revolutionary armies soon became the most feared military force in Europe. As Goethe could not then have realized, a bright and ambitious twenty-three-year-old artillery lieutenant colonel in the Ajaccio volunteers named Napoleon Bonaparte was then in the provincial backwater of Corsica, learning the art of leadership that later carried these forces across Europe from Iberia to Russia.

In 1792, the French revolutionary army emboldened the spirit of revolutionary France. It was also a product of the distinct environment of France in revolution. Although the spirit of 1792 burned with an intensity that France could not hope to maintain, Valmy and Jemappes shone as validation of the French experiment and the value of republican forms of government over monarchical ones. As a visible statement of that conclusion, the French Republic executed Louis XVI in January 1793. That act, and the revolutionary sentiment that it announced, led France to an intensification of war with a host of foes that included Austria, Prussia, Piedmont, Britain, Spain, and Holland. Europe was on the road to a twenty-two-year period of almost constant war.

As French revolutionary fervor spread, so, too, did French military practices. Austrian Prince Clemens von Metternich once quipped that when France sneezes the rest of Europe catches a cold. Never was this statement more true than in the late eighteenth and early nineteenth centuries. The wars of Louis XIV (ruled 1643–1715) had already established France as a premier military power. French defeats in the Seven Years' War had tarnished that reputation, but only a bit. At the time of the French Revolution, France still commanded the respect of friends and foes alike. When France underwent a revolution and major military reform, therefore, change became almost inevitable across the European continent.

Valmy and Jemappes ushered in these reforms, and with them a new era in European history. Valmy gave French revolutionaries the strength to abolish the French monarchy and solidify a republic in the continent's most powerful nation. That act led not only to years of near-constant war, but to reactions across Europe that ranged from a desire to imitate to a desire to destroy the new French system. War soon became "an integral part of the politics of the revolutionary state" and, by extension, an integral part of the entire European continent.[6] The soldiers who formed the French revolutionary armies not only brought war to Europe; they began an entirely new era in the history of soldiers' daily lives by changing the soldier's relationship to his state, his society, and to warfare itself. These changes eventually produced reform across Europe, making 1789 a major watershed both in European history and in the history of soldiers' daily lives.

THE CITIZEN-SOLDIER AND HIS ENTRY INTO MILITARY SERVICE

Soldiers and their relationship to society formed a major problem for Europeans at the end of the eighteenth century. To most Enlightenment thinkers, soldiers represented an instrument of the state, most often used to coerce people both at home and abroad. As servants of the monarch, often more loyal to their officers than to their nation, they stood out as the antithesis of liberty and a glaring example of all that was wrong in the ancien régime. Soldiers, moreover, legally belonged to their superior officers in a state not far removed from serfdom. The officers, drawn almost exclusively from the nobility, thus oppressed their soldiers just as the Second Estate more generally oppressed the Third.[7] Symbolic of this state of affairs, companies frequently derived their names from their commanders, and larger units similarly held seigniorial names that underscored their titular ownership by the king and, through him, his small coterie of upper nobles.

The dominance of the nobility in the French army's leadership repeated itself across Europe. Of the 10,000 officers in the French army from 1781 to 1789, only 46 had been promoted from the ranks. Military service became especially important for lesser nobles, who had claims to important aristocratic titles but often had little money. Proud service in the army could provide a social compensation for a noble from an impoverished family. Russian Boyars and Prussian Junkers, who possessed titles and estates with especially unproductive land, turned to military service as validation of their status within society. British nobles, many of whom had long since lost economic predominance to the growing English middle class, followed a similar route.

For wealthy nobles, a military commission might serve as a way to establish a career for a second or third son. The system of primogeniture, common in Europe, transferred land and title to the eldest son, thus ensuring the long-term financial and social stability of only one child. Younger sons, especially from families unable to bequeath them much money, needed meaningful employment. The church and the military became obvious pathways to secure futures. The word "cadet," used to describe a student in a military school, comes from a French word meaning youngest son. Arthur Wellesley, the future Duke of Wellington, was the fifth son in his family, his rival Napoleon Bonaparte was the second surviving son in his, and Jean Baptiste Rochambeau (who led the French army that assisted the American rebels at Yorktown, Virginia in 1781) was the third son in his, to cite just a few examples. In many parts of *ancien régime* Europe, commissions were acquired by purchasing them. Wellington's father began his son's military career by purchasing a lieutenant colonelcy for him.

The tremendous expense of being an officer further prohibited commoners from entering the officer corps in large numbers. Horses, parties, and a luxurious officer's mess were part and parcel of an officer's life. Senior officers were expected to lead the lives of gentlemen, host influential visitors, wear elaborate, hand-tailored uniforms, and appear dashing on the equestrian field or the parade ground. For relatively poor officers, this burden proved quite severe. Many fell heavily in debt, sometimes to their wealthy brother officers. Still, they lived a life of material comfort, waited on by servants and enjoying the finer aspects of their elevated social status.

Officers also enjoyed the privileges that accrued to membership in a continental social and political elite. They lived by a code based in medieval chivalry and usually gave and received mutual courtesies, even in battle. If captured, they could expect to be feted as if they were on a social visit, drinking their captor's best wines and eating his food until a parole or a pardon could be arranged. Officers lived in a system of mutual respect and understanding, behaving as gentlemen whenever possible. Wellington's refusal to permit a sharpshooter to fire on Napoleon at Waterloo in 1815 ("certainly not!" he is supposed to have remarked) represented just one famous case of ethical reciprocity between fellow officers. An officer who violated this code, by contrast, could expect harsh treatment in return for his breach of the pact of honor.

Life in the ranks bore few parallels to life in the officer corps. As we have already seen, before 1789, few men entered military service out of any sense of patriotism. Instead, their motivations were more personal. For the majority who became soldiers, military service was a way to escape poverty, debt, prison, or a local problem such as impending illegitimate fatherhood. Across Europe, military service attracted men who found themselves the victims of such circumstances, or of a recruiting sergeant who bought them one too many drinks at the local tavern. More than one young European male awoke to find himself not only with a bad hangover, but also a commitment to military service for six, eight, or, in some Russian cases, twenty-five, years. In times of crisis, a central government might call on local communities to supply a given number of young men to serve. A father's dispute with the town mayor or simply an unlucky number in a draw might lead to military service.

In most western European nations, governments set the term of military service at six to eight years on the theory that when an individual's term of service expired, he would be too old to take an apprenticeship or to learn a civilian trade. He would, therefore, have little choice but to reenlist. When the second six-year term expired, the soldier's problem would only have grown more acute because he would have even fewer options. Armies therefore attracted thousands of men who had no other viable career choices and remained in the army only reluctantly. Thousands of men deserted each year, especially at harvest time when they could find seasonal agricultural work, but many of them later faced up to their punishments and returned to the army after having failed to establish themselves in civilian life.

Many men, however, risked those punishments rather than submit to military service. Areas near international borders, large forests, or remote mountains often sheltered large and well-organized bands of deserters or draft evaders. In many cases, such men received significant support from civilians who provided food, work, and information about the movements of the local police. Society at large, especially in the countryside, rarely saw men avoiding military service as cowards. Quite the contrary, a man's creativity and courage in evading the "impôt de sang" (blood tax) could demonstrate considerable heroism.

Even with all of the methods of coercion possessed by modern states, therefore, armies often found themselves short of manpower. Since an attachment to country did not much matter in motivating men to serve, armies frequently turned to hiring foreign mercenaries. The French army on the eve of the revolution had 23 foreign regiments out of a total of 102. The British hired Hessians, German soldiers loyal to their king, and other mercenaries and sent them to America to fight rebels because of a shortage of trained English manpower. Americans loathed the Hessians, whom one observer called "a set of cruel, unfeeling people," in large part because of their foreignness in a war of national independence.[8] George Washington's daring raid on the Hessian base at Trenton, New Jersey, on Christmas Eve in 1776, gave the Americans a tremendous morale boost similar to the one Valmy later gave the French.[9] Nevertheless, the concept of the foreign mercenary retained a key place in European armies. The best of the mercenary units came already trained in the latest tactics and armed with modern weapons. Several German, Swiss, and Italian communities specialized in the art of preparing mercenary units and generated much of their public revenue from the practice of sending their unwanted young men to fight someone else's wars.

Despite the advantages of mercenaries, no army sought to rely on them too heavily. They came from the same general social material as native soldiers, but they had even less connection to the communities they served than did native soldiers. They had terrible reputations for all sorts of criminality, drunkenness, and pillaging. If their pay did not arrive with the speed or regularity they expected, they might take compensation for their lost wages by plundering the very communities that they had been hired to protect. Most governments therefore preferred to impress and conscript men closer to home.

Because large numbers of soldiers could usually be hired, rounded up, or coerced to serve when needed, officers had little incentive to treat them well. Consequently, the life of the average European soldier during the ancien régime period was nothing short of dreadful. Intense discipline, poor living conditions, nonexistent medical care, and terrible food characterized daily life. A regimental commander who showed a degree of paternal welfare for his men and their well-being was rare indeed. On the contrary, several commanders rented their units out to perform agricultural labor and pocketed the proceeds to fund their lavish lifestyles, although this practice fell into disfavor in western Europe in the second half of the eighteenth century.

Most officers saw their men as unreliable rabble prone to excessive drink and irresponsible behavior. Frederick the Great of Prussia (ruled 1740–1786) often said that he wanted his soldiers to fear their officers more than they feared the enemy. Only through brutal discipline, he believed, could soldiers be made reliable both on the battlefield and in the barracks. Any loosening of that discipline, he believed, would unleash the inherent barbarism in the nature of his soldiers. His observation summed up the general attitude of Europeans toward soldiers and the lives they led. To most Europeans, soldiers appeared little better than common criminals, and as such, they deserved similar treatment.

More than one tavern displayed signs forbidding soldiers to drink in their establishments. To most innkeepers, soldiers brought violence, prostitutes, and in all likelihood an unwelcome visit from the local police that created problems far in excess of the profits to be realized from the relatively modest sums soldiers were able to spend. Communities regularly resisted hosting soldiers, even when ordered to do so. Wealthy towns collected money from their residents in order to pay for housing soldiers in neighboring towns that needed the business. Such towns believed that the money was well spent as a kind of insurance policy that protected their property and their daughters from soldiers. Even the relatively popular French army created by the *levée en Masse* struck observers as "unkempt, disorderly, [and containing] more than the normal amount of ruffianism."[10]

REFORMING SOLDIERS' ROLES

Even before the French Revolution, several progressive European thinkers had begun to think about reforming the system. French officer Jacques Antoine Guibert argued that contemporary military systems not only turned men into criminals, but also made them inferior soldiers. In his *Essai général de tactique*, published in 1772, Guibert argued for the abolition of the traditional French army in favor of a true citizen army.[11] Influential philosophes like Jean-Jacques Rousseau and the Baron de Montesquieu had made similar arguments, but they were based on the belief that a citizen army would not endanger domestic liberty as a standing army isolated from its society would. "Every citizen," Rousseau wrote, "should be a soldier by duty, none by trade."[12] As influential as the philosophes were in the civilian world, they held little sway in the army.

Guibert's arguments, by contrast, came not from a philosopher detached from the daily needs of an army, but with the authority of a well-respected serving officer. He contended that a popular army, built on the principle of service to the nation, could fight a new style of war. Motivated by patriotism, such men could move quickly without direct and constant supervision from mistrusting sergeants and officers. They could also live off the land, thus freeing them from the cumbersome magazine system, because their commanders could trust them not to desert and because civilians would freely give their food and fodder to men fighting for the general welfare. Such an army would be both swift and deadly. It could achieve surprise and fight brilliantly, sweeping aside the large, but unmotivated forces in front of them.

Although his arguments seem to foreshadow Valmy and the army that France eventually built, Guibert was no prophet. He believed that the people of western Europe were too materialistic and too soft to make the sacrifices necessary to form the army he had envisioned. His gruff personality and a second book that repudiated many of the conclusions in his first did not incline many members of the French nobility to experiment with his ideas. As a result, until 1789, France retained the basic structure of the ancien régime system. Despite his more influential ideas on tactics and his election to the prestigious Académie Française in 1785, Guibert had little real influence on the composition of French armies.

The French Revolution, however, opened up French society, and by extension the French army, to experimentation of all kinds. Guibert's ideas overlapped in many important ways with those of the revolutionaries, even if Guibert's politics and his death in 1790 prevented him from playing a role in implementing them. The powerful notion of a citizen force with citizen leaders had obvious appeal to French republicans, although few of them knew exactly how to build such an army and most were much more concerned with establishing domestic political institutions than they were with army reform.

The army, moreover, stood out as a particular problem to revolutionary thinkers. Removing France's absolute monarchy would serve no purpose if the army remained a bastion of reaction powerful enough to deny Frenchmen the rights they had so recently won. Nevertheless, the French could not reduce or eliminate their army because to do so would leave the revolution vulnerable to foreign enemies as well as domestic anti-revolutionary revolts like the one that began in the Vendée in western France in March 1793. The army and its soldiers thus had to serve two, sometimes conflicting, goals: they had to protect France from enemies at home and abroad while securing civil liberties and protecting the rights of French citizens.

Guibert, Rousseau, Diderot, and other Enlightenment thinkers provided an intellectual way out of this traditional democratic conundrum. A citizen army, the republicans argued, would not threaten civic liberty because the soldiers would not oppress their own communities. Full believers in the revolution and its cause, soldiers would fight for liberty both at home and abroad. France could thus have an army whose soldiers were motivated neither by fear of their officers' brutal discipline nor by hopes for the spoils of conquest but, as Guibert had envisioned, by patriotism and ideology.

Although such a system seemed perfect on paper, it proved difficult to create. A wholesale reform of the army might only serve to chase needed expertise out of the officer corps and the ranks. A zealous volunteer army might fight for what was right, but it might equally stand no chance against the long-term professionals that formed the armies of France's enemies. The French thus had effectively built two systems by the time of Valmy. The first system was based around its traditional army, although the officers now had to swear their allegiance to the nation, not to the king. Thousands of officers had left France, but many of them were incompetents who owed their positions to their noble pedigrees. Thousands of more qualified officers stayed on, providing the army with continuity and a core of professional leaders. The second system centered around the National Guard, an enthusiastic, purely voluntary force that attracted the most ardent supporters of the revolution.

In part because so many revolutionary soldiers left the regular army to join the National Guard and in part because of the abiding political unreliability of the regular officer corps, the French merged the two systems in 1793. Consistent with revolutionary ideology, the new French system treated its soldiers as citizens first and soldiers second. Although the division of officers and men remained, the gap between the two groups narrowed significantly. Soldiers addressed one another as "citoyen" (citizen) rather than by rank, and officers commonly used the more respectful "vous" when speaking to their men rather than the familiar "tu." Military units also dropped their seigniorial names in favor of more mundane, but more republican numbers. The Royal Roussillon Regiment thus became the 54th Infantry Regiment.[13]

The new French army accordingly recognized that its citizens soldiers deserved the rights and privileges of all citizens. Soldiers no longer needed their officers' permission to marry and promotions at the lower ranks were often decided by balloting. The men of a unit nominated three of their own when a promotion to corporal or sergeant opened and the officers chose from among those three. Soldiers also acquired the right to be politically active, as long as their politics were sufficiently supportive of the republic. Jacobin political clubs appeared in many units, giving the men a forum to discuss the issues of the day. Nationalist celebrations, songs, and entertainment reminded men of the importance of the revolution. Men deemed to have the right ideology stood the best chances of promotion to the next level.

Military service itself became more humane. Soldiers saw less of the traditional harsh discipline meted out to men deemed to have violated their unit's regulations. The lash and other similar devices virtually disappeared. Peer pressure and what one scholar has termed "revolutionary discipline" replaced traditional methods.[14] Instead of fearing punishment, men hoped for advancement. Revolutionary ideology preached the need to open leadership positions to men of all social backgrounds. The need for officers to lead a growing army, combined with the number of Royal Army officers who left France, led to rapid promotions and, by necessity, to a greater emphasis on talent. Parisian promotion boards understood talent to mean both technical proficiency and revolutionary mind-set, characteristics that men of all social classes could possess. Napoleon later completed this process, telling his men that in every private's haversack was a marshal's baton. Any man in the French army, he told them, could rise as high as his talents could take him.

Commensurate with the idea that soldiering was a socially important, indeed vital, occupation, the soldier's material conditions also improved. Pay rose to a respectable, if still not overly generous, level and the quality of food generally improved as well. French governments made inconsistent but symbolic progress in providing for better pensions, health care, and payments to widows and orphans. The famous Les Invalides military hospital in Paris, built for the officers and noncommissioned officers of Louis XIV's army, opened its doors to men of all ranks. This material improvement had the twin advantages of improving the image of the soldier and reducing his need to pillage the communities where he was garrisoned for basic sustenance. The French soldier, once widely denigrated as a criminal at worst and a servant at best, had become a professional and an artisan in the minds of his countrymen.

In 1791 and 1792 these changes sufficed to draw large numbers of Frenchmen into military service. In 1791 more than 100,000 men volunteered for military service in just two months, giving the French army 169 new battalions. This group came as close as Europe in this period ever did to the ideal of the citizen-soldier. King Louis XVI's failed attempt to flee France in June of that year, followed by the declaration of war against Austria, produced motivated soldiers who saw a genuine connection between their personal goals and those of the society at large.

The class of 1791, however, proved to be the exception rather than the rule. Even most of those men left the army after completing their one year of military service. These men understood military service as the responsibility of all Frenchmen. In effect, they assumed that if all Frenchmen believed equally in the values of the revolution, then it was time for the next cohort of young firebrands to take up the colors and win the next Battle of Valmy. The soldiers of the class of 1791 were ideologically disinclined to understand military service as a lifetime occupation. Having done their part, they expected to return to their jobs and families and make room for the heroes of the future.

Unfortunately for France, the younger brothers of the men of 1791 proved unexpectedly reluctant to pick up the standard from their older brothers. A call by the French government in 1793 for 300,000 men resulted in only half that number entering the army, although the 1793 class of 150,000 men class was still much larger than the 1791 class of 100,000. To recruit the 150,000 men of 1793, the French government had resorted to methods reminiscent of the ancien régime. The central government gave quotas to local communities who responded with the same inconsistent methods that they had used before the revolution. Drawing numbers by lot was the most common method of determining who would serve, but even this method was far from fair. Wealthy men could buy substitutes and personal connections could also ensure an exemption.

To many Frenchmen, especially in the western and southern provinces that were relatively safe from invasion, the new system seemed little different from the old system. In its own way, the new system struck many men as capricious and essentially unfair because the local nature of the recruitment process distorted the national goals of the system. Men of privilege therefore still avoided military service with little consequence. Central government attempts to use propaganda to reinforce the importance of patriotism and volunteerism only underscored the wide gap between the promise and the reality of national ideology and military service. The large numbers of men who failed to report or who quickly deserted highlighted the depth of the problem.

The French government responded with a call to arms that returned to the themes of volunteerism, national emergency, and the responsibility of all French citizens to do their utmost to ensure the success of the revolution. The *levée en Masse*, issued in August 1793, ended any speculation about who owed service to France:

> From this moment until that in which our enemies shall have been driven from the territory of the Republic, all Frenchmen are permanently requisitioned for service in the armies. Young men will go into battle. Married men will forge arms and transport supplies. Women will make tents, uniforms, and serve in hospitals. Children will pick up rags. Old men will have themselves carried into public squares, to inspire the courage of warriors, and to preach hatred of kings and the unity of the Republic.

The *levée en Masse*'s beautifully straightforward simplicity did not create perfect equity, but it did establish the principle of universal service. Its logic, moreover, eliminated foreign mercenaries and substitution. More than 300,000 men answered its call, providing more than enough men for the immediate future. Within a few years, France had an army of more than 1,000,000 men, far larger than any other European nation except Russia could possibly have fielded. Small numbers of foreigners still served in the French army, but they were no longer mercenaries; they were volunteers who believed in the French Revolution and its appeal to universalism. The eleven separate French armies contained an uneven mixture of hardened veterans and disorderly conscripts, but their sheer size made them a force that the rulers of Europe could not ignore.

France added an additional element to this system with the passage of the Jourdan Law of 1798. The law brought modern conscription to France, making all men liable for military service at age twenty and immediately adding another 400,000 men to the rolls. The inability of the central government to track evaders led to the widespread use of substitution and, in some cases, local subterfuge allowed some men to avoid serving, but the principle of rational, national service had gone one step further down the road to the modern age. As the Napoleonic government grew more administratively efficient and therefore better able to account for its citizens, the central government in Paris also became better able to control the decisions made at local levels. These changes lowered evasion rates significantly. The logic of the *levée en Masse* had met modern bureaucracy, taking much of the power to determine who would enter military service out of the provinces and into the hands of administrators in Paris.

Napoleon's rise to power brought with it a surge in patriotism and an internal stability that led to even wider and more constant military recruitment. By strengthening the power of the state and making localities more answerable to the central government in Paris, Napoleon made local chicanery in the draft system, evasion, and desertion all much less likely to succeed. In 1801 he negotiated a Concordat with the Catholic Church that effectively ended the crisis of conscience felt by practicing Catholics over serving a republic that had expressed avowedly anticlerical sentiments. France under Napoleon moved even further toward developing a truly national ideology that both

This cartoon depicts the greatest fear of Britons: the possibility of Napoleon evading the powerful Royal Navy and landing an army on the coast of England. Although he never did so, similar fears emerged in the years before World War I, only this time the army Britons worried about wasn't French, it was German. Courtesy of the Library of Congress.

privileged the rights of citizens and demanded their participation in a system that relied increasingly on war.

Few European states had the necessary ideological or material bases to follow the French pattern. Few saw any immediate need to do so. Traditional European armies could still defeat the new citizen armies on the battlefield, although those victories were becoming fewer and fewer. Militarily, the members of the First Coalition were not yet willing to copy the French too closely and thereby abandon a system that had served them for decades. Most aristocrats concluded, with passably good reason in most cases, that the French system would not stand the test of time and that once the revolutionaries had been defeated, their amateurish system would be discredited and European warfare would return to its traditional patterns.

Social and political factors may have been even more important than military ones in the First Coalition's determined resistance to change. Governed by conservative regimes and led by traditional aristocracies, the armies of Europe saw the French model as the virtual antithesis of everything that they held dear. In what they saw as the natural order of society, only gentlemen of the nobility had the requisite knowledge, breeding, and judgment to govern. They looked aghast at the excesses of the revolution, most notably the execution of eighty four French aristocratic senior officers in the period of the Great Terror. To them, the French model evoked hatred, disgust, and fear much more than a desire to imitate.

As a result, European armies outside France changed much less fundamentally than did their French counterparts. In most societies, soldiers continued to come from social classes deemed by the aristocracy to hold little redeeming social or economic value. As a result, criminals, orphans, economically unnecessary serfs, vagabonds, and the indigent continued to be overrepresented in the ranks. In effect, these systems were the polar opposite of the French system. Instead of recruiting men closest to their societies in the hopes of forging close links, the armies of Austria, Prussia, Russia, and the Italian and German states looked to enlist those men with the weakest connections to their societies.

Most continental armies, therefore, still relied on the press gang, the decision-making processes of local officials, and the hiring of mercenaries to fill their armies. Several of them rewarded volunteers by privileging them for promotion to the rank of noncommissioned officer, but all of them looked upon their soldiers as failed civilians. In the dialect of the Kingdom of the Two Sicilies, the word for prisoner became synonymous with the word for soldier, a clear indication of the status of the common soldier.[15]

The expansion of the army posed further challenges for traditional regimes. The larger the army, the greater the need for officers. Although the elite could easily prevent the basest commoners from becoming officers, a large army would inevitably have to turn to the growing European middle classes to fill the officer corps. This idea filled many traditionalists with dread. Many aristocrats saw little practical difference among non-nobles, no matter what the difference in their backgrounds or their educations. Only in the most technologically demanding (and not coincidentally the least prestigious) fields, such as artillery, did the men of the middle class make important inroads into leadership positions. The most socially elite branches, such as the cavalry, normally had the highest-ranking nobles in their officer corps.

This cartoon attacks an American plan to create a professional reserve army in place of local and state militias. Fears of a standing army being used to deny civilians their civil liberties led the Van Buren Administration to give up the idea, but images of soldiers as oppressive tools of central governments remained prevalent in the United States and in Europe. Courtesy of the Library of Congress.

An innate distrust of standing armies ran deeply in the Anglo-Saxon world as well. Britain and the United States both benefited from the luxury of distance to keep their enemies at bay. The British, of course, also had the tremendous security provided by the first-class Royal Navy. Consequently, neither nation developed a large standing army. Both preferred militia systems inconsistently populated by volunteers who drilled when they wanted to and who largely set their own standards of efficiency. Despite the evident failures of this system in combat, most notably on the American side in the War of 1812, they retained a social cachet that led politicians to support their retention.

Such regular armed forces as the British and Americans fielded generally fought wars of expansion. For the British, the 1707 Act of Union largely ended fighting between the English and the Scots (indeed, the Scots quickly became an indispensable source of manpower for the British army), but conflict in Ireland and a global empire always drew away a large proportion of British soldiers. For the Americans, the persistent westward expansionist demands of a growing nation coming into its own led the regular army into conflict with native peoples until their final subjugation following the Battle of Wounded Knee in 1890. None of these crises led the British or the Americans to turn to conscription in this period, although both sides in the American Civil War (1861–1865) used it briefly with dissatisfying results.

Across Europe and the United States, then, a wide variety of systems existed to entice or coerce men into military service. Each of them came with advantages and disadvantages, but they all reflected the general social assumptions of their societies' ruling classes. The dynamism in France continued to challenge traditional European models of military manpower accession. The increasing size of the French armies practically forced France to expand at the expense of its neighbors in order to provide food not only to the army, but to a civilian population increasingly deprived of peasant labor as more and more men entered the army. War, as Napoleon believed, should nourish war.

Such was the system that Napoleon inherited when he assumed effective control of the French state in November 1799. The soldiers of the French army were by that time experienced, talented, motivated, and unusually numerous. Under Napoleon, France grew increasingly interested in expansion for ideological, practical, and megalomaniacal reasons. Still, even Napoleon's great string of early victories did not produce an unending enthusiasm for the army. Contemporary observers noted that popular acceptance of military service ebbed considerably as the casualty figures from Napoleon's campaigns mounted. One indication of this trend is the increasing cost of substitutes. Whereas in 1800 an average substitute purchased in the southern city of Avignon cost 416 francs, in 1806 an average substitute cost 2,880 francs and in 1813 a substitute cost 4,900 francs.[16] France also turned increasingly to its allies to provide manpower. Nevertheless, levies for manpower almost always met their goals. Potential recruits seemed to have mirrored the spirit of serving soldiers who, as Napoleon famously remarked, complained but still marched.

To defeat Napoleon and contain France, the states and societies of Europe had to adapt to the new French system or at least imitate some of its forms. The traditional military powers of Europe largely chose from the French those elements that posed the least threat to established practices. The British continued to resist the idea of conscription, although bills to that effect appeared regularly in Parliament. In classic British fashion, the government chose to improve the market conditions of military service in the hopes of enticing more men into volunteering. Changes included the introduction of a pension system, shorter enlistment terms, and minor ameliorations of the traditionally brutal British system of military discipline. Even these changes, though, were insufficient to "overcome the opprobrium which had traditionally attached to the red coat."[17] As a result, men continued to enter the British army because of the traditional motivations of sheer financial desperation, an overly indulgent night at the tavern, or a desperate need to get out of town quickly.

Wellington once famously referred to the men of the British army as the "scum of the earth." His judgment may have been a bit too harsh, but most Britons did not volunteer for military service unless all options in civilian life had been exhausted. In Wellington's words, "men enlist from having got bastard children—some for minor offences—many more for drink." Indebtedness also appears to have played a key role, as evidenced by the practice of the British government to remit the debts of enlistees up to £30. The army thus became, in the words of one observer sympathetic to Wellington's views, the preserve of "the dissolute, the idle, and the unfortunate."[18]

Part of the problem with attracting men into military service sprang from the general disregard that Parliament and the War Office showed toward army reform. Bureaucratic weaknesses in the British army led to problems of supply and administration that made the lives of British soldiers worse than they need have been. British strategy therefore counted a great deal on fighting the wars against Napoleon by subsidizing the much larger armies of the continent. The British army fought well and played a critical role in the ultimate defeat of Napoleon, but there was much truth in the quip that politicians in London planned to fight France to the last drop of Russian blood.

Until 1806, Prussia, the most powerful of the German states and the state with the proudest military traditions, largely tried to fight Napoleon with its existing system. In the early years of the revolutionary and Napoleonic wars, the Prussians fielded an army characterized by a sharp and deep division between officers and men much more reminiscent of England than France. The ranks included large numbers of Poles and non-Prussian Germans. Discipline was among the harshest of any European army. In virtually all respects, the Prussian army from 1789 to 1806 represented the features of the ancien régime as closely as any.

In 1806, however, the Prussians received a nearly complete fall from grace at the twin battles of Jena and Auerstadt. While part of Napoleon's army marched to Jena on October 14 and routed one Prussian army, a smaller force of 27,000 men under Louis Nicolas Davout, one of Napoleon's best commanders, headed fifteen miles north to Auerstadt. Sitting on the Prussian lines of communication to Leipzig thirty miles to the northeast, Davout and his men knew they would be attacked. Commanding the Prussians once again was the Valmy veteran the Duke of Brunswick. He had at his disposal 63,000 men and, as at Valmy, should have swept the French from the field.

Davout and his men courageously withstood Brunswick's assaults for more than six hours. After the Prussians had worn themselves out, Davout counterattacked. The unfortunate Brunswick suffered from a wound that forced him from the battlefield and led to his death. Prussian king Frederick William III assumed personal command, but the Prussians had already begun to disintegrate. More than 25,000 Prussian soldiers surrendered and another 25,000 lay dead or wounded. The French had suffered just 8,000 casualties. Within ten days, Napoleon was in Berlin and Frederick William had retreated all the way to Moscow in search of asylum.

The resulting Treaty of Tilsit (July 1807) rubbed salt in Prussian wounds. The Prussians agreed to cede to France all German territory between the Elbe and Rhine rivers. Prussia also agreed to pay an indemnity to cover France's war expenses and reduce its army to a mere 42,000 men. For a nation with such proud military traditions, the twin humiliations of battlefield disgrace and diplomatic ignominy proved to be too much to bear. Shaken to its foundations, the Prussian army sought reform. The most important changes came in recruitment and the type of men Prussia sought to turn into soldiers.

Prussian leaders tried, ironically, to build an army using the same kinds of men that the French had used to defeat them. Prussia looked to create a new army based on national sentiment and patriotism similar in broad outline to the one that Davout had used to win with inferior numbers at Auerstadt. The Prussian ruling class abolished serfdom and spoke in national terms in the hopes of creating soldiers that would fight with the same zeal shown by Napoleon's forces. As soon as Napoleon's military fortunes began to ebb, the Prussian army grew by employing a system closer to universal conscription than any previously introduced in Prussia. As in France, many middle-class men (and a few women as well) volunteered out of a sense of "aggrieved nationalism" to chase the foreign invaders out. Frederick William's "call to his people," issued in April 1813, showed how far the Prussian military system had evolved. Contrary to the traditional system that emphasized tight control by officers, the call urged maximum effort from Prussians of all classes to defeat the French. "All means [of fighting] are hallowed," the statement read. "The most severe are in fact to be preferred, since they get it over most triumphantly and quickly."[19] The goal was the creation of popular resistance within state control and guidance.

As France had done, Prussia opened its officer corps by privileging talent over birth for promotion. Counting on patriotism to motivate men, discipline became much less harsh, a welcome innovation for Prussian soldiers. The Prussians simplified drill, which meant much less marching, and focused on education and marksmanship. In the new Prussian army, "No longer were soldiers to be mere automata driven to fight by fear of the lash, nor conditions in the army so severe that the population would not willingly join its ranks."[20] Reformers expected these changes to produce an army of talented, motivated men fighting for national goals out of a desire to liberate their homeland.

If the Prussians envisioned a people's war that evoked the spirit of the French armies in 1792, the Spanish took the concept one step further. Lacking a popular central state that could rally the people, and possessing an army that had failed to institute the reform it knew it needed, Spanish resistance to Napoleon's invasion of Iberia centered around more popular responses. An uprising in Madrid in May 1808, sparked a national movement aided by the British and led in part by Spanish priests who feared the anticlericalism of French republicanism. The intense resistance of Spanish bandits and irregulars led to such problems for Napoleon that the campaign acquired the nickname "the Spanish ulcer."

Spanish irregulars so impressed and terrified contemporaries that the term "guerrilla" entered the English language and continues to be synonymous with irregular warfare. Many of these men were members of organized criminal bands seeking to enrich themselves by robbing from French supply columns. Others wore uniforms and accepted some basic level of military discipline within an improvised command arrangement. One such group grew to more than 13,000 men. Guerrillas harassed French forces, threatened supplies, terrorized commanders, and engaged in a war of atrocity with French soldiers that appalled their nominal British allies.

Guerrillas depended on support from local populations, most of whom were willing to help Spanish forces trying to eject the French. Guerrillas therefore shared common national and ideological roots with the armies of Europe, but they differed strongly in their methods. Although they were generally successful in tying down French soldiers and greatly complicated French operations elsewhere, they were also brutal, lawless, and hard to control. As a result, they did not inspire a desire for imitation. Rather, they horrified most non-Spaniards who witnessed them in action and led to a desire to avoid such auxiliaries at all costs.

MILITARY RECRUITMENT AFTER NAPOLEON

The desire to contain and defeat the powerful forces of Napoleon had therefore led to a variety of experiments and reforms in European armies. These changes impacted the daily lives of European soldiers as they became more important to the system as individuals. Their material conditions, morale, and linkages to society more generally

Another cartoon showing Europe's fears of Napoleon. The Emperor is surrounded by drunks and gluttons while his elite soldiers stand guard. Courtesy of the Library of Congress.

became more important to the officers charged with their care. Perhaps more importantly, soldiers themselves understood that their military service gave them a special call on the resources of the state.

Nevertheless, European ruling classes largely envisioned returning to traditional, conservative systems after the final defeat of Napoleon in 1815. The return of Louis XVIII to the French throne marked the initiation of the Congress of Vienna system designed to reinstate as closely as possible the social and political order of Europe as it had existed before 1789. Most Europeans, exhausted by so many years of war, were anxious to return to peace and rejoiced at the general demobilization of European armed forces. Smaller armed forces meant that fewer men of the post-Napoleon generation had to leave their homes and jobs to serve in the army.

For the rulers of Europe smaller armies meant the opportunity to eliminate the passionate, popular armed forces of the revolutionary and Napoleonic periods. In their place came smaller, more professional armies constituted of long-term volunteers and conscripts. In France, thousands of officers easily transitioned from the Napoleonic army to the new Royal Army of the restored Bourbons. Marshal Davout, the great hero of numerous Napoleonic victories, entered the French peerage in service to the French monarchy as the Duke of Auerstadt.

Across the continent, soldiers became increasingly distant from the societies that they served, especially in comparison to the revolutionary and Napoleonic periods. The general absence of war on the European continent converted armies and soldiers into a domestic constabulary designed to put down strikes and stand on guard against future revolutions. As often as possible, troops remained in barracks and on bases, isolated

Europe in 1815, after the Treaty of Vienna.

from the citizenry, but located close enough to large cities to be ready to respond to urban distress. Strict discipline, spartan living conditions, and an insistence on obedience to the government became the general conditions of soldiers' lives. Small armies also allowed for the luxury of eliminating expensive foreign mercenaries, who all but disappeared in this period. Conscription calls lightened accordingly, permitting most Europeans with means to avoid service through occupational deferments or the purchase of a substitute.

The revolutions and urban revolts of the 1830s, immortalized in Victor Hugo's famous novel *Les Misérables*, demonstrated to conservatives that the process of isolating soldiers from society had not gone far enough. The French king, Charles X, sparked the rebellions by dissolving the elected Chamber of Deputies and disenfranchising three-quarters of the French electorate. In 1830 and 1832 numerous soldiers and even a few entire units showed marked sympathies with urban crowds and demonstrators, reawakening in conservative minds frightful memories of 1789. An 1832 law in France therefore eliminated the reserves, leaving France with the long-term, well-disciplined regular army that conservatives sought. These forces remained generally more obedient to their officers and rulers during the continent-wide rebellions of 1848.

The experiences of domestic rebellion led to a widening gulf in European minds about the best way to organize armed forces. Conservatives and monarchists argued for following the pattern of long-term volunteers, loyal to their units and obedient to properly constituted political authority. Workers, revolutionaries, and republicans argued for the creation of national guards with close links to their societies that mirrored the military systems of the French Revolution. Armies that truly represented their societies, they argued, would serve the will of the people, not the will of a small ruling class. With few European wars and limited military budgets, however, such a vision remained a utopian ideal, although the appeal of such ideas remained powerful well into the twentieth century.

The Crimean War of 1854–1856 demonstrated to many Europeans that they had paid far too little attention to their armies in the years following the defeat of Napoleon. In general, the French, British, and Russian armies performed poorly with uninspired leadership and unmotivated soldiers. The British still had officers who had purchased their commissions. The lack of conscription inside Britain forced the British army to fill the ranks with mercenaries from Germany and Switzerland. Their Russian adversaries did use conscription of a press gang sort that made soldiers out of criminals, orphans, and the poor. Sons of soldiers were required to serve in the Russian army by law, creating an embittered hereditary caste of men who knew little beyond the world of the barracks. Opposition to military service became so intense that many Russian villages hired "cripplers," men who amputated toes and fingers of potential conscripts in order to make them ineligible for military service. Other young men knocked out their front teeth, thus making it impossible for them to tear open paper rifle cartridges. Russian officers were often hired Germans who, lacking noble pedigrees, could not attain commissions in the Prussian army.

The Crimean War led to some minor changes in recruitment and enlistment practices. Appalled by the poor performance of their officers, the British finally abolished the system that permitted men to purchase their commissions. Nevertheless, the nobility continued to dominate the officer corps, especially at the most senior ranks. Several British War Office boards urged reform of the army, although the character of the men in the ranks did not constitute a major area of concern. Few British officers envisioned using a radically different system for recruiting the "other ranks." Soldiers therefore still largely came from the urban poor and stayed in service for long periods of time.

Russia's defeat in the Crimean War led it to undertake potentially fundamental social reform with military consequences. Russia abolished its age-old practice of serfdom in 1861 in part to develop a sense of affinity between serfs and "Mother Russia" and in part to reduce the number of soldiers needed for internal security. The abolition of serfdom, however, did not change the desperate lives of most Russian peasants and did not incline them to volunteer for military service in larger numbers. Most Russian enlistment terms were for twenty-five years and therefore most Russians looked upon military service as little different from a lifetime prison sentence.

Although some European men in this period clearly joined the army in hopes of finding adventure or making a name for themselves, most men did so because they felt that they had little choice. The initial wave of enthusiasm for the revolution in France in 1791 and 1792 produced armies closest to the citizen-soldier ideal, but even in France patriotism only went so far. The extreme lengths to which men went to avoid military service, including self-mutilation, escape to the mountains, and desertion from the ranks, indicate the general unpopularity of military service in this period. Senior officers seem to have cared less about the quality of their men than their quantity. Soldiers needed to have a basic skill set, of course, but their officers saw them as more or less expendable.

The extremely low regard in which Wellington and so many of his colleagues held soldiers also reflected their own class biases. Members of an aristocracy that depended on control of the military for their very survival, officers saw their own men as servants at best, potential revolutionaries at worst. Stern discipline, they believed, was critical to the process of converting the rabble into minimally reliable soldiers.

NOTES

1. Jean-Paul Bertaud, *The Army of the French Revolution: From Citizen-Soldier to Instrument of Power* (Princeton, NJ: Princeton University Press, 1988), 40.

2. Both quotations are from Christopher Hibbert, *The Days of the French Revolution* (New York: Morrow Quill, 1980), 179.

3. Geoffrey Best, *War and Society in Revolutionary Europe, 1770–1870* (Montreal: McGill University Press, 1982; 1998), 78.

4. Quoted in Hibbert, *The Days of the French Revolution*, 143.

5. Alan Forrest, *Soldiers of the French Revolution* (Durham, NC: Duke University Press, 1990), 6.

6. Forrest, *Soldiers of the French Revolution*, 5.

7. The Three Estates system divided France into the First Estate (the clergy), the Second Estate (the nobility) and the vast Third Estate encompassing the 95 percent of French society that belonged to neither the First nor the Second Estate.

8. Harry M. Ward, *The War for Independence and the Transformation of American Society* (London: Routledge, 1999), 89.

9. For more, see David Hackett Fischer, *Washington's Crossing* (Oxford: Oxford University Press, 2004).

10. Best, *War and Society*, 88.

11. A good general introduction to Guibert can be found in R. R. Palmer, "Frederick the Great, Guibert, Bulow: From Dynastic to National War," in *Makers of Modern Strategy from Machiavelli to the Nuclear Age*, ed. Peter Paret (Princeton, NJ: Princeton University Press, 1986), 91–119.

12. Quoted in Bertaud, *The Army of the French Revolution*, 40.

13. Forrest, *Soldiers of the French Revolution*, 28.

14. Best, *War and Society*, 75.
15. Best, *War and Society*, 30.
16. Alan Forrest, *Conscripts and Deserters: The Army and French Society During the Revolution and Empire* (Oxford: Oxford University Press, 1989), 59.
17. Charles Esdaile, *The Wars of Napoleon* (London: Longman, 1995), 145.
18. Peter Burroughs, "Crime and Punishment in the British Army, 1815–1870," *The English Historical Review* 100, no. 396 (July 1985): 545–571, quotation at 548.
19. Best, *War and Society*, 162 167.
20. Esdaile, *The Wars of Napoleon*, 207.

Two

✯ ✯ ✯

TRAINING AND LEADERSHIP

> Mind the square; you know I often told you that if you ever had to form it from line, in the face of an enemy, you'd be in a d—d ugly way, and have plenty of noise about you… by G-d, if you are once broken, you'll be running here and there like a parcel of frightened pullets!
> —*British Colonel Wallace to the men of his 88th regiment.*[1]

FROM CIVILIAN LIFE TO MILITARY LIFE

The previous chapter discussed the many ways that men found their way into military service. This chapter will discuss the often painful transition from civilian life to military life that hundreds of thousands of European and American men experienced in the nineteenth century. Separation from extended families, sweethearts, and friendship networks was only one part of that transition. The other part involved initiation into the strange and insular world of the military's basic social and tactical units, the regiments, battalions, and companies. The very foreignness of the army and its unfamiliar ways often provided a rude shock to many young men.

Regiments, most often commanded by colonels, formed the largest units with which men normally identified. The regiment provided the insignia men wore on their collars and the unit lore and history that men learned in the mess hall and the barracks. A typical regiment contained between 1,600 and 2,000 men at full strength, although in peacetime a regiment might have as few as 500 to 600 men. Colonels headed a staff of regimental officers for leadership and administration, but the real heart of a regiment was its noncommissioned officers, headed by the nearly omnipotent regimental sergeant major, arguably the single most important individual in the unit. The regimental sergeant major had the most direct contact with the men and he was likely to be the man to whom the troops looked as the final authority on all matters official and unofficial. His word was often law even when it contravened official policy. Even the officers relied upon him for accurate information on the men in the regiment and for translating their general orders into practical instructions to the men.

Regiments in turn formed, in ascending order of size, brigades, divisions, corps, and armies, but these units were usually far too large to place demands on men's loyalties. A unit to which so many thousands of men belonged lost its special status. The division formed the most important operational unit for most nineteenth-century armies because it was sufficiently large to include all three principal arms: infantry, artillery, and cavalry, as well as its own administrative, logistical, and medical functions. Sizes and compositions varied, but typical British divisions in the latter years of the Napoleonic Wars contained approximately 6,000 men each. Under Napoleon, the French combined divisions to form corps in order to provide a greater level of flexibility on campaign. Few men, however, identified closely with the division or the corps.

Instead, men's loyalties moved down through smaller units constituted of men who knew one another intimately. Below the regiments came battalions, the standard tactical unit, and the company. Organizations in peacetime and war often looked very different from one another and each nation had its own way of developing its orders of battle. The Austrian case in the 1830s, however, was fairly typical. Each regiment had three battalions and each battalion had six companies. Each regiment had its own sergeant major (in German, the *Feldwebel*), whose staff included four sergeants, twelve corporals, and eight lance corporals. In peacetime, the number of noncommissioned officers might fall considerably short of the full contingent, while at maximum wartime strength the number of noncommissioned officers might double.[2]

On a personal level, joining the army meant joining a regiment. That progression involved an elaborate process of induction, training, and initiation. This system ultimately aimed to shape civilians into long-term, often life-long, members of the unit. First, however, a man had to make the initial transition from civilian to soldier. Systems of military training often intentionally made the transition from the civilian world to the regiment even more painful. Part of the logic of military training has traditionally revolved around the assumption that a man's civilian belief and support systems have to be torn down before he can be rebuilt in the mold of a soldier. In essence, military training has long presumed that a man must lose his individuality in order to become a functioning part of a larger whole. He must, the theory holds, also lose much of his association to a given locality, ethnicity, or religious affiliation in order to better serve the nation as a whole. For peasants with an extremely localized worldview, this system could cause tremendous hardship and emotional dislocations.

The process of changing men from civilians into soldiers also aimed to make individuals more or less replaceable. Men might leave the army for a wide variety of reasons including desertion, discharge, disease, and death. In some cases, there might be enough notice to train a replacement, but in other cases, most notably on the battlefield, a man might have to step quickly into the position filled by a fallen comrade. Men therefore had to become interchangeable parts within their battalions and regiments.

The relatively low level of skill in the armies of this period facilitated the operational requirements of interchangeability. Forcing men to think and act as cogs in a larger machine helped men to make the mental transitions necessary to develop this component of a soldier's world.

Military training systems have often also involved changing the peasant's religious and moral convictions. Not all soldiers, of course, were religious. The French revolutionary period had an especially well-pronounced current of anticlericalism that either denigrated religion or encouraged men to keep their faith a private matter. Until Napoleon's negotiation of a Concordat between the Catholic Church and the French government in 1801, few units welcomed chaplains and even for many years afterward priests were regarded as unwelcome interlopers. Members of religious minorities often faced official and unofficial pressure as well.

Nevertheless, many men, especially those from traditional communities, took their religious convictions seriously. Convincing such men to take weapons training whose sole aim was to violate the commandment against killing was not always easily accomplished. A man did not have to be religious, moreover, to be appalled by the gambling, smoking, drinking, and womanizing that many men in military units engaged in as a matter of course.

Furthermore, the new soldiers of the period from 1789 to 1870 were often products of "nations" that had not yet developed any important sense of commonality. Men of a given unit, although all from the same political entity, often spoke different dialects or even mutually incomprehensible languages. They often practiced different religions, and sometimes placed their own loyalties to their localities over loyalties to an amorphous nation that few of them really understood. In the most extreme cases, such as the multiethnic states of eastern Europe, men occasionally saw their fellow soldiers as their real enemies by virtue of long-standing acrimonious histories between national sub groups. Men often had little hatred for enemies hundreds, or even thousands, of miles away, but contempt for neighbors born of familiarity often burned brightly.

Asking such men to work together for the greater good of the regiment or the nation presented significant, often insurmountable, challenges. As late as 1944, American soldiers moving through northern France remarked on the "tribalism" they observed. One French resistance member told an American tank operator that his loyalty was not to France, but to his home region. "He spoke Breton and fought for Brittany," observed the American quizzically. "Hitler could keep Normandy for all he cared." Americans also observed Sicilians who spoke about "Italians" as if they were a completely alien entity.[3] Distinctions between neighboring Bretons and Normans, Sicilians and Calabrians, Flemish and Walloons made little sense to Americans, but mattered deeply to Europeans, even as late as the middle of the twentieth century and beyond, as the non-violent division of Czechoslovakia demonstrated after the Cold War.

The extraordinary diversity of European societies thus greatly complicated the process of military training. Some states tried to solve the problem by separating their armies into units based upon ethnic background. The Austrian army thus had distinct German, Slavic, and Hungarian regiments, although German officers often dominated the senior positions in all of these units. This system kept men serving and living alongside people who spoke their language and shared their customs. It did, however, greatly complicate administration. The Austro-Hungarian army eventually developed three bureaucracies that worked in three languages. Austro-Hungarian army regulations recognized eleven languages for the purposes of training: German; Hungarian; Czech; Slovak; Slovene; Croat; Serb; Ruthene; Italian; Polish; and Romanian. Even then there were at least a dozen more large minority groups in the empire who spoke a language unrecognized by the army.

Even in armies that separated their regiments and battalions along ethnic lines, overcoming linguistic and religious problems proved to be a significant barrier. Combining regiments recruited and trained from different ethnic backgrounds into larger formations was no guarantee of success. Brigading regiments from diverse backgrounds did not necessarily ensure their cohesion on the battlefield. Even inside smaller units, sergeants and corporals often had to translate their orders from the national language into several regional languages and dialects before the men could understand and execute them. Getting men from such diverse, and often antagonistic, backgrounds, to see themselves as members of the same army (to say nothing of larger national loyalties) proved to be the much greater challenge. The training process therefore aimed to break these barriers down and force men to see one another first and foremost as comrades whose lives might ultimately depend on their ability to work together.

Armies, therefore, had to do more than train men for battle. They had to reshape their soldiers' entire worldview and often undo much of what a man had learned from his civilian background. As we will see, the armies of nineteenth-century Europe became more than military instruments. They also became national schools, teaching men to think of themselves as French first and Provençal, Breton, or Gascon second. Nationality remained at this point a vague concept that had no necessary pull on men's loyalties. Historian Benedict Anderson's description of nations as "imagined communities" with few organic linkages is not far from the mark.[4] Karl Marx's notion of nations as "false consciousness" struck even many non-Marxists as an apt description of a process still very much in development.

Armies therefore became instruments through which men learned national awareness. In an age before compulsory schooling, it is no exaggeration to say that the army was the most important institution through which governments could directly influence large numbers of their male citizens and subjects. In the army, men learned to recognize national symbols, appreciate a shared (if often constructed) history, and, perhaps most importantly, to appreciate how their nation differed from those on their borders. The simplest way to teach this lesson involved teaching what the nation was not. Thus as the French revolutionary armies moved through Germany and Spain, Germans and Spaniards often concluded that they did in fact share more in common with their fellow nationals than they did with the much more foreign French.

Multiethnic empires like the Russian, Austro-Hungarian, and Ottoman could not even pretend to historical and cultural constructions upon which a large majority of subjects might agree. Instead, these empires treated the army as a bond common to many, if not all, males. If the Austro-Hungarian state could not make a Polish subject forget his "Polishness," for example, it might still be able to use military service to teach him the value of at least coincident loyalty to his ethnic group and the larger empire. In this way, the empire, through its army, might serve as a glue to bind together its dizzying number of ethnic, linguistic, and religious minorities.

Some empires fared better at this process than others. In Great Britain, the army served as a means for Welshmen, Scots, and even Catholic Irishmen to demonstrate loyalty and learn to become "British" by service, if not always by sentiment.[5] The voluntary nature of military service in the British case helped to solidify the relationship between man and state. In the case of the Scots, military service soon became a clear mark of their contribution to the empire and their identification with its goals. Although the higher ranks remained dominated by Englishmen, the British army came to depend on the Scots, who served in numbers disproportionate to their representation in Great Britain as a whole. While never losing their Scottish identity, Scotsmen used military service to become as "British" as any group. They therefore fought for the interests of king and country, but many did so while wearing kilts.

Armies aimed to train men to remain loyal to the state regardless of their concurrent commitments to class, ethnicity, or religion. In the period between the Napoleonic Wars and the Wars of German Unification, the Prussian army worked to develop in its men a concept of *Soldatengeist*, a type of professionalism that emphasized an ultimate loyalty to the state, the monarch, and the army.[6] Whatever a man's personal attachments to his place of birth, the process of professionalization attempted to subsume all identities under the larger identity of soldiering. The Prussians, of course, were not alone in this development. Some version of *Soldatengeist* existed in every army on the continent. Obedience itself therefore became a mark of military professionalism in its own right.

Across Europe, definitions of nationhood came from the center. Elites in London, Paris, and Berlin determined the proper dialect, customs, and history for men to learn. For men from rural, peasant backgrounds, this transition forced a nearly complete reversal of their own traditional identities. Little wonder, then, that many men returned to their native villages after years of military service only to find that they no longer felt that they fit in. The military had become their home; however much they might not have liked it, it had become the only world that many men any longer understood. Through military service they had developed, often through simple osmosis, a national identity not always present in their native communities.

In an era before mass compulsory education, the army often had to teach soldiers basic skills. Few armies thought that their men needed to know how to read and write; literacy was only a goal for officers and most noncommissioned officers. Still, new soldiers needed to learn basic skills and, in some cases, to learn which foot was their left and which was their right. As chapter one demonstrated, many communities saw military conscription as a means to be rid of their least useful elements. Many of these men were among the least educated members of their communities and we can presume that some of them must have had physical and mental deficiencies as well.

After leaving their families, many recruits faced an initial journey to a training camp sometimes hundreds of miles from home. For peasants who had rarely been more than a day's walk from their family's land, even a journey of a few miles could be disorienting. Many men faced much longer journeys as armies often intentionally chose to train soldiers far from their home communities. Such a system gave men an appreciation of the scope of the nation, physically removed them from the influences of their friends and families, and made desertion considerably more difficult as men with strange dialects and customs stood out and were more likely to be reported by locals to the police.

Because soldiers often proved reluctant to fire on crowds from their home communities, separation placed soldiers among strangers, improving the chances that they would fire as ordered in the event that they were called upon to quell a local disturbance.

LINE, COLUMN, SQUARE: THE IMPORTANCE OF DRILL

Once in military service, European men soon learned that their lives were dominated by hours upon hours of marching, formation, and drill. The hours, weeks, and months of drill repeatedly instilled in men's minds the need to obey orders, reflexively and without questioning them. As a result, punishments for even minor infractions on the parade ground could be quite severe. Although drill was one of the most despised forms of military training, officers placed special emphasis on it for a variety of military and nonmilitary reasons explained below. The end result of this system for soldiers' daily lives was an existence based on obedience, discipline, and punishment.

Most officers saw drill as essential to the development of the small and large unit tactics necessary for battlefield success. Infantry tactics in the nineteenth century required military units to execute relatively complex maneuvers with speed and coolness, even when under intense fire. Before the French Revolution, the most common tactical deployment, the line, also required the greatest discipline. Infantry battalions marched into the battle area, then men fanned out into a line two or three rows deep with the individual rows separated by just a few paces. In theory, well-trained and well-disciplined men in these lines could fire by rows, with the front rows on their knees and the back rows standing tall. Alternatively, a front row could fire, then move to the back while the next row advanced and fired its volley. This system, when properly executed by trained soldiers, allowed each row to fire, reload, and repeat the process ad infinitum. As long as the men retained the formation's cohesion and could be supplied with powder and ammunition, they could continue to pour out a nearly continuous rate of fire. The wall of fire that the line produced also served to protect the men of the line from enemy infantry charges.

Line tactics, however, required men to have the discipline to stand and face the fire of the enemy. Lines were particularly vulnerable to artillery, which could break significant holes in the rows and thereby lessen the degree of fire the rows could produce. Once broken up, the lines became vulnerable to cavalry charges as well. Despite these weaknesses, the line remained a favorite formation of officers in the French revolutionary and Napoleonic wars because of the sheer volume of fire it could produce. Clever and competent commanders found ways to protect their lines, thus increasing their efficiency. For example, by carefully placing infantry on the "reverse" or hidden slope of a hill, a commander could protect his infantry from the low-trajectory fire of infantry and artillery.

The line was a poor formation for attacking, as it demanded that men advance at the same pace over inconsistent ground and sometimes in the face of fire from the enemy's line. To resolve this dilemma, the French introduced the infantry column. Already in vogue among commanders in the middle of the eighteenth century, the column saw its perfection in the 1790s with the energetic armies produced by the *levée en masse*. The column involved lining up squares formed by individual battalions or companies to create a formation that was deep and revealed only its narrow front rank to direct enemy fire. Columns could therefore move forward in force while exposing a smaller portion of their fronts to enemy fire.

The column was the formation best-suited for moving men into hostile or contested space with the least risk of mass casualties. The individual component units of the column, moreover, could break off to form smaller attack units or even deploy into line. If the enemy showed signs of wavering, a large-scale attack by a column or columns might provide the mass necessary to deliver a coup de grâce. Well-trained armies could even divide large columns into several smaller ones to attempt an envelopment or a flanking maneuver. Columns also offered a relatively easy way to move large numbers of reinforcements to endangered sectors of the battlefield.

Columns, however, had imperfections of their own. Because a relatively small number of men faced the enemy directly, a column had much less firepower than a line. The extended rectangular shape of columns, moreover, left long flanks exposed to attack on their weakest points. They were especially susceptible to being surrounded by enemy cavalry. Thus infantrymen had to know how to form squares, whose masses of men and steel offered protection against horses. Commanders might also angle the squares to form diamonds depending on the direction of the enemy attack.

A square protected its officers and noncommissioned officers in the center to provide guidance, leadership, and a broad side of a saber to wavering men. Solidly developed squares formed of well-trained men could even move in unison. Ernest and Trevor Dupuy cite an instance during the Peninsular War when the veteran British Light Division formed itself into five individual squares and moved more than two miles while constantly under attack from enemy cavalry.[7] The division retained its cohesion and lost just thirty-five men during its retreat. Of course, the very mass that provided protection against cavalry left the square dangerously exposed to artillery.

To add even greater complexity to the tactical problems of line, column, and square, commanders often tried to combine them. This formation, known as *l'ordre mixte*, involved deploying battalions or companies in column formation on the flanks, sometimes with an additional column placed in the center. To connect the columns, other units deployed in line. When used creatively and effectively, the columns protected the line's flanks, reducing the danger of envelopment by cavalry, while the line provided the needed firepower on the battlefield. *L'ordre mixte* combined the strengths of the line and column while at the same time compensating for their most serious weaknesses.

Although it looked graceful on maps and elegant in theoretical exercises, *l'ordre mixte* often proved to be quite difficult to execute in actual battle conditions. Variations in terrain and the nature of the enemy often complicated the translation of the theory into practice. This formation, moreover, was cumbersome and required well-drilled infantry to make it work. In the hands of an extraordinary commander like Napoleon, it could prove devastating. If not executed with great skill, however, it could lead to chaos and confusion at a critical point in a battle.

The most adept officers therefore had to learn to use instinct and education to know when to deploy units into line, column, square, and *l'ordre mixte*. More importantly, such tactics depended upon having well-drilled infantrymen who could quickly and unhesitatingly execute the movements necessary to shift from one formation to another. Soldiers had to know their place during each transition and in each of the many variations of the basic formations. They had to learn to move quickly, efficiently, and in unison with the other men of their units. They also had to respond to commands despite the noise, smoke, and confusion of the battlefield. Consequently, drill became a constant fixture in the lives of the soldier's training regimen.

Teaching men tactical formations through drill was a long and painstaking process. Many military observers estimated that men needed three years or more of drill before they became disciplined and proficient at the technical aspects of warfare. To prove the point, some of the era's most tactically skilled armies had spent long periods before their most successful campaigns doing little but training. Several French units of the 1805–1807 period, the foundation of Napoleon's famous *Grande Armée*, had spent two years in Boulogne preparing for an invasion of England that never came about. As a consequence, they performed exceptionally well in continental campaigns, providing France with its most dramatic victories of the period. Similarly, the British army that fought with marked skill on the Iberian Peninsula from 1809 to 1813 had been rigorously trained in England for years without interruption.[8] Over time, as armies had to replace the losses of long-term veterans with less well-drilled recruits, their tactical sophistication declined, in many cases so much so that certain tactical maneuvers became impossible for commanders to execute.

Drill also served a number of nonmilitary purposes as well. Most officers, even in the French revolutionary armies, held a reasonably healthy suspicion of their men. Part of this fear was understandable, as they had taught the same men whose lives they made miserable to fire weapons in mass formations with cool efficiency. For their own safety and for the larger good of the unit and the state, soldiers had to be disciplined enough to use their weapons only when, and only against whom, they were ordered to do so. Obedience had to become instinctual and unyielding. Drill helped to instill that obedience at an almost Pavlovian level. In the most ideal cases, the mere presence of an officer or a noncommissioned training officer (like a drill sergeant) inspired an involuntary and reflexive submission.

Discipline also served to keep men with their units when on campaign. Although brutal discipline might impel some men to desert from their units, commanders believed that it kept a great many more where they could be monitored. Men on long marches, officers believed, needed strict discipline and fear of punishment to keep them from falling out of line to seek female companionship, a tavern, an orchard, or a peasant's livestock. For this reason, few armies before the French Revolution dared to let their men forage for food, water, and fodder for fear that they might never return. Instead, armies moved slowly and deliberately to protect long and cumbersome supply wagons.

Drill also had a moral and psychological justification. Commanders in this period attempted to win battles not simply by killing large numbers of men on the other side. Large set-piece battles, even when successful, were costly, far-flung affairs that were hard to control. Maintaining unit cohesion, tactical formations, and supply systems long enough to kill thousands of men while keeping one's own casualties light was a tricky and delicate business. Even victorious armies lost large numbers of veterans who were difficult to replace. For these reasons, long, drawn-out battles, while sometimes necessary, were not the principal objective of the military art. Most commanders sought more effective and cheaper ways to win battles.

The most reliable way to win a cheap victory was to break the enemy and force him to flee. Once enemy formations began to disintegrate they could be pursued and picked apart by advancing infantry and cavalry. Once cut off from avenues of retreat, human survival mechanisms often took over, leading men to surrender with little resistance rather than fight on. Once an army was convinced of its defeat, the battle normally ended. The goal, then, was not only to break the enemy physically, but, more importantly, to break him psychologically, converting well-disciplined infantry into the "parcel of frightened pullets" that Colonel Wallace warned his men about. Flank attacks, encirclements, and surprise could all achieve this task if used cleverly. Panic and the loss of unit cohesion largely explain the period's penchant for astonishingly lopsided victories, such as at Austerlitz in 1805 when an outnumbered Napoleon inflicted 26,000 casualties while taking just 9,000 and at Auerstadt the following year when the French inflicted nearly 50,000 casualties (half of them prisoners) at the cost of 8,000 men lost.

Leo Tolstoy described how such panic, if left unchecked, might spread through a unit. During the 1805 Austerlitz campaign, the failure of officers to keep soldiers informed about actions in their sector led to "an unpleasant impression of mismanagement and misunderstanding" of undetermined origin running through the Russian ranks. The sense of disorientation spread "imperceptibly and irresistibly, like water flowing over a valley" from unit to unit as rumors grew and became increasingly exaggerated. The presence of Austrian allies in the sector led to a natural desire on the part of the Russians to attribute the confusion and uncertainty to failures on the part of the German-speaking units. The end result, according to Tolstoy, was that the Russians arrived on the battlefield already disillusioned by their leadership and their allies and in a poor state to bring the fight to Napoleon, who stood confidently on a hill with "gleaming eyes" fixed "intently" on the Russians in the valley below him.[9]

As Tolstoy showed, panic might fragment a unit before it even saw battle. Strict discipline aimed to keep men in line despite rumors and half-truths. Once in battle, men had to hold their positions reflexively and instinctually. The more men who broke and ran, the greater the chance of the contagion affecting entire units. The panic of even a few men could lead to disaster for an entire army. Officers and noncommissioned officers were not above shooting or running down their own retreating men in order to force the others to stand and fight, but as a policy it was neither popular nor efficient. Using drill and other methods to develop group identities over a span of months or even years offered a much better insurance policy against an army breaking and running in battle.

Drill and its attendant miseries served another important role, that of building *esprit de corps*. Once in battle, men do not fight for ideology or abstract principles, but to protect their own lives and the lives of their comrades. The more cohesive the unit, the more likely soldiers are to fight for one another. They do not have to like one another personally, but they do need to learn to work well together. Like a sports team, the individual players may despise and envy one another, but if they can learn to focus on the task at hand they can develop into an effective organization. As such, abnormally close relationships between soldiers were often discouraged out of fear that loyalty to one individual on the battlefield might supercede loyalty to the entire unit.

Initiation and in-group rituals cemented these small-group dynamics and drill often played an important role. Many initiation and training programs involve unnecessary

Few soldiers, especially soldiers from democratic societies, enjoyed the spit and polish elements of soldiering. Saluting proved to be especially contentious for Americans. During the early months of the Civil War many locally raised units used handshakes instead. Courtesy of the Library of Congress.

and seemingly silly rituals. Fraternities, sports teams, and military organizations alike all ask people wanting to join them to run a literal or figurative gauntlet to demonstrate their willingness to accept the mores of the group. Some aspects of drill served this purpose as well. By having undergone the ritual, an individual distinguished himself from those who either chose not to participate or attempted to do so but had failed. The rituals create an in-group and an out-group. Membership in the unit thus involves more than an external identification. It involves a process of internal identification with comrades as defined by shared experiences.

On the larger level, then, drill separated soldiers from civilians by virtue of giving them a distinct experience and a shared corporate body of knowledge. All soldiers from an army shared in common a method of drill and the knowledge of having endured a strict system for teaching it to them. The ability to drill became one of the first marks of a man's passage through this rite of manhood and professional status. Even if they hated the process by which they learned it, drill provided a visible demonstration of accomplishment and one in which many men took pride. Once a new class of recruits, unfamiliar with drill, arrived in camp, the soldiers became veterans by virtue of the abilities they had acquired more than simply by their time in service.

Furthermore, drill kept men busy and expended their energies. If idle hands are the devil's workshop, then it is easy to imagine the fears officers had of what their young soldiers might do with an excess of free time. Drill was an easy and inexpensive way to keep men busy. It also might wear them out enough to prevent them from getting too drunk or crazy in their off hours. Early morning drill thus played a significant role in keeping the amateur drinkers from going too far the night before.

Consequently, the daily lives of soldiers involved drill, drill, and more drill. Soldiers marched in drenching spring rains, blazing summer sun, biting autumn winds, and frigid winter snow. They marched even after they had worn out their boots and when their uniforms were evidently ill-suited to the weather. Some units drilled as much as eight hours per day, building up their soldiers' physical fitness for future campaigns as they did so, but leading many men to develop lifelong hatreds of their drill instructors and the very sight of a parade field. Still, there was no way around it. To be a soldier meant spending more time drilling than engaging in almost any other activity, sometimes including sleeping.

THE SOLDIER'S DAILY LIFE AND EDUCATION

Like college fraternities, smaller military units such as regiments were exclusive (even if in the latter case they were at the same time involuntary) and somewhat secretive. Also like fraternities, small military units had their own distinct and specific rituals. Units therefore became different from one another by virtue of more than just the insignia on their uniforms. They developed mannerisms that set them apart and had shared customs that only members of the unit would know. Like a special handshake or password between men of a secret society, these rituals rewarded those who had completed training with the soldiers of their units. The more arduous the training and the more elite the unit the more insular the units became.

Membership in certain units therefore carried a special cachet. For some men, this cachet came from the locality where the men were recruited. States often (though not always) tried to recruit as exclusively as possible from a contiguous geographic area like a parish or a town. The theory was that men recruited from a shared region entered military service with an *esprit de corps* and a small-unit dynamic already in place. They would therefore be more willing to endure military service and survive the horrors of the battlefield if they already had strong and deep attachments to their comrades, many of which had been developed from their childhoods. The familiarity of locally recruited units often helped men endure the hardships of the transition to military life and the most arduous periods of military training.

Local recruitment served another important function. If men were all from a given locality, it stood to reason that most of them still had important familial and economic ties to that locality; they therefore had an additional incentive to perform well in military service. If they did not, they or their families could expect to face ostracism from the home community. One study of American soldiers in the Civil War suggests that officers and noncommissioned officers had to be careful in the ways that they ran their units lest their men write home that power had gone to the officer's head. In some cases, men even urged their parents to boycott a soldier's parent's business until he changed his ways.[10]

Other units acquired their cachets from their battlefield exploits. These units attracted men who had either volunteered for military service out of a genuine desire to join the army or men who became increasingly attracted to the military once they got a taste of it. Getting into such units was not always easy and competition to be members of particularly well-known units could be intense. To be sure, many men simply wanted to endure their enlistment requirements with as little fuss as possible, but for those men who wanted more, service in Napoleon's Imperial Guards or Britain's Coldstream Guards regiment (whose motto was "Second to None") could provide a distinction that a man could carry with him for the rest of his life.

Whether in an elite unit or not, many men took pride in soldiering even if they were glad to be done with it. Mastering the art of soldiering carried with it a clear mark of a man's virility and his association with the practitioners of the soldier's craft from the days of antiquity. The combat veteran had survived an ordeal that most men never knew. Being on the same battlefield with Napoleon, Wellington, or Blücher gave a man a lifetime of stories to tell to his friends at the tavern and to his grandchildren around the hearth. Service on a battlefield like Austerlitz, Waterloo, or Gettysburg made him a part of history itself. Like coal miners or steel mill workers, they had accepted a difficult and dangerous way of life and had survived.

Music and Training

Training illiterate soldiers and developing *esprit de corps* depended on using methods familiar to the men. Music often played a critical role in these processes, and musicians were vital elements to the armies of the nineteenth century. Young boys often received their first taste of military life through service as a bugler or a drummer and such boys soon became valued members of their units. Whether children or adults, musicians served several important functions in armies. On chaotic battlefields, loud music often served as the only reliable means of delivering orders because musical instruments could deliver messages more loudly and over a greater distance than could human voices. Buglers could therefore tell men when it was time to advance, when it was time to deploy into a given formation, and when it was time to retire.

Music also performed ceremonial functions in many places. Most formally, music accompanied official functions to lend an air of fanfare to observances such as holidays, reviews, and parades. Large and ostentatious military bands became nearly indispensable for any large unit and many smaller ones. Each regiment in the Austro-Hungarian army had ten full-time, professional musicians assigned to it, supplemented by soldiers with musical ability. A drum major commanded the musicians and a bandmaster assumed responsibility for the musical training and the professional development of the musicians. In battle, the band wore the same uniforms as soldiers and often advanced with their battalions when the latter charged.[11]

The French government placed an equal reliance on bands to "overcome the homesickness and apathy" of military life. Hometowns often hired conductors and musicians, many of them retired soldiers, to accompany men on march and play music familiar to the men. Other units collected money from their meager wages to hire traveling musicians from local areas to march with them for a few miles. They played familiar music to make soldiers feel better about the distances they were placing between their military posts and home. They also played to give the men some pleasant entertainment in their off-duty hours. As one contemporary from Brittany recalled, "By dances in the evening they (the soldiers) forget the fatigue of the road and think themselves close to the fields where they were born."[12]

Music often formed a critical component to the process of educating and politicizing soldiers. Official army bands played anthems that preached the special virtues of the nation, the army, and sometimes individuals like Napoleon. In the French revolutionary period songs often carried themes of anticlericalism, equality, liberty, and the need to export the revolution to oppressed peoples across Europe.[13] Music was therefore an important component to education as well as entertainment. It became an officially sanctioned means to transmit approved political, social, and cultural messages from the government to the men.

Less formally, music provided an eagerly sought source of entertainment in the barracks, camps, and taverns where men spent so much of their time. Like their marching songs, folk songs reminded men of home and helped them to pass the time. They also provided an unofficial occasion that drew men of the unit together. In a time when many men could not read, songs took the place of books, telling stories of adventure, romance, and history. A soldier who could play a flute or a guitar for his comrades increased his social standing in his regiment exponentially. An officer who could serenade ladies on a piano showed his skill as a gentleman.

Music also helped men learn how to perform the necessary maneuvers on the drill field. Historian William McNeill has argued that music and the coordinated rhythmic movement that music inspires played a critical role in creating cohesion in military units. Shared movement, he argues, created a sense of community that in turn led to bonding. Such bonding increased the likelihood of a unit and its constituent individuals standing together in an emergency.[14] Ancient Chinese military texts suggest that this concept had been well understood for centuries. It certainly proved to be valuable to the armies of nineteenth century Europe. More practically, music helped men develop the ability to march in unison and may have even helped some of them to hate the ordeal a little less on occasion.

Military music thus formed an essential element of soldiers' daily lives. Some of these songs soon spread from unit to unit, sometimes changing words and tunes as soldiers adapted them to their own unit's specific circumstances. One of the most famous military songs of this period emerged as the result of a request from the mayor of Strasbourg to one of his musically minded engineers. The mayor believed that the French soldiers marching off to war in 1792 needed a new marching song. The engineer, Claude-Joseph Rouget de Lisle, wrote "Chant de guerre pour l'armée du Rhin," the "War Song for the Army of the Rhine." It was the only song he wrote that ever caught the imagination of his contemporaries, but it became one of the most famous songs ever written.

One of his contemporaries, François Mireur, heard the song in Marseille as he was organizing an army to march to Paris in support of the revolution. The men of Marseille sang the song with such vehemence that it has since become known as "La Marseillaise" in their honor. Its first stanza is one of the most recognizable pieces of music in the world:

> Arise children of the fatherland
> The day of glory has arrived
> Against us tyranny's
> Bloody standard is raised
> Listen to the sound in the fields
> The howling of these fearsome soldiers
> They are coming into our midst
> To cut the throats of your sons and consorts

In 1795, "La Marseillaise" became the French national anthem. During the period of the Restoration, Louis XVIII banned it, as did Napoleon III during the Second Empire, but the song's enormous popularity and the emotion associated with it led to its reinstatement in 1879. In 1887, notably under the auspices of the French Ministry of War, the government decided upon the official version most often heard today.

"La Marseillaise" is a stirring national anthem, complete with bloody images of a vengeful enemy coming "to cut the throats of your sons." It is, however, first and foremost a soldier's song. Its message tells citizens to "form your battalions" to fight against "mercenary phalanxes." A later stanza reads:

> Tremble, tyrants and traitors
> The shame of all good men
> Tremble! Your parricidal schemes
> Will receive their just reward
> Against you we are all soldiers
> If they fall, our young heroes
> France will bear new ones
> Ready to join the fight against you

No political speech could have better expressed why men had joined the French army or what they had hoped to achieve through their military service.

Political Education and Discipline

Political speeches and indoctrination also formed critical components of soldiers' daily lives. In part, this process was an inevitable outgrowth of conscript armies increasingly tied to a nationalist mission. National armies had to understand what they were fighting for and what the nation meant as a whole. The removal of most foreigners from armies during this period underscored an approach to military organization that emphasized forging careful linkages between states, individuals, and societies.

Nevertheless, as we have seen, only a minority of soldiers understood the larger national and international questions on the minds of the mostly middle-class nationalist reformers. The army therefore became a focus of political teachings both to inspire men to accept and even welcome their military service as well as to instill in men a national, patriotic sentiment that they could take back to their hometowns after they left military service. This complete "root and branch" redevelopment of the army aimed, in some cases, to eliminate undue aristocratic and clerical influences.[15]

As with so many other reforms in this period, the main impetus came from France. In 1793, Valmy and Jemappes hero General Charles Dumoriez surrendered the forts under his command and threw in his lot with the Austrians. Dumoriez acted partly out of blind ambition, believing that he had done as much with the French army as he could, and partly out of a sense of disenchantment with the same revolution he had done so much to safeguard. He was not alone; at the time of his change of allegiance France had less than 2,000 of its pre-revolutionary officers still in the nation's service. The increasing fire with which the revolution burned chased out thousands of France's aristocratic officers.

Dumoriez's act of treason shocked revolutionary France and convinced the Jacobin government that the army itself needed close political monitoring. Aristocrats and senior officers came in for the most scrutiny. In 1794 the Jacobins purged most of those aristocrats who remained or made their lives sufficiently uncomfortable to convince them to emigrate. This process created a young officer corps that was mostly middle class, but also able to boast that one in four officers was of peasant origin. By 1794 only 5 percent of the French army's soldiers had experience in the French Royal Army. More than 20 percent of the army's generals were former sergeants.[16]

Removing the aristocrats, however, did not solve all of the army's problems. A domestic revolt in the Vendée in western France reminded revolutionary leaders that not all Frenchmen fully supported the revolution and its goals. Because the army had to serve as the premier instrument of national defense from both enemies abroad and reactionaries at home, the political reliability of the army became a question of paramount concern. Officers had to develop a mentality that made them first among equals. They could not use their rank and power to form a new aristocracy that might replace the one the revolutionaries had just purged. They had to lead by patriotic action, not class interest.

To control the officer corps, the French government relied on the promotion system. By carefully monitoring the political views of their officers, senior French officials could favor for promotion those men most loyal to the government and the ideals of the revolution. Relatively minor deviations from fashionable political ideologies in Paris might be forgiven in a man of talent, but excessive reactionary beliefs would almost surely hold up a man's promotion. Because the political winds shifted so violently so quickly many officers learned to stay as far from political questions as possible. Others learned to play the game, following political trends and making political alliances.

With aristocrats and their predictable political preferences losing their grip on the officer corps across Europe, states took a greater interest in the political beliefs of their officers. Some, like Great Britain, tried to develop a nonpartisan ethos while others, like Prussia, made political faithfulness a prerequisite for advancement. In France the problem of political reliability remained more controversial than anywhere else, leading to numerous scandals including the infamous Dreyfus Affair and the "fiches" scandal of the early twentieth century, to be covered in future chapters.

Officers were not the only problem. Soldiers, the second part of the political matrix, had to show no loyalty to their officers or to their units. Their loyalty had to be first and foremost to the nation. The French government assigned military magistrates to units to distribute revolutionary newspapers and lead classes on the issues of the day. Jacobin clubs became common in French units, with the men encouraged to debate their "brother" officers. Revolutionary discipline aimed to win over men's minds in the hopes of building morality and national patriotism. The more the army developed these traits, reformers hoped, the less the army would have to resort to old-style discipline and the better a fighting force it could become. Its performance under Napoleon suggests that many of these reforms bore fruit.

After the Napoleonic period, the focus of education became increasingly professional. Armies, especially their officer corps, worked to build an ethos of service that stressed loyalty to the government and nonpartisan politics as essential components. Of course, officers still held political (most often conservative) preferences, but they often took pride in not acting on those preferences. Throughout the nineteenth century and into our own time, soldiers acted from the principle of obedience to legally and properly constituted political authority. This attitude helps to explain the loyalty of the overwhelming majority of men during the continental crises of 1848 as well as during numerous smaller incidents.

One of the most fundamental changes a man noticed upon his entry into a regiment was the nearly absolute loss of personal freedom. His life now rested in the hands of virtually omnipotent military professionals who had already completed the transition from the civilian world to the army. These men had nearly limitless authority to inflict punishments of all sorts. Punishments varied tremendously, depending on the crime committed and the sentiments of local and national authorities. In cases involving the most serious and sensitive charges, soldiers normally were tried by military courts-martial. Commanders most often turned a soldier over to the formal military justice system to face charges brought by civilians such as rape, destruction of private property, and theft. Only in rare cases did soldiers face the civilian court system. These charges usually involved the destruction or theft of property. The notoriety of nineteenth century prisons in general, and military prisons in particular, often served as their own deterrents.

Much more commonly, offenses and punishments were handled inside the regiment. Officers held an authority to punish that was "largely unchecked" by any civil power or court.[17] Keeping punishments inside the unit allowed commanders to issue disciplinary action without having to admit to the larger system that their leadership had failed. A wide variety of punishments existed, from flogging to confinements to a trip behind the barracks with a sergeant. Other, more informal punishments existed as well. Some men actually preferred these punishments because without official charges they could not lose rank or pay beyond nominal fines. Men whose colleagues found them unsatisfactory faced a variety of physical and verbal abuses and, in extreme cases, ostracism. Forcing a man out of his unit often involved a ritualistic process of "drumming him out." Removing the buttons and insignia from his uniform symbolically cut his ties to the unit. The system motivated other men to improve their performance in order to avoid the humiliations associated with being drummed out.

The number of offenses in the regiment and the power of regimental officials to dispense punishments meant that officers and sergeants had to learn to use that power judiciously or risk losing the respect of their men. For most soldiers, temptations abounded. The army did not just remove a man's liberty. It changed everything about him, from the clothes he wore to the food he ate. Many young, homesick men looked for the first chance to desert and return home. Commanders often had to be more lenient than the law demanded to return these men to camp. Treating such boys in the same manner as a trained veteran who fled in the face of the enemy simply made no sense, although some men might be flogged or otherwise punished to set an example.

In many cases, the crimes committed by soldiers were similar to those committed by civilians. Thus, military courts, just like their civilian counterparts, had to punish men who stole, raped, and murdered. But many other military offenses had no direct civilian analogues. These offenses were more commonly violations of a unit's disciplinary code than violations of a society's judicial code. They included sleeping on duty, going absent without leave (a crime that became the more serious charge of desertion if a man stayed away too long), and insubordination. Putting soldiers through a civilian judicial system to adjudicate these offenses struck most observers as imprudent.

Combined with the desires of the army to regulate its own affairs without civilian interference, the separate nature of military justice led to a clear and distinct separation between the military and civilian justice systems. Thus, the major reforms of the civilian justice system, led by Great Britain's Jeremy Bentham (1748–1832), had little impact on the military system. Bentham's arguments that criminal justice should follow rational, scientific, and utilitarian principles fell largely on deaf military ears. Instead, military justice remained quite distinct and was the preserve of senior officers and unit commanders.

Military officers understood the problem of justice as an extension of the need to enforce discipline in their units. Given the low opinion in which most officers held their men, many of them ascribed incidents of military indiscipline to being functions of the "moral degeneracy" of soldiers' lower-class origins. "Men of loose and unstable principles must constitute a *very* large element in our army," commented a British officer in charge of prisons in 1869. "Poverty forces these characters to enlist, and exposed to the low temptations of our garrison towns, they naturally revert to their former habits."[18] A small number of army reformers were more sympathetic, arguing that the abrupt transition from civilian life to the highly regimented world of the military caused disruptions in the lives of young men, leading many into petty acts of insubordination that should not be punished in the same manner as serious crimes.

As a result, most military justice systems developed two tiers. Serious crimes against persons and property were handled by official courts-martial as were crimes that threatened unit cohesion like desertion in the face of the enemy or inciting disobedience to orders. Courts-martial had the authority to impose a death sentence for the most heinous of offenses, but they also had a range of other options that included sending men to corrective units in inhospitable areas. These "condemned corps" were usually to be found in unhealthy locations like West Africa. One of France's most notorious prisons was located on the appropriately named Devil's Island off the coast of French Guyana. Courts-martial could also impose sentences of flogging, usually conducted in the full view of the men of the condemned soldier's regiment in order to, in the French phrase, "encourage the others" to behave in line with their officers' expectations.

Smaller offenses were usually handled less formally at the battalion or regimental level. Drunkenness and absences without leave were the two most common misdemeanors in a typical unit. Officers had a virtually unlimited range of options to punish their soldiers for such transgressions. They included restricting men to barracks; placing them in solitary confinement (often in rooms without windows or outside light); restricting men to diets of salted water and moldy bread; removing a man's alcohol ration; forcing men to parade in full dress uniform; and instituting fines. Officers could also order floggings without the sanction of a court-martial, but the cruelty of the system and its apparent inability to correct minor transgressions led to public condemnation of it in Britain and elsewhere. Over time the number of lashes an officer could order became restricted and the practice itself fell into disuse in many (though by no means all) units.

Soldiers had few official means to redress the often capricious and cruel ways that sometimes sadistic officers punished their men. Many soldiers deserted, especially those men assigned to overseas units with enticing frontiers. Deserting got men out of their units, but it also came with the risk of more punishments if the men were caught. Most men therefore had little choice but to accept their punishments, however they felt about their ultimate justice.

SPECIALIZATION AND WEAPONS TRAINING

The next chapter will deal with weaponry and its technical aspects. Here we will be concerned with how men learned to use those weapons. Although it might seem unusual or counterintuitive, few soldiers in this period received much training in marksmanship. Until the middle of the nineteenth century, smoothbore muskets were so inaccurate that it hardly repaid the effort to teach men to fire at individual targets. The limited number of weapons, spare parts, gun oil, and even ammunition also argued against spending too many hours on marksmanship training. More commonly, men learned to fire weapons in volley because armies presumed that a mass of fire might compensate for the inaccuracy of the weapons themselves. Men thus spent much more time practicing the numerous steps required to load their weapons than they did the steps required to aim and fire them.

Training in small arms thus revolved more around when to fire the weapons than the selection of targets. The famous American dictum that urged men to "wait until you see the whites of their eyes" has become a symbol of American courage, but it also had the more practical effect of reminding men not to fire at targets until they came into range. The time required to reload smoothbores further emphasized the need to teach men not to fire prematurely lest they give the enemy time to advance unopposed. Volleys were most effective if men fired in unison and on the orders of an officer or sergeant. In the heat of battle, fire discipline often broke down and men fired as quickly as they could reload, but the well-timed volley remained the ideal.

The bayonet, by contrast, absorbed a great deal of weapons training for many men in this period. Inexpensive to practice, bayonet training theoretically inured men to the idea of killing by repeating the steps required to push cold steel into another human being. Originally conceived as a defensive weapon to protect infantry from enemy cavalry charges, the bayonet became a preferred offensive weapon of the French revolutionary armies.[19] By inspiring their men to finish battles with the bayonet, French officers hoped to spread a formidable reputation for their units and instill fear in their enemies, thus increasing the chances of French foes breaking and panicking on the battlefield.

The bayonet charge was to be the final phase of the battle. With enemy formations broken by effective use of artillery and infantry, the way became clear for a decisive push. The bayonet's job was to deliver that final contribution to victory. Relatively simple to use, it fostered a warrior culture and gave meaning to the phrase "driving the point home." The overlap between a presumed revolutionary warrior ethos and the bayonet as a weapon of the revolution created an ideological justification for what was at base a tactical necessity. The bayonet, however, found a home in all of the European and American armies of this period, showing that more than the revolutionary ethos was at work.

Several European armies in the latter years of the Napoleonic period experienced increasing difficulty in training new recruits to form column, square, and line. Without precise formations, the inaccuracy of small arms rendered them much less useful. The bayonet, however, still had utility. Austria was among the states that concluded after 1815 that the firing line did not suit mass conscript armies. Rather, the Austrian and other armies aimed to win battles by shock tactics using "attacks pushed home at bayonet-point by closed formations."[20] Until the widespread introduction of rifles in the 1850s, commanders preferred to win with mass and steel rather than rely on the inaccuracies of bad weapons in the hands of mediocre marksmen.

Before the battle could reach the bayonet phase, however, armies had to rely upon specialized soldiers, many of whom were volunteers. The most innovative of these specialized units were the skirmishers, or light infantry. Such men moved in front of their formations in "clouds," pairs, or as individuals. Their mission involved "anything which required daring and initiative" and was described by a contemporary officer thus:

> When an army advances in the presence of the enemy the Light Infantry are in front; retreating, they are in the rear; foraging, they protect; landing, they are the first to jump out of the boats; embarking, they are the last to leave the shore.[21]

Tactically, skirmishers acted like twentieth-century paratroopers, moving inside and behind enemy formations to spread confusion and attack targets of opportunity. Most commonly, skirmishers aimed to harass enemy formations by opening fire from concealed locations. Shooting from several angles, they might cause a panic in the other side's line or column. They might also target individual enemy officers or soldiers. Enemy artillery batteries were common targets as were supply wagons and the other side's skirmishers.

Almost exclusively done by volunteers, skirmishing required a high degree of specialization and training. Skirmishers operated in open space normally with no officer or sergeant nearby to give them orders. They thus had to be men not prone to panic, able to operate on their own initiative, and, perhaps most importantly, men who could be trusted to return to their units. The French had the best early success with skirmishers because they tended to have the most highly motivated men. Voluntary French National Guard units, the most ideologically committed to the revolution and its principles, often contributed large numbers of men to light infantry units. Other armies copied the idea of light infantry with varying levels of success. In general, armies formed of volunteers or highly motivated conscripts, like the British and the Prussian, had the best skirmishers after the French. Armies with the most draconian recruitment and disciplinary systems, like the Russians and the Austrians, had less-effective skirmishers.

Whether called skirmishers, Jägers, Hussars, Rangers, or Grassins, they were a true elite whose training did not always mirror that of common infantry. Because they depended upon the accuracy of their fire, skirmishers received the best small arms and the most regular weapons training. Indeed, in many armies they were the only men trained to hit specific targets at a variety of ranges. They also needed training in screening an army, moving separately through a contested battle space, and protecting their own unit's resources from enemy skirmishers. Skirmishers became the forerunners of the modern special forces units that all sophisticated armies have come to rely upon.

Artillery formed another specialization in early nineteenth century armies. Because of the highly technical aspects of the "queen of battle," artillery officers tended more often to be of middle-class origin. Even the most traditional armies recognized that the nobility lacked the requisite mathematical and scientific knowledge to lead artillery units. Ballistics, meteorology, and geography all figured into the art and science of ranging and sighting field guns. It was difficult and intricate work that required a cool head and a calculating mind.

The mental work of artillery units belonged to the officers, but the physical challenges of life in an artillery unit belonged to the enlisted men. Heavy and cumbersome guns and ammunition wagons had to be manhandled onto the battlefield. Horse artillery added mobility and glamour to the branch, but even then most of the hard chores still had to be done by manpower. Artillery service involved working through smoke, heat, and noise that was unusual in a relatively quiet age. Although service in the artillery was statistically safer than service in the infantry, artillery batteries could easily find themselves the targets of the enemy's light infantry and, because of their responsibility to stay with their relatively immobile guns, often found themselves dangerously exposed.

The rifle, with its vast increases in range and accuracy, forced a change in infantry training at midcentury. Officers wrestled with exactly how to implement the new weapon into existing systems. With marksmanship now possible for almost any soldier, armies switched the rifle's focus from a weapon for skirmishers to a weapon for the entire army. Armies could now effectively create entire units of sharpshooters. Armed with a rifle, even the worst shots in a battalion could still be more accurate than the best shots of the Napoleonic period who carried smoothbores. Marksmanship therefore became a focal point of weapons training. The rapid yet calm process through which men loaded their weapons became central as well. The more bullets a man could load, the more he could fire.

The advent of the rifle did not eliminate the need for the bayonet. Commanders, like Robert E. Lee at Gettysburg, still aimed to finish battles with a charge. Bayonets, moreover, retained their role in the tactical defense, protecting infantry from enemy cavalry and infantry attacks. Most commanders were loathe to abandon the bayonet and the martial spirit that training with it allegedly instilled. The sight of a battalion of men marching in formation with the sun glistening off their bayonets continued to hold a fascination for many military professionals well into the twentyth century.

As this chapter hopefully has made clear, senior commanders cared relatively little for the individuality of European soldiers. In fact, they aimed to remove individuality through a rigorous and intentionally disruptive process of training and initiation that tried, insofar as possible, to create soldiers that were replaceable and interchangeable. Underlying these beliefs, of course, was a presumption that other factors, most notably senior leadership and mastery of technology, were the keys to battlefield victory.

To summarize, from 1789 to 1870 two important changes in the nature of training occurred. First, armies came to play a key role in developing a sense of national consciousness. Through military training and national service, men came to understand on a personal level the value of the nation and their service to it. Not all men agreed, of course; to many soldiers, military service represented an unwelcome interruption of their civilian lives. Still, even in these men the years of exposure to military training and its methods created a sense of nationalism. This process remained incomplete by 1870, but it formed an important basis to military training in the following decades.

Second, military service, especially after 1848, developed an important emphasis on professionalism. As war and military service grew correspondingly more technical, military service became the preserve of men who served for long periods of time and dedicated themselves to education and specialization. Loyalty to state, regime, and nation formed crucial components to this developing sense of professionalism. Consequently, by 1870 professional armies with an emerging national sense had become the rule in Europe. As the events of that year soon demonstrated, the mix, when combined with new weapons, proved a dangerous and heady brew.

NOTES

1. Quoted in Rory Muir, *Tactics and the Experience of Battle in the Age of Napoleon* (New Haven, CT: Yale University Press, 1998), 74. A pullet is a young chicken.
2. Darko Pavlovic, *The Austrian Army 1836–1866 (1): Infantry* (Oxford: Osprey, 1999), 7.
3. See Peter Schrijvers, *The Crash of Ruin: American Combat Soldiers in Europe During World War II* (New York: New York University Press, 1998), 243.
4. Benedict Anderson, *Imagined Communities* (London: Verso, 1983).
5. For an interesting case study, see Peter Karsten, "Irish Soldiers in the British Army, 1792–1922: Suborned or Subordinated?" *Journal of Social History* 17 (1): 31–64.
6. Dennis Showalter, *The Wars of German Unification* (London: Arnold, 2004), 81.
7. R. Ernest Dupuy and Trevor Dupuy, *The Encyclopedia of Military History from 3500 B.C. to the Present* (2nd. rev. ed.) (New York: Harper and Row, 1986), 735.
8. Muir, *Tactics*, 75.
9. Leo Tolstoy, *War and Peace* (New York: Modern Library, 2002), 301–305.
10. Gerald Linderman, *Embattled Courage: The Experience of Combat in the American Civil War* (New York: Free Press, 1987) and his *The Mirror of War: American Society and the Spanish-American War* (Ann Arbor: University of Michigan Press, 1974) provide wonderful examples of the close connections between units and the communities from which they were recruited.
11. Pavlovic, *The Austrian Army*, 21–22.
12. Jean-Paul Bertaud, *The Army of the French Revolution: From Citizen-Soldier to Instrument of Power* trans. by R. R. Palmer) (Princeton, NJ: Princeton University Press, 1988), 125.
13. Bertaud, *The Army of the French Revolution*, 139.
14. William H. McNeill, *Keeping Together in Time: Dance and Drill in Human History* (Cambridge, MA: Harvard University Press, 1995).
15. Alan Forrest, *The Soldiers of the French Revolution* (Durham, NC: Duke University Press, 1990), 24.
16. Bertaud, *The Army of the French Revolution*, 169–182.
17. Showalter, *The Wars of German Unification*, 19.
18. Peter Burroughs, "Crime and Punishment in the British Army, 1815–1870," *The English Historical Review* 100, no. 396 (July 1985): 545–571, quotations at 547 and 548. Emphasis in original.
19. Bertaud, *The Army of the French Revolution*, 155.
20. Showalter, *The Wars of German Unification*, 55.
21. Both quotations are from Muir, *Tactics*, 52.

Three

✶ ✶ ✶

WEAPONS, UNIFORMS, AND DAILY NEEDS

> Hundred of bodies, drenched with fresh blood, of men who two hours before had been filled with various lofty or pretty hopes and desires, now lay with stiffened limbs in the damp, flowering valley separating the bastion from the trench, and on the even floor of the mortuary chapel in Sebastopol. Hundreds of men crawled, twisted, and groaned, with curses and entreaties on their dry lips, some among the corpses in the flowery valley, others on stretchers, cots, and on the bloody floor of the hospital.
> —*Leo Tolstoy describing the effects of rifles on Russian charges at Sebastopol during the Crimean War (1854–1856).*[1]

TECHNOLOGICAL CHANGE AND INDUSTRIALIZATION

Most of the significant changes in weapons technology in the period from 1789 to 1870 had their origins in the preceding decades. Engineers and gunsmiths had worked out the basic innovations in nineteenth-century weapons design years before their general implementation in European and American armies. During the nineteenth-century these changes reached fruition and caused exponential transformations in the ranges, rates of fire, and accuracies of weapons. Developments in technology, moreover, rapidly outpaced changes in tactics, operations, and strategy. Neither soldiers nor their commanders fully understood these changes and how they came to impact soldiers' daily lives, often leading to tremendous bloodshed on the nineteenth-century battlefield.

The armies of 1789 were not armed with radically different weapons from those of Frederick the Great or Louis XIV, despite the theoretical work designers had already done to improve basic artillery and infantry weapons. By 1870, however, all armies that pretended to great power status had radically updated their stocks of weapons. Nineteenth-century armies used weapons that represented several generations of technological leaps from those in use in decades past. As a result, the armies of 1870 employed small arms and artillery pieces with vastly increased lethality at correspondingly longer ranges. Armies, like the Austrian army of 1866, that failed to keep pace with these developments fell behind with a consequent effect on their soldiers' chances at survival on the battlefield.

The mere possession of better weapons, however, has never offered a guarantee of victory on the battlefield. Several armies carried advanced weaponry into battle yet managed to fritter away their technological advantage through poor leadership or a doctrine that had not evolved to take advantage of the new technologies. Better weaponry did, however, put one army at a distinct advantage over its opponents. It might also compensate for poor decisions made on the battlefield. More advanced weapons, in other words, gave an army more room for error and a better chance to recover from errors already made, but weapons, no matter how advanced, did not decide battles or wars by themselves.

From the perspective of the average soldier, new weapons came with the attendant need to master them. All armies faced steep learning curves to introduce new weapons into their armies, train or retrain men in their use, divine how the new technology would impact future battlefield movements, and adjust their doctrine and tactics accordingly. Veteran soldiers might have faced this process several times in their careers. Deciding on new weapons and incorporating them into field units involved a mixture of forethought, experience, and a reading of tea leaves that was less scientific than intuitive. Some armies did better than others. Those that failed to adapt often found themselves relegated, at least temporarily, to the second tier of European powers.

All soldiers in this period had to train and fight within the framework of these rapid changes in weapons. The high level of casualties in the American Civil War and other conflicts was partly a function of relatively inexperienced men working with new and powerful weapons whose military consequences commanders and soldiers often badly misunderstood. The men themselves often failed fully to grasp the ways to use the new weapons to greatest tactical and operational advantages. Shifts in technology often necessitated shifts in mentality that proved difficult, especially for old-dog veterans resistant to learning new tricks.

Building a better weapons system in a workshop did not lead, of course, to its immediate implementation. Most weapons required decades to move from design to widespread use and many weapons failed to the make the transition at all. But combining entrepreneurial and artisanal know-how with the emergent manufacturing technologies of the industrial revolution created a dynamic system capable of producing large numbers of almost anything, including weapons. Factories, moreover, could produce weapons, ammunition, and spare parts to exacting standards. The so-called American system of mass production enabled the production of weapons with the use of tools and dies that allowed for a precise interchangeability of parts.[2] Eli Whitney of cotton gin fame played a key role in these developments after he decided to turn his hand to arms manufacturing.

As a result of industrialization, for the first time in military history, large numbers of weapons were produced by factories rather than by artisans. The result was arms production on a scale and scope theretofore unimaginable. With a continental and worldwide capitalist system that provided funding and technical expertise, innovative industrialists built a weapons industry in Europe and the United States that provided armies with a wide variety of the weapons choices. In 1810 the German industrialist Friedrich Krupp started what became one of the most successful of these firms. Other firms followed suit in almost every nation with an industrial base. Operating in a free enterprise environment, in peacetime they sold their goods to almost any nation able to pay the bills. Driven by profit during an era of great (and small) power competition, the best firms made enormous profits which they in turn invested in the development of new factory equipment and the production of the next generation of weapons.

As a result of this burgeoning industrial manufacturing sector, weapons systems changed much more quickly than had been possible previously. But changing an army's standard small arm or artillery piece always involved difficult negotiations and contentious decisions. Adopting new weapons was an expensive process and budgets did not always allow armies to buy the kinds of weapons they most wanted. Governments with competing military, social, and economic demands often decided that their armed forces could wait a few years before acquiring new weapons, especially if the era was one of relative peace. Neither did armies welcome the idea of saving money by buying newer weapons in smaller quantities and giving them only to select units. Such a process left armies with many calibers of ammunition and many different spare parts to stock, vastly complicating already inconsistent supply systems.

Generals, moreover, tend by nature to be conservative. They dislike discarding a tactical and training system that they have spent years developing simply because of an (often still unproven) innovation in weapons technology. As a result, they tend to resist making major changes until the new system has had a chance to prove its efficacy on the battlefield. The more complicated the technology, the more reluctant senior officials normally were to change. New technologies often required new mind-sets that did not meet the wishes of superannuated senior officers who desired little more than to hold onto their sinecures for as long as possible. All officers understood that new weapons offered no panaceas for their army's ills and most developed a healthy suspicion of the smooth-talking arms salesmen.

Moreover, as discussed earlier, most officers held their men in relatively low esteem. Many of them thus preferred undemanding weapons systems because they doubted the abilities of their own men to master complex ones. Better, they argued, to have a simple system for simple men than a complex system that might break down in the fog and friction of combat due to the incompetence of the men charged with carrying it out. New weapons might appear elegant and glitzy in carefully staged demonstrations, but few generals were willing to risk their armies and their own reputations on the gamble that their men could perform half as well when the bullets began to fly.

Investing in new weapons systems, moreover, did not always pay dividends. A nation might invest heavily in a particular weapon only to find that it had become obsolete in the time it took fully to integrate the weapon into the army's tactics and doctrine. The laborious process of convincing parliaments and monarchs to authorize the funds for another round of rearming would therefore have to begin all over again. Generals who constantly appeared before appropriations bodies claiming that their rivals had trumped the technologies for which they had pleaded just a few years earlier could end up sounding like Chicken Little, always warning that the sky was falling. Generals had to reserve their own moral and political capital for weapons systems that they believed they truly needed.

To add a final complication to this process, a weapon might be superior in some areas, but not in all areas, forcing commanders to decide which aspects of military technology they most valued. To cite just one example among many, the Prussians introduced the revolutionary needle gun beginning in 1841. Although faster loading than the commonly used weapons in Europe at the time, the needle gun had a shorter range and less stopping power due to the escape of gasses at the breech. The Prussians accepted the rifle, but had to make corresponding adaptations to their doctrine and tactics in order to take advantage of the weapon's positive traits while compensating for its negative traits.

To follow the example further, the decision to adopt the needle gun had direct impacts on soldiers. Above all, Prussian soldiers had to learn to practice "fire discipline." They had to learn not to fire their weapons at targets beyond the effective needle gun range of 600 to 650 yards. Opponents with longer-ranged weapons could therefore stand off at 700 yards or more and fire on the Prussians without them being able to respond. Because of the limited range of their rifles, Prussian soldiers had to overcome the human desire to fire back in self-defense. They also had to learn to advance into the teeth of enemy fire in order to close the range and make their weapons effective. The tactics, of course, came with attendant changes to systems of training.

These problems notwithstanding, all of the nations of Europe invested heavily in weapons lest they fall too far behind their rivals. Prussia's rapid victories over Denmark in 1864 and Austria in 1866 demonstrated the perils of going to war with obsolete weapons. The inability of smaller states to keep up with the technological capabilities of larger states helps to explain military support for the unifications of Germany and Italy and the amalgamation of the Austro-Hungarian Empire. If there was not necessarily safety in numbers, at least there were larger budgets and greater industrial resources.

From Muskets to Rifles

The French revolutionary armies went to war armed primarily with flintlock muskets, a technology that had been the centerpiece of armies for more than a century. As its name implies, the flintlock ignited gunpowder by the striking of a flint onto a piece of steel to send a shower of sparks down upon a flash pan. Flintlocks represented a significant step forward from the matchlocks they replaced because the flint could produce a spark in inclement weather. The barrel of the musket was smooth, facilitating the rapid loading of ammunition that normally consisted of round balls of iron or steel.

Easy to load, flintlocks had both the virtue and the drawback of being notoriously inaccurate. Upon firing, the ball rattled inside the barrel and flew out at an unpredictable angle. Such a weapon was less than ideal for precision marksmanship, as not even the best shots in the army could reliably expect to hit a man-sized target at ranges as close as fifty yards. Nevertheless, as discussed in chapter two, the inaccuracy of the musket obviated any need to teach men marksmanship and thus greatly simplified infantry training for the vast majority of soldiers; quantity of fire mattered most on the battlefield. The heavy projectile (later versions of the British "Brown Bess" smoothbore fired a .73 caliber round) ensured that if the round did find a human target it would knock it down and most likely keep it down.[3]

The flintlock was a relatively simple weapon, but its simplicity did not guarantee availability to all soldiers who needed it. The massive expansion of armies in the period from 1789 to 1815 struck a European continent that was still largely agricultural. To the extent that it was a manufacturing society, the modes of production were still predominantly artisanal. The end result was a demand for weapons that nascent industries could not always match. In September 1793, one French regiment marched to war with just 600 muskets and an astonishing 200 rounds of ammunition for its 2,600 men. Recruits from the La Rochelle district went to war with no weapons at all.[4] The lack of proper gun oil led to weapons wearing out prematurely, especially in the hands of men who had only a rudimentary knowledge of how to use and care for them. Soldiers therefore often received inadequate training in the use of the very weapons they carried with them into battle.

In many cases, men brought their own weapons to war with them. Although this system vastly complicated supply, it came with notable advantages. Not the least of these advantages was the reduced cost to the state of arming its soldiers. More importantly, many of the privately owned weapons were markedly superior to those made in state armories and private factories. Individual weapons were more likely to be rifles instead of muskets. Rifles, unlike muskets, contained a barrel with a twisted groove cut on the inside. The result was a projectile that, when heated, expanded and fit snugly into the groove. The projectile thus spun, rather than rattled, out of the barrel, providing stability in flight and vastly better accuracy and range.

Privately owned weapons were more likely to be rifles because their owners used them for sport or for acquiring food. Rifles had been in common private use in western Germany beginning around 1600. German emigration to Pennsylvania brought the weapon to North America where it proved to be well adapted for use in heavily forested wilderness. Although never used in large numbers, the rifle demonstrated its military utility in the French and Indian Wars (1756–1763) in the hands of men accustomed to relying upon it to eat. If they could hit squirrels and turkeys with their rifles, they could surely hit a brightly uniformed French or British soldier. As Americans went west, they took the rifle with them, where it soon adopted the name Kentucky Rifle to reflect its frontier pedigree and identity.

The rifle's longer range and greater accuracy made it an evidently "better" small arm than the smoothbore musket. Nevertheless, it came with significant disadvantages. Because the rifle's accuracy depended upon a snug fit between the projectile and the groove, the ammunition had to be custom made and pushed carefully down the barrel with a wooden or iron ramrod. Loading times were therefore longer and the entire loading process had to be completed with greater intricacy. In the hands of inexperienced soldiers, the ramrods themselves could warp the barrels. Soldiers, moreover, now needed training in another crucial step necessary to maintain their battlefield effectiveness. Rifles also normally lacked the capability to carry bayonets because they were designed for hunting, not warfare, and turkeys rarely charged at hunters en masse.

Rifles were also more expensive to manufacture because the grooves had to be cut precisely by expert craftsmen. Failure to bore the barrels uniformly rendered ammunition either too big or too small. If the barrels were too small, by even a few millimeters, then the ammunition would not fit down the barrel. If the barrels were too big, then the projectile would not properly expand to produce the desired spinning effect. Thus, there were plenty of good reasons for even forward-minded commanders to recommend the retention of the smoothbore musket, despite the inability of most soldiers to hit the proverbial broad side of a barn with it.

The French and Indian Wars and the American War for Independence showed European observers the value of rifles in the hands of their owners. Their success in America led to their slow incorporation into European armies where elite units such as the German *Jägers* already knew of their capabilities. Providing rifles to skirmishers seemed a worthwhile expenditure and made the most tactical sense, as skirmishers had the most evident need for the added accuracy. Skirmishers were the closest European analog to the individual frontiersmen who made such deadly use of the rifle in America. The German *Jäger* battalions were the first to include large numbers of rifles, followed by British light units and Napoleonic *chasseurs à pied*. At Waterloo, a British rifle brigade virtually destroyed three French artillery brigades single-handedly, a feat impossible to conceive for musketeers.

Mass incorporation of rifles had to await the full flourishing of the industrial revolution. Industrialization greatly reduced the cost of manufacturing the guns themselves as well as the ammunition, oils, spare parts, and ramrods necessary to sustain the system. Manufacturing parts and ammunition by industrial methods also guaranteed uniformity of size, shape, and quality. Once armies were convinced of the rifle's utility and states authorized the funding, factories could also rebore muskets to convert them into rifles. Most importantly, industrialization vastly increased the amount of materiel that firms could produce. Firms like Krupps, which initially focused on civilian production, quickly converted to weapons manufacturing as a large, or even exclusive, aspect of their businesses.

Industry also reduced the costs of innovation and experimentation. Accordingly, the 1840s to the 1870s witnessed more changes in the nature of weaponry than had the entire previous century. The most important innovation of the period involved the development of better ammunition. The Minié ball, developed by a French officer but first introduced into the British army in 1851, contained four (later three) grooves, a conical shape, and a hollow end. On firing, the grooves heated to form flanges that expanded into the grooves of the rifle. Rifles had now found the ideal ammunition, although Minié balls still had to be rammed down the muzzle. A percussion cap contained the fulminate, thus removing the need for the less reliable flints, which normally had to be changed after about twenty uses. Minié rifles dominated the battlefield in the American Civil War and were responsible for the majority of that conflict's casualties. Custom made for military purposes, the Minié rifles, unlike their Kentucky Rifle forebears, carried bayonets.

Improving the Rifle

For all of their advantages, Minié rifles were still slow and cumbersome to load. A German designer, Johann Nicholas von Dreyse, solved that problem in 1836 after twelve years of experimentation on a breech-loading small arm. His needle gun vastly improved loading times by introducing a bolt action at the breech. Into that breech soldiers fed a paper cartridge containing fulminate, gunpowder, and projectile. On pulling the trigger a needle broke open the paper cartridge inside the breech setting off the fulminate and then the gunpowder. The needle gun vastly increased the number of shots a soldier could fire and it also allowed him to load the gun while lying down, an important advantage for skirmishers and soldiers who sought cover. Prussia ordered its first 60,000 needle guns in 1840 and completed the transition to the new rifles shortly thereafter.

Whether Minié-inspired muzzle loaders or needle gun–inspired breech loaders, the transition to rifles changed the focus of infantry training. All soldiers, not just skirmishers, received heavy doses of marksmanship training because they now carried accurate weapons. For most men, target practice was a welcome alternative to the drill field, but marksmanship training focused on more than targeting and ranging. Men still had to learn how to deploy into various formations and orders. In many cases, formations became smaller and more dispersed to allow men to take advantage of their rifles and reduce their exposure to the newer, and deadlier, rifles that their enemies carried.

Needle guns were one of the century's most significant steps forward, but they were still premature "first-generation" technologies. The breeches failed to seal perfectly, leading to much of the propellant gas escaping and thereby reducing the power and range of the projectile. In the hands of a trained soldier, the Austrian Minié rifles exceeded the range of the needle gun by as much as 300 yards. Prussian soldiers often fired their needle guns from the hip to avoid the singing of skin and facial hair that accompanied the escaping hot gases, thus negating the very accuracy the needle guns were designed to provide. The ease of loading, moreover, often led excited men to fire too quickly and too randomly, expending their standard supply of sixty cartridges in about fifteen minutes.[5] Rifles therefore depended on a supply system that could manufacture enough cartridges, move them into the operational theater, and resupply men in the heat of battle.

Despite these shortcomings, Prussian soldiers put needle guns to deadly use against the Danes and Austrians, both of whom were still using Minié-inspired muzzle loaders. Especially when used to repulse enemy charges, the needle gun proved devastating. As long as Prussian troops could hold their fire long enough to draw the enemy into range, they could dissolve enemy forces with unprecedented rates of fire. In numerous battles and smaller engagements of the Austro-Prussian War of 1866, the superior Prussian rate of fire carried the day on both the offense and the defense. At the decisive battle of Sadowa (also called Königgrätz) that July the Prussians inflicted 45,000 Austrian casualties while taking only 10,000. Poor Austrian leadership contributed to their defeat, but all observers noted the awesome effect of the needle gun.

Prussian soldiers could not count on the same advantage in small arms during their war with France in 1870–1871. By then the basic design of the needle gun was more than thirty years old, which effectively represented several generations of technological improvement in the rapidly changing military atmosphere of the mid-nineteenth century. In 1866 the French had introduced a much better rifle, the chassepot. Although based on a paper cartridge like the needle gun, it had a more effective seal at the breech, in large part because of the introduction of a rubber gasket, the materials for which came from France's new colony in Indochina. The chassepot therefore had a greater range and better accuracy than the Prussian weapons. In the end, however, the superiority of the chassepot did not lead to battlefield triumph, providing yet another case study of the lack of a positive correlation between modern technology and victory.

Artillery Development

Artillery development followed a similar pattern from smoothbore to rifling. By the time of the French Revolution, France was already famous for having the best artillery in the world. Much of the credit for this development falls to Jean Baptiste de Gribeauval, a French officer who began a major artillery reform in 1765. He standardized French field pieces, based on the weight of the projectile fired, into four-, eight-, and twelve-pound guns. The use of better iron and bronze alloys allowed for the guns to become lighter, and therefore more mobile, without sacrificing strength. Elevating screws assisted in sighting and ranging and crews were specially trained to move the guns by both manpower and horsepower. Artillery became an elite branch inside the French army, attractive enough to compel a young and ambitious Napoleon Bonaparte to dedicate the early part of his career to its mastery.

Artillery pieces in the nineteenth-century fired a wide variety of ammunition. Simplest and most familiar was a round shot of iron designed to break formations as it bounced or skipped, like a bowling ball moving through pins. The French eight-pound gun introduced in 1839 fired a 106.1-mm ball at a muzzle rate of 363 meters per second. Its effective range exceeded 3,800 yards. The twelve-pound gun introduced in 1853 fired a 121.3-mm ball although its speed and effective range were slightly inferior to those of the smaller guns. The effect of such cannon balls on masses of infantry, like squares, and on buildings could often be devastating.

Other types of ordnance were developed for use against infantry. In 1784 a British officer named Henry Shrapnel innovated the shell that soon bore his name. The shrapnel shell contained a number of lead pellets with a charge designed to burst in the air, scattering a hail of the deadly metal pellets down onto the soldiers below. In the open field it was a terrifyingly effective weapon. Other types of shell included the case shot shell, which might contain several hundred such pellets. Grape shot canisters carried fewer numbers of much larger pellets. Artillery pieces might also be filled with any metal available, including rusty nails, to provide an effect similar to that of a gigantic shotgun.

Artillery proved particularly adapted to the French army and those armies that closely imitated it. The removal of the aristocracy from the French army from 1793 to 1815 opened military careers to the talents. Artillery, with its need for mathematical precision, was the branch best suited to the educational abilities of the emerging European middle classes. States that lacked a large, educated middle class, such as Russia, generally fell behind in artillery development. Soldiers who could demonstrate the ability to master the skills needed to succeed in artillery could expect unusually rapid promotions, especially when compared to their comrades in infantry and cavalry.

Theoretically, artillery barrels could be rifled in much the same way that small arms could be. But since artillerists normally aimed at mass formations and large targets like buildings, rifling did not seem to most officers to merit the costs involved. Instead, armies invested in the much less expensive process of improving the carriages and caissons that carried the guns themselves. Artillery ammunition also became more perfectly spherical and of uniform diameters appropriate to the size of the gun.

Industrialization, however, allowed for innovation in artillery as it had with rifles. Following its war with Austria, Prussia completed the introduction of Krupp-manufactured rifled and breech-loading steel artillery pieces that it had begun in 1859. Although expensive, the new rifled artillery pieces were "the kind of expense that, in the minds of most [parliamentary] deputies, the army should be making." The Prussian parliament and war ministry therefore had little trouble finding the funds to make the transition despite the expense.[6]

Even with the problems associated with the introduction of a new and untested system, the Prussian guns were a step above anything the Austrians and French could offer in return. Made of cast steel, they were more durable and lighter than the soon to be obsolete bronze smoothbore and rifled pieces in wide use in Europe and the United States. The new steel guns had considerably longer ranges and fired much more powerful shells. In the Franco-Prussian War, German gunners often fired their new guns with near impunity at ranges too far away for the French to respond adequately.

The French had one other weapon that they brought to bear in the 1870–1871 war, but even the French high command was not sure how to use it. The *mitrailleuse*, a hand-cranked weapon consisting of twenty-five barrels that fired in sequence, offered Europe's first attempt at a rapid-fire weapon. Similar in broad outline to the American Gatling Gun, the *mitrailleuse* had a maximum theoretical rate of fire of three plates, or seventy-five rounds, per minute. Although capable of sweeping the field (when it did not jam or misfire), the French made a crucial mistake by assigning it to the artillery rather than to the infantry, where it could have done the most damage. As a result, it played virtually no decisive role in the Franco-Prussian War.

The impact of such technological development on the daily lives of soldiers in Europe and the United States largely depended upon the abilities of their commanders to recognize the tactical and operational changes that new technology impelled. Most importantly, the next chapter will discuss how the area of engagement, or less euphemistically, the killing zone, expanded exponentially. Those armies and commanders that failed to understand the impact of new technology created an important, and deadly, lag between technology and tactics. In far too many cases, battlefields became the laboratories and soldiers the experimental material in a bloody process of learning how technology changed the experience of war.

MARCHING ON ITS STOMACH: FEEDING THE ARMIES

Napoleon famously observed that an army marches on its stomach. Logistics, the science of supplying armies with all of the items that they need to be effective, has been a regular concern of armies since the Roman Army in the First Punic War (265 to 241 B.C.E.). As the Romans understood, an army lacking in food, ammunition, and clean

This image gives a sense of how soldiers were attired during the Crimean War. Note the difference between the uniform and equipment of the officer on horseback and those of the enlisted soldiers. Courtesy of the Library of Congress.

drinking water cannot be effective. An army that has to spend its time focusing on basic necessities cannot focus as much attention as necessary on the enemy. Men might even desert if their hunger or thirst became sufficiently acute. Logistics thus formed an essential element in the military systems of European armies in the nineteenth-century.

Providing appropriate clothing, food, and medical care to soldiers often proved to be as difficult for states as providing weapons. Converting men into soldiers in the nineteenth-century most often meant removing peasants from their fields in the prime of their producing years. Nearly every man brought into the army therefore meant one less man to grow food. The new soldiers thus had to be fed by a decreasing agricultural population. Many societies were operating at subsistence levels or with only minimal surpluses even before the development of large armies with mouths to feed. Times of drought or flood increased these pressures tremendously.

One obvious solution to the problem of logistics involved having soldiers live off the land as they marched forward. In another famous Napoleonic phrase, the emperor urged that, ideally, "la guerre nourrit la guerre," war feeds war. He meant that by living off the enemy's land, an army could force its foes to expend their resources while easing the pressure on one's own land. Living off the land had several other advantages. Most importantly, it eased the pressures on the state to provide food for its soldiers, especially as those armies moved farther from home and secure supply bases. Living off the land also allowed men to move more quickly because units did not have to protect their long, slow supply wagons.

Historian Alan Forrest has argued that living off the land became the only way for the French state to feed its enormous volunteer armies in the 1790s. Having brought hundreds of thousands of men into the army through volunteerism, the *levée en Masse*, and conscription, the French state found that it could not produce enough food for them. Expansion into Belgium, Italy, and Germany thus became a logistical imperative almost as much as an ideological or strategic necessity. In 1794 the French army seized half of all Belgian grain in order to feed itself, fulfilling Napoleon's belief that war should feed war.[7]

Indeed, finding food became a main determinant of Napoleonic strategy and troop movements. In 1796, Napoleon forced the communities of the Italian Cisalpine region to provide food and supplies for his men that surpassed 160 million francs in total value. In 1806 he kept his armies in Germany after the decisive twin victories at Jena and Auerstadt so that German fields rather than French fields could provide the food for the men of his victorious army. The decision may have been an impolite way to treat France's new German allies, but it spared French farmers from the burden of having to find food for more than 200,000 hungry soldiers.[8]

Theoretically, Europe in the nineteenth century should have been better able to support armies than in decades past. In the eighteenth century Europe had experienced an agricultural revolution that included the introduction and incorporation of new world crops like potatoes, peppers, corn, and tomatoes. Technological developments, including better plows and fertilizers, also helped to improve crop yields. Diets became more varied and caloric intake levels generally increased. Nevertheless, a famine in the 1780s demonstrated that, improvements notwithstanding, the precarious nature of agriculture had not changed. For military purposes it also showed the risks of depending too much on the ability of armies to find adequate supplies on the march.[9]

Living off the land had many variations, depending on the desires of the occupying army and the behavior of locals. In the best cases, armies paid for what they needed and sometimes paid more than current local market rates. If peasants knew that they would be paid generously then they would be more likely to bring their products to market voluntarily because they were assured of a handsome profit. Armies sometimes set up markets and fairs to concentrate supply and facilitate purchasing. If armies simultaneously used this method to feed their men with some sensible regularity and disciplined those men who took it upon themselves to seize food from locals, then the occupying force might enjoy reasonably harmonious relations with locals.

Having men pay for their food depended on a consequent development in military administration. Sometimes armies purchased food from a central fund, but just as often they relied on the men themselves to buy their supplies individually. To pay for their food, the men obviously needed money. Regular pay thus had the important role of not only keeping the men happy, but of supplying a primary means to feed them. Providing regular funds to men on campaigns hundreds or thousands of miles deep in enemy territory, however, severely stressed the administrative capabilities of states and armies.

Even if the army could deliver money to its men on a regular basis, it did not always have sufficient funds to pay market price or above. In less ideal circumstances, armies paid what they wanted to pay rather than what peasants thought was fair market value. Armies might also pay in their own currency or in a special military scrip that peasants could not use in their home communities. In such conditions, peasants often hoarded their food to sell it on the local market or the black market. As much as they might have liked to do so, armies rarely had the manpower to scour the countryside to compel recalcitrant peasants to force their cooperation in the invaders' system. Even powerful armies found themselves at a disadvantage when negotiating with peasants on their land and their terms.

Armies always had the option of simply taking what they wanted. They could do so on an organized basis, sending official armed foraging parties out to obtain food by any means available. Alternatively, they could let the men fend for themselves. Neither system was ideal both because of the hostility it generated and because of its basic inefficiency. Peasants had over the years built a well-deserved reputation for their skills in hiding assets from tax collectors. Those skills easily transferred to hiding food from invading armies, especially when peasant communities worked together to resist having their livelihoods simply taken away by soldiers. As a result, peasants had far more places to hide grain and livestock than armies had soldiers to find them.

Living off the land created operational military problems as well. Dispersing men to search for food ultimately depended upon a commander's faith that his soldiers would return to their units in a timely fashion. Once off on a foraging party, soldiers were normally away from supervision and could find any number of temptations and reasons not to come back to their camps. The higher ideological motivation of French revolutionary armies made them most likely to find their food and return. Even many French revolutionary soldiers, however, might just as easily seek out their sustenance in a tavern or delay their foraging missions by days or weeks.

Even if commanders could trust their men to return, a region still had to have enough food to sustain the soldiers moving through it. Living off land that could barely support its own local population was an invitation to disaster. No amount of browbeating or bribing could entice a region's peasants to give up food that they did not have. An army proverb dictates that amateurs think about movement, but professionals think about logistics. Army campaigns therefore often depended upon moving units through areas believed to have agricultural surpluses.

Food, being such a basic necessity, constantly occupied soldiers' thoughts and actions.[10] Soldiers often spoke and wrote about what they ate in the parts of Europe they marched through. Campaigns through fertile agricultural areas brought promises of a varied diet, especially if the campaign coincided with harvest season. For this reason, many soldiers preferred to campaign during the fall when the weather was mild and living off the land was normally easiest. Orchards heavy with fruit or fields filled with grains solved an army's supply problem. Jakob Walter, a German soldier who served in Napoleon's *Grande Armée*, noted that the mere sight of "beautiful villages on the Main River, surrounded by vineyards, fruit trees, and grain fields" was enough to put everyone in his unit "in a happy mood."[11]

Marching through poor country, on the other hand, could prove to be a significant disappointment to men with grumbling stomachs. Walter wrote about his disenchantment with part of the German principality of Württemberg because its light, sandy soil only produced "oats, potatoes, and rye, seldom any wheat." Potatoes were an excellent source of calories, but took time to cook and in some communities were still more closely associated with animal feed than food fit for humans. During the same campaign Walter had complained about having to spend eleven weeks in a region that could produce only potatoes, beans, and mutton.[12]

Even marching through good agricultural country was no guarantee that the food would find its way into soldiers' pots. In extreme cases, a state might destroy its own food supplies in order to complicate the logistical dilemmas of an invading army. The most famous case from this period occurred in Russia in 1812, when retreating Russian soldiers burned crops, slaughtered animals they could not move, and poisoned water wells as they moved eastward. These actions eliminated any chance for the men of Napoleon's *Grande Armée* to live off the land as they advanced. French logistical lines, moreover, stretched for thousands of miles through unfriendly territory, difficult terrain, and poor weather, leaving men hungry and malnourished. Thousands of men literally starved to death. Napoleon's inability to feed his men in Russia played a large role in the ultimate failure of his campaign.

The social problems involved with living off the land multiplied if an army had to live off its own land. If peasants understood a linkage between themselves, the nation, and the army, they might voluntarily offer their food and even their wine to passing soldiers. If they did not, however, they might look upon their own nation's soldiers, especially those from distant regions, as no more worthy of support than soldiers from an invading force. Crafty peasants were no less so because the soldiers demanding food and shelter spoke their language. Involuntarily requisitioning, purchasing, or seizing food and supplies from one's own peasants was an unpopular and often counterproductive means to acquire food, shelter, and other essential supplies like firewood.

All armies relied to some extent on living off the land, but few were willing to do so exclusively. The states of nineteenth-century Europe thus developed extensive logistical networks and supply systems. Periodic mobilizations of large numbers of soldiers, however, revealed how easily a national system of logistics could be overtaxed. In many cases, states contracted with private firms to solve these problems, although that system proved to be far from perfect. In other cases, they took over supply themselves. During the French Revolution, the Jacobins nationalized all industries and declared that saltpeter, a necessary component for the manufacture of gunpowder, was a national resource and could not be privately owned.[13]

Technological Advances for Food Provision

Most urgently, armies needed ways to produce food that could be preserved, stored, and carried for long distances. The quest to find ways to feed armies over large distances led to several important innovations. In 1795 the French government offered a cash prize to any citizen who could invent a better way to preserve food. A Parisian candy, wine, and pickle maker named Nicholas Appert took up the challenge. Although Appert was fifty years too early to take advantage of Louis Pasteur's discovery of microorganisms and their role in causing food spoilage, he knew that exposure to air caused wine to go sour. He deduced that a similar process operated on food and guessed that if he could expel air from food containers he could stop or at least delay the spoiling process. Eventually, Appert learned to put partially cooked food in glass containers that he then immersed in boiling water to expel the air. Once sealed, the food inside had a much longer shelf life. Using this system, Napoleon's Egyptian army carried with them preserved partridges and vegetables that stayed edible for four months. In 1810, Appert collected his prize money from the emperor himself.

Other inventors developed equally useful processes for feeding armies. Another Frenchman perfected a system for deriving sugar from beets that was chemically identical to cane sugar. Being suited to growth in a cold climate and in poor soil, beets provided a ready source of sugar for France during the period of the British blockade, which shut off the importation of sugar cane from the Caribbean. At the same time, England's Peter Durand developed a system to manufacture reliable food containers from tin plate, a material that was both inexpensive to acquire and light enough to carry on campaign. By 1812, Durand's system for canning food had become a commercial process that provided a ready source of nonperishable food to the British army and navy.

With the emphasis on portability over palatability, army food hardly excited soldiers' taste buds. Chronic shortages of salt, fats, and spices made the food bland and, much like modern institutional cooking, its preparation in mass quantities had an astonishing capacity to remove whatever flavors it might once have contained. Camp cooks, moreover, rarely had any training or experience in cooking for large numbers of men. As a result, cooks quickly became the bane of many units' existence and the target of many jokes and much sarcasm. Other foods were prepared in distant field kitchens and brought forward to units. The tough, almost solid, biscuits known to American Civil War veterans as hardtack were common in Europe as well. Their near inedibility received opprobrium in many veterans' memoirs from both sides of the Atlantic. The biscuits often had to be soaked in liquid to even make them soft enough to chew. They were also susceptible to being infested by maggots or eaten by rodents.

Recognizing the shortcomings in army food, many states contracted with firms to provide supplements to those soldiers who wanted them. Soldiers frequently had the option of paying out of pocket to buy food from locals or from sanctioned and unsanctioned camp followers called sutlers. Sutlers remained a part of the American logistical system until 1866. Their food was often tastier and fresher than that provided by the army field kitchens, but sutlers were under no obligation to go into battle areas and were often unreliable. Their mere existence, however, shows the limits of the nineteenth-century food system.

Sutlers were most important for the food and alcohol they provided, but they performed other services as well, from laundry to mail delivery. Many sutlers were wives of older veteran soldiers serving in nearby units. The system thus allowed families that wanted to stay together to do so with some reasonable regularity. Although the evidence is rather sketchy, it also appears that the camps of sutlers included prostitutes and other camp followers whose potentially pernicious moral and sanitary influence on soldiers worried many army commanders.

Nevertheless, armies came to rely on the sutler system to fill in the gaps in their own supply and logistical administrations. Over time, they came to be more carefully regulated. A French ordinance of 1801 only allowed women "employed as washerwomen, vendors of victuals and drink" to accompany units. The restriction probably intended to outlaw prostitution although it is impossible to gauge its ultimate success or failure. The same ordinance limited the number of female sutlers to four per battalion. Brigade commanders had the authority to choose sutlers based upon those women who were "most agile and useful to the corps" and "whose conduct and morals are known to be most regular," another hint at the existence of prostitution. Most commanders chose wives of their senior enlisted men to be sutlers both to reward their most trusted men and in the hopes that men would not seek romantic liaisons with the wives of their superiors.

Officially sanctioned sutlers received certificates and identification cards that permitted them to travel into army areas. Sutlers had to stay four miles away from the army itself and were expressly forbidden to enter combat areas, although in reality many women risked their lives to feed the men of their units during battle.[14] Most armies tried to force men to trade only with the officially licensed sutlers, but numerous unofficial camp followers were always nearby. Without them armies would often have had difficulty in finding the food they needed.

The need to acquire more and better food could lead men to a series of informal, sometimes illegal, measures. Combining resources, trading, and even stealing between units and individual soldiers became common methods of supplementing official rations. In times of peace, men might perform extra work for local peasants in exchange for food. In times of war, when logistical systems broke down, men often resorted to extreme measures. Jakob Walter recalled that in the *Grande Armée* during the Russian campaign "much of the humanity of man … vanished because of hunger." Outside Smolensk he heard of men being murdered by their own comrades "for the sake of bread" and watched men steal food from anyone close at hand.[15]

Less extreme, but still illegal, measures became commonplace as well. Sentries from opposing armies sometimes met to trade surpluses in their rations or to acquire foods from the other side to diversify their own diets. During the American Civil War, northern soldiers often traded their coffee, which they had in relative abundance, for Virginia and Carolina tobacco. Similar exchanges occurred in European armies as well, despite efforts by commanders to discourage the barter system and punish offenders.

When food was scarce, armies often made decisions on which units received their rations and which did not. Elite units normally received the best quality and quantity of food. Combat units often fared better than those in the rear areas. In an alliance war, states often looked to secure food for their own troops first and cared for their allies second, if at all. French administrators thus looked out for French troops; in the *Grande Armée* soldiers in French regiments received better food than did the men in the regiments belonging to Napoleon's German allies.

Even given the poor taste, inconsistent delivery, and unappealing appearance of army food, for many men army rations represented a significant improvement from their civilian caloric intakes. An American soldier from the War of 1812 was authorized 20 ounces of meat (usually beef) and 18 ounces of flour (baked by field kitchens into bread) per day. By the time of the Mexican War, the army had added 2.4 ounces of beans, 1 ounce of coffee, 2 ounces of sugar, and salt. The quality of the beef varied significantly and few soldiers were surprised on days when their own ration fell short of the standard, but for men accustomed to sparse yeomen and peasant diets, the meat and flour rations were reasonably generous.

The most obvious shortfall in the soldiers' diet came in the area of fresh vegetables. Vitamins A and C were particularly lacking. Thus, vegetables became one of the comestibles that armies most commonly looked to acquire on their march. Vegetables added important nutrients and, it should be noted, an element of color to bulk meals that could acquire an unappetizing monochromatic appearance. Canned vegetables helped to compensate somewhat, but fresh vegetables purchased or taken from local farmers provided the best source.

Along with food, armies assumed the responsibility of providing their men with water, tobacco, and alcohol. Assuring large quantities of fresh, reliable water in an era before understanding of microbes and parasites proved to be a significant challenge. Poor water quality could lead to outbreaks of a series of debilitating diseases including diarrhea, dysentery, and cholera. Water, an essential source of life, could also cause entire units to go out of the line and into hospital. Boiling the water to make coffee or tea might render it safe to drink, but it was no sure guarantee either.

Thus, some armies encouraged their men to drink fermented or distilled beverages which, even though they might cause dehydration or drunkenness, did not often cause the longer-term health problems associated with contaminated water. Rum, produced from nonstaple products like molasses and sugar, became a standard beverage in armies and navies, as did beer, a relatively lighter (in terms of alcohol content) beverage. American soldiers in the nineteenth-century could generally expect one gill (equivalent to four ounces) of rum, brandy, or whiskey daily. Sutlers and local tavern owners were usually nearby to sell soldiers alcohol of all types over and above that supplied as their ration.

Alcohol became a central feature of virtually every army and a common component of soldiers' daily lives. Commanders might forgive a few drunken excesses, but most were aware of the larger threat to good order and discipline that excessive alcohol consumption might fuel. The great lengths they had to go to in order to secure their units' rum rations from their own men were but one example of the often pernicious effects of alcohol. Still, efforts to limit the alcohol intake of soldiers in this period, especially in the days before, during, and after a rigorous campaign, normally proved to be futile. Soldiers found ways to buy, trade, or even produce their own, sometimes toxic, alcoholic beverages. It was much easier for commanders to deal with the frequent incidents of inebriated soldiers getting themselves into trouble than it was to take the unpopular step of trying to restrict or remove their men's alcohol ration.

Over time these attitudes changed. The general trend in the nineteenth-century moved toward providing men with less alcohol. In 1832 the American army substituted coffee and sugar for the traditional rum ration. In 1862 the American navy and in 1865 the United States army quartermaster stopped ordering and distributing alcohol of all kinds. Even in Europe, where temperance movements had always had less effect on society, the trend was similar, if not identical. In 1823 the British cut their alcohol ration in half, although it was still the rough equivalent of four double whiskeys per day. In 1850 the British army officially made a connection between alcohol and indiscipline and cut the ration to one-eighth of a pint of rum per day, although the army made efforts to compensate by procuring better quality rum for its men.

These reforms normally went unheeded in times of war and especially in units experiencing combat. Men continued to turn to alcohol's depressant characteristics to help them deal with the realities of combat. A strong mug of brandy helped sentries shake off the cold, at least temporarily. Alcohol also provided social opportunities for the men of a unit. In this vein, sergeants or junior officers could at least temporarily break down the status barriers between them and their subordinates by offering them a drink. Extra alcohol rations might also serve as an incentive or a reward for men who accepted a particularly arduous duty.

UNIFORMS

States often fared no better in clothing their men than they did in feeding or arming them. Just as local communities often ran out of weapons and food, so too did they run out of cloth and leather. In 1793 and 1794 the French army had tremendous problems locating enough red and blue cloth to make uniforms for all of their new recruits.[16] Many men thus marched off to war in their civilian clothes. With French industry still in a relatively primitive state, the manufacturing capability of the state could not quickly compensate; neither could the numerous small cottage industries and family clothiers make up the deficiency.

Shoes and boots were also in great demand, especially given the amount of time soldiers spent on their feet. Until the new French Republic could devise effective bureaucratic solutions to manufacturing and distribution problems, it relied on France's most famous military method for dealing with problems, improvisation.[17] In 1793 the French state responded to the demand for military footwear by requiring every shoemaker in France to produce five pairs of shoes every ten days for the army. Nobles who stayed in France were required to give up their sturdy shoes or to provide money to have more shoes made. Émigrés who left France had all of their property seized by the state, with their shoes often ending up in the army.[18]

Improvisation, of course, came with serious drawbacks. Few shoemakers were accustomed to making footwear that could withstand the hours and hours of drill that soldiers demanded of their boots; nor could the system easily account for significant variations in sizes. Boots quickly wore out or caused their owners to develop painful blisters, only further increasing the agony of drill. All too often, boots and shoes came in one size, requiring small men to wear several pairs of socks and large men either to cut their boots open or try to purchase a better-fitting pair from a sutler.

Military uniforms served a variety of purposes. Most obviously, uniforms, along with flags, facilitated the process of finding one's allies and enemies quickly and reliably on a battlefield. Nineteenth-century battlefields were confusing places, with noise, smoke, and chaos as defining features. The bright uniforms of the early decades of this period were designed to allow men to spot one another through the smoke. The inaccuracies of smoothbore muskets meant that the bright colors did not place men into as much harm as might appear at first glance. The danger of such men exposing themselves to the enemy did in brightly colored uniforms not become a serious military problem until the appearance of large numbers of rifles in the middle of the nineteenth-century. The French Army, as we will see, kept its brightly colored uniforms as late as 1914.

For most of the nineteenth-century vivid colors served important roles in clarifying an already confusing battlefield. They should not, therefore, be read as a sign of the incompetence of military clothing designers or of the generals who ordered the uniforms. Because battle normally involved masses of men lining up in open fields at close ranges, the bright colors did not normally expose men to unnecessary hazards. In some cases, such as in the French and Indian War and the American War for Independence, brightly clad soldiers became obvious targets for darkly clothed skirmishers and irregulars, but these conditions presented themselves in Europe with sufficient rarity to impel armies to retain their bright uniforms.

As rifles came to replace muskets, so too did bright colors give way in some armies to earth tones and patterns designed to make men appear less conspicuous. Throughout the 1840s and 1850s the Austrian army, usually criticized for its backward approach to military matters, made significant changes to its uniforms.[19] Austrian uniforms became darker and began to use more grey, although the pants still remained blue. Hats became smaller and less colorful as well.[20] Coarser, duller fabrics also had the virtue of being easier to manufacture and the removal of bright dyes from uniforms rendered them less expensive to obtain.

Uniforms also helped men identify specific units (most commonly regiments) within the army. To cite just a few examples from the nineteenth-century, Great Britain's Dragoon Guards wore blue tunics and blue pants with yellow stripes. The uniforms of the Hussars were broadly similar but with a double yellow stripe on the pants. Artillerists, sappers, and engineers also wore blue tunics, but with red stripes on the trousers. Light infantry more often wore red uniforms with grey or green pants. These distinctions allowed experienced men and officers to identify the types of units and specialties in their areas quickly and reliably.

An American soldier says goodbye to his wife before leaving for the Mexican War in 1847. The bright colors and tall hat made him easier to identify on the battlefield and, given the general inaccuracy of contemporary weapons, did not necessarily expose him to greater danger. Courtesy of the Library of Congress.

Ethnic minorities used uniforms to set themselves apart from other soldiers in the army and to underscore their own heritage. The Scottish Lowland Brigades of the British army wore blue tunics like the rest of their comrades, but they wore Scottish tams on their heads and distinctive green plaid trousers on their legs. Their bands, which naturally contained bagpipes instead of bugles, customarily wore kilts, as did some of the regimental officers. Similarly, Austrian Serezan regiments wore colorful Turkish-inspired overcoats and footwear as did the Algerian-inspired Zouaves of the French army.

Similarly, uniforms allowed for easy identification of men by rank. In most armies, officers wore the most elaborate uniforms, often with white pants to emphasize their removal from the dirtiest aspects of soldiering. More colorful and much larger hats also set officers apart.[21] Noncommissioned officers, most often the tactical leaders of smaller units, also needed distinguishing uniforms. Prussian sergeants were easily identified by an extra row of lace on the front of their sashes.

Many units used their uniforms to advertise their own rich histories and heritages. A few examples will illustrate the general pattern. The men of Britain's Royal Sussex

Regiment wore plumes above the crests on their hats to commemorate their victory over the plumed French Royal Rousillon Regiment at the Battle of Quebec in 1759. The Royal Welsh Fusiliers wore a ribbon of hair that they attached to the back of the necks of their tunics to signify their having been the only unit in the British army given permission by the king in 1834 to continue to wear long hair as a reward for their service in Nova Scotia. The famous French cap called the képi originated in units with service in Algeria. Uniforms thus became another way to reflect the creation of in-groups and out-groups among soldiers, a process that began during the training process covered in chapter two.

Many soldiers took great pride in the ways that their uniform underscored their attachment to their unit, but most were more concerned about their uniform's practical value. Here military clothing more often than not fell short. Few armies could afford to distribute summer- and winter-weight variants. As a result, the uniforms were normally far too hot for summer duty and far too cold in winter. Artillerists, working with hot guns, were especially prone to remove their tunics in combat on hot days. In winter time, the failure of the uniforms was particularly acute and many men suffered unnecessarily due to avoidable problems like frostbite, hypothermia, and even common colds. Other men sought out any warm clothing they could find, including furs and blankets. An army of men so attired, of course, ceased to be "uniform."

Poor uniforms could undermine the fighting capacity of an army. New recruits and recalled reservists suffered the most from cheap uniforms purchased from the lowest bidder or a contractor with connections in the Ministry of War. The Prussian army did not even issue underwear, causing men extreme discomfort during long marches.[22] Many uniforms quickly fell apart, exposing soldiers to the elements. The failures of supply led to more frequent losses of men to disease and, in many cases, a serious depletion in unit morale as the system seemed to care little for the basic needs of the men. On more formal occasions soldiers sometimes wore more elaborate "parade" or "mess" uniforms. Unlike combat uniforms, formal uniforms had to be kept at a high level of cleanliness, with buttons polished and old, worn belts replaced. As their names imply, they were to be worn for ceremonial functions only. Officers' uniforms were especially elaborate and often tailor made.

A soldier needed much more than weapons, food, and clothes. The infantryman's knapsack kit was designed to provide him with everything he might need both on campaign and in combat. On the march,

A British soldier prepared to attack during the Crimean War. The British kept their red tunics and tall hats much longer than they should have. Note also the backpack the soldier had to carry with him into battle. Australian War Memorial Negative Number ART50001.

however, it was just one more item to burden him down. By the time of the Franco-Prussian War, the French kit included: a rolled tent; two tent poles and pegs; a mess tin; a bayonet and ring; a cartridge pouch; a water canteen; and a cup.[23] The infantry had to carry their heavy weapons as well. If a soldier wanted to bring anything else, like a blanket or a bottle of brandy to warm himself at night, it had to be carried over and above this load. Small wonder, then, that retreating men often discarded everything not deemed essential to their survival.

The weight of the soldier's equipment had the perverse side effect of forcing him to consume everything he plundered rather than take it on the march. Thus, when soldiers found full cellars in peasant homes, they were likely to binge. After stuffing themselves with as much food and drink as they could handle, they often crept off to sleep in order to be ready to resume the march the next day. Soldiers often resented the sight of food they had to leave behind, especially when they did not know for sure when they would eat their next meal. For the same reason, men most often had to leave behind money because most monetary systems then depended on coins which were too heavy to transport in bulk.

Outfitting a soldier with uniforms and kit could be quite expensive. In 1831 it cost the considerable sum of between £300 and £400 to equip a junior officer in the British army.[24] Some of the funds to equip officers came from the officers themselves or from their families. On the other hand, the state had to pay to equip the enlisted men, most of whom were far too poor to supplement their uniforms with their own money. States normally contracted with private firms, although this system had its flaws. In the West, firms often produced products of inferior quality and the relative shortage of companies large enough to meet the demand left states with little leverage. In the states of the East, notably Austria and Russia, corruption and nepotism reached such levels that neither the state nor the contractors even took the effort to disguise them.

The preceding chapters have examined the effort and expense needed to recruit, train, and equip large numbers of soldiers. These exertions ultimately aimed at one goal: producing sufficient numbers of men with the arms and competence needed to fight and win the nation's wars. The next chapter will examine the experience of battle from 1789 to 1870 from the perspective of the soldier. Combat was a rite of passage for all soldiers and an experience that men who survived it never forgot.

NOTES

1. Leo Tolstoy, *Sebastopol* [1855], quoted in Geoffrey Wawro, *Warfare and Society in Europe, 1792–1914* (London: Routledge, 2000), 60.

2. See David Hounshell, *From the American System to Mass Production, 1800–1932: The Development of Manufacturing Technology in the United States* (Baltimore, MD: Johns Hopkins University Press, 1984).

3. French smoothbores carried a .69-caliber round, slightly smaller than the British, but still quite powerful. The larger British guns had the advantage of being able to use captured French ammunition because the latter was small enough to fit down the barrel. The French, by contrast, could not use the larger British ammunition left on the battlefield.

4. Jean-Paul Bertaud, *The Army of the French Revolution: From Citizen-Soldier to Instrument of Power* (trans. by R. R. Palmer) (Princeton, NJ: Princeton University Press, 1988), 242–246.

5. Wawro, *Warfare and Society*, 83. Wawro also notes that many Prussians regretted the choice of the needle gun and that American Confederate commander Gen. Robert E. Lee preferred slower-loading Minié rifles because "what we want is a firearm that cannot be loaded without a certain loss of time, so that a man learns to appreciate the importance of his fire."

6. Dennis Showalter, *The Wars of German Unification* (London: Edward Arnold, 2004), 101.

7. Alan Forrest, *Soldiers of the French Revolution* (Durham, NC: Duke University Press, 1990), 131.

8. Hew Strachan, *European Armies and the Conduct of War* (London: Routledge, 1983; 1993), 54.

9. For more on the military impacts of agricultural changes, see Strachan, *European Armies*, 41.

10. Food, or the lack thereof, is a dominant theme of the six letters from German soldiers of the Napoleonic period reprinted as an appendix to Jakob Walter, *The Diary of a Napoleonic Foot Soldier* (ed. Marc Raeff) (London: Penguin, 1991).

11. Walter, *The Diary of a Napoleonic Foot Soldier*, 33.

12. Walter, *The Diary of a Napoleonic Foot Soldier*, 17.

13. Forrest, *Soldiers of the French Revolution*, 137–138.

14. Linda Grant de Pauw, *Battle Cries and Lullabies: Women in War from Prehistory to the Present* (Norman: University of Oklahoma Press, 1998), 136.

15. Walter, *The Diary of a Napoleonic Foot Soldier*, 66.

16. Bertaud, *The Army of the French Revolution*, 242.

17. Forrest, *Soldiers of the French Revolution*, 142.

18. Bertaud, *The Army of the French Revolution*, 245.

19. Napoleon supposedly denigrated the Austrians as always being one idea, one year, and one army behind. For a recent scholarly critique of the Austrian army, see Geoffrey Wawro, *The Austro-Prussian War: Austria's War with Prussia and Italy in 1866* (Cambridge: Cambridge University Press, 1996). Showalter, *The Wars of German Unification* is less scathing.

20. Darko Pavlovic, *The Austrian Army 1836–1866 (1): Infantry* (Oxford: Osprey, 1999), 25–32.

21. Information on the British army uniforms comes from Frank Wilson, *Regiments at a Glance* (London: Blackie and Son, n. d.), and Mike Chappell, *Wellington's Peninsula Regiments (2)* (Oxford: Osprey, 2004).

22. Showalter, *The Wars of German Unification*, 39.

23. Stephen Shann and Louis Delperier, *The French Army 1870–1871: Franco-Prussian War (1), Imperial Troops* (Oxford: Osprey, 1991), 36.

24. Wilson, *Regiments at a Glance*, 21.

Four

✶ ✶ ✶

"SEEING THE ELEPHANT": SOLDIERS AND THE NINETEENTH-CENTURY BATTLEFIELD

> This beautiful grain region without woods and villages could now be compared to a cleared forest, a few trunks here and there looking grey and white. Within a space an hour and half['s march] long and wide, the ground was covered with people and animals. There were groans and whines on all sides. The stream separated the battlefield into two parts. On the left of the water stood a row of a few houses which looked as if transformed into a chapel for the dead. Over the river there was a wooden bridge that had been burned. On account of the congestion before and during the burning, the banks on both sides of the bridge were filled with dead piled three and four deep. Particularly the wounded who could still move hurried to the river to quench their thirst or to wash their wounds; but the suffering brothers had no help, no hope of rescue: hunger, thirst, and fire were their death.
> —*Jakob Walter describing a battle in Russia 1812.*[1]

MOTIVATION, MOBILIZATION, AND CAMPAIGNING

The fighting and winning of wars is, of course, the primary reason that states develop and maintain armies. War, according to Napoleonic wars veteran and Prussian military theorist Carl von Clausewitz (1780–1831), acts as an extension of politics by other means. Recent studies have emphasized that war reflects a state's cultural and social patterns as well.[2] War is therefore the ultimate expression of a state's goals, values, and beliefs on several levels. Moving beyond these definitions of war, and recalling the discussions of previous chapters, we can also conclude that the use of military force to achieve desired state aims defined all of the training, equipping, and preparation of armies in this period.[3] The importance of war to statecraft in this period can hardly be exaggerated. For most of the nineteenth century, war and the preparations for war were the largest items in European budgets and the most important single issue on the minds of European rulers.

Motivation

Victory or defeat on the field of battle could shape the destinies of armies, of rulers, and of entire nations, and dramatically shaped the lives of the individuals who fought in them. Not all soldiers fought in wars and not all who served in wartime saw active combat; Rory Muir estimates that in 1805 fewer than half of Napoleon's soldiers "took part in any serious fighting."[4] For those who were involved in combat, however, war was a defining moment in their life course, separating them not only from civilians, but from other soldiers who did not see combat. The transcendent experience of battle, what American Civil War soldiers called "seeing the elephant," was therefore every bit as decisive and dramatic as an individual event as it was as a national and state event.

Warfare created sharp distinctions between those who understood it on a personal and visceral level and those who did not. Paradoxically, many combat veterans came to see themselves as having more in common with combat veterans from enemy armies than with civilians from their own nation. For this reason, many combat veterans held little bitterness or resentment toward their former adversaries, especially as time eroded the rationales that created the wars in the first place. To most soldiers, enemy combatants, unlike civilians, were men who, like themselves, had undergone the test of battle and had survived.

Some soldiers, though by no means all, developed their motivation from a personal ideological connection to larger state goals. Alan Forrest argues that the men of the French revolutionary armies were infused with a sense of "messianic idealism" and that the soldiers of France from 1792 to 1814 understood that war "was about absolutes of good and evil, that the people were fighting a war for liberty and against tyranny, for their revolution against the reimposition of monarchical absolutism."[5] In a similar vein, James McPherson argues that for Civil War soldiers on both sides, "abstract symbols or concepts such as country, flag, Constitution, liberty and legacy of the Revolution figured prominently" in the ways that men explained why they had joined the army and why they believed it was necessary to fight.[6] McPherson and others have shown that as Northern soldiers marched through the South, what they saw of slavery and its effects reinforced their ideological commitment to the war and spurred them on to fight even harder to destroy the evil institution of slavery.[7]

To be sure, the men of the French revolutionary armies and the American Civil War had more highly developed senses of ideology than did the men of most armies throughout history. Coming from a revolutionary society and indoctrinated by heavy doses of Jacobin propaganda, French revolutionary soldiers fought an ideologically based war, even if the soldiers themselves most often understood the ideology in personal terms. The same could be said of the men who volunteered for the Union and Confederate armies in the United States in 1861.

But these men were an exception to the larger pattern. Over the course of a man's military service, ideology became less important, even to the soldiers of revolutionary France. As the goals of Napoleon's foreign policy came to be less and less defined by the need to defend the revolution and the borders of France from outside aggression, the soldiers of France lost the ideological edge that had served them so well in the 1790s. By 1800, few Frenchmen carried with them any sustained interest in liberating their European brothers from the yoke of ancien régime tyranny. Despite his emphasis on the ideological motivations of the early French volunteer armies, Forrest contends that the vast majority of Frenchmen came to see military service in the Napoleonic armies as a "*corvée* [labor tax] to be endured" and only on rare occasions as "an honor or privilege."[8] Although they were capable of fighting well, Napoleon's men lacked any larger philosophical connection to the regime and came to be known as the *grognards*, the grumblers.

Most soldiers, even most French soldiers of the revolutionary period, therefore, only derived partial motivation from ideology. Volunteers were more likely to derive their motivation from ideology than were conscripts, but even most volunteers lost an element of their idealism as a more detached military professionalism took its place over time. Few veteran soldiers concerned themselves much with larger political questions, most of which were well beyond their control. Much more commonly, men fought for more immediate reasons, such as defense of one's homeland or the desire to protect one's family. These goals needed no overarching ideology to make themselves perfectly well understood. Moreover, while ideology might serve to entice men to join the army, it did not normally sustain men in battle; instead, much more concrete needs instinctively took over men's minds.

The most important motivators of men on the nineteenth-century battlefield differed little from the factors that had motivated the generations of men who came before and after them. Men fought, as they always had, primarily for their comrades. The battlefield therefore provided the payoff for the months and years of training and development of small unit dynamics in companies, battalions, and regiments. Soldiers fought to protect the lives of the men they had come to know and to ensure the respect of those same comrades. This process depended upon a concept sociologists refer to as "task cohesion." According to this theory, men of an organization who rely upon one another for success identify so strongly with the unit that they will go to great lengths to protect it, even if they do not have close personal attachments to the unit's members. In other words, it matters little if the men like one another; it only matters if they can act in unison toward a common goal.

Mobilization and Campaigning

Before men could fight, however, they had to mobilize. Mobilization refers to the time period between a declaration of hostilities and the actual departure of a unit for the theater of battle. Most large military operations, especially those that suggested the imminence of combat, were preceded by weeks or months of rumors about national and international affairs and their potential impact on the unit. Veteran soldiers knew that most rumors would turn out to be false, but men living in an environment with restricted access to essential information on a topic so vital to their lives naturally hung on to any information, whatever its source. Official channels did not always produce the most reliable information. Tavern owners, sutlers, and camp followers often knew what the army was going to do before the men did.

Mobilization was a complex but vital process. Unit leaders had to ensure that their soldiers had all of the equipment that they needed and that the equipment was in the best possible condition. Worn out uniforms and boots had to replaced before the unit set off on long marches and malfunctioning weapons had to be repaired before they could be used in combat. Sufficient supplies of all of the accoutrements of an army had to be located, obtained, and catalogued. These supplies included such diverse items as blankets, flags, musical instruments, ammunition, saddles, horses, and wagons. Perhaps most importantly, unit leaders had to round up all of the unit's men and ensure that they were fit for the coming campaign. Sergeants often spent the first few days of the mobilization process dragging men out of taverns and scouring the countryside for men on leave.

Mobilization also involved locating and refitting reservists. In theory, reservists were supposed to maintain contact with their local garrisons and provide up-to-date information on their residences or general whereabouts. In reality, this system often functioned inconsistently and ineffectively. Men forgot to inform their local barracks when they moved and officers usually found more pressing tasks, even in peacetime, than tracking down the movements of reservists. Even when reservists did report for duty, they often had to be retrained in weapons systems introduced since their departure from active duty. Civilian habits reacquired in the years spent out of the army had to be drummed out of men anew. Jakob Walter recalled being mobilized in 1812 (the third mobilization of his career) and spending five days being inspected and equipped for campaigning amid rumors (unfounded) that they were marching to the Baltic Sea in order to be transported by ships to Spain.[9]

Soldiers in the Napoleonic period marched from their mobilization centers to the battlefields. If soldiers were lucky, their units furnished animals and supply wagons that assumed the burden of transporting not only heavy unit equipment like artillery pieces but individual equipment like knapsacks and rifles as well. Supply wagons thus greatly eased the burdens of the campaign, especially for reservists who had become unaccustomed to long marches. A few hours' ride on the back of an empty supply wagon was a rare treat that allowed men to rest their feet, close their eyes, and recover from blisters acquired along the way. Less fortunate men had to march for hundreds of miles while carrying all of their weapons, food, blankets, and ammunition.

Weather, the receptivity of local populations, and the quality of food found along the way all played key roles in determining the quality of the marching. Few men knew where they were or where they were heading, so it is not surprising that more immediate concerns occupied their attention. Despite the rumors of a safe and easy water transport to Spain, Jakob Walter and his comrades must have been able to deduce that their eastward march through Germany pointed toward a campaign in the relatively impoverished regions of eastern Europe. Still he wrote of "singing and dancing" during the early days of his unit's march through Germany, owing to fine weather and abundant food.[10]

Over the course of the nineteenth century, armies began to pay more systematic attention to transporting men across long distances via railroad. During the American

Civil War the Union used its much larger railway network to transport men from local recruitment and training centers to the theaters of battle. Railroads also provided the Union with an operational flexibility that allowed its armies to compensate for their longer, more extended exterior lines of communication. Not coincidentally, many of the Union's senior commanders had extensive experience in railroad operations in the years before the war. General George McClellan, commander of the Army of the Potomac from July 1861 to November 1862, had been a chief engineer and a president of railroad companies in Ohio and Illinois. Understanding the significance of rail networks, Union generals designed military operations that often targeted Confederate rail centers like Chattanooga and Atlanta.

In Europe, Prussian leaders realized the military value of railroads almost immediately, using them to concentrate forces in order to defeat the Revolution of 1848. In the years that followed, Prussia's General Staff assigned many of its most talented officers to solving problems related to the incorporation of railroads into Prussian mobilization and logistical schemes. Prussian military funds frequently provided needed capital for the construction of civilian railroads and retired Prussian officers often took important jobs in the railroad industry, leading to systematic methods for the sharing of civilian and military expertise. In the Seven Weeks' War with Austria in 1866, lateral rail lines allowed the Prussians to supply armies spread out over greater distances.[11] Prussian chief of staff Helmuth von Moltke (the elder) became so convinced of the value of the railroad to the future of military operations that he declared, "Build no more forts. Build railroads." The Prussians used railroads to overwhelm France in 1870, concentrating large numbers of men with dizzying speed. Using six main rail lines, they moved 426,000 men from the Austrian frontier to the French frontier in just four days.

Many soldiers appreciated the ways that rail transportation was changing the nature of military strategy and operations. Of greater and much more immediate concern to most soldiers, however, was the change that railroads introduced into their movement while on campaign. Railroads were the first major innovation in overland military transportation since the Roman Empire's creation of a network of paved roads. While revolutionary, the technology did not always have revolutionary impacts for the soldiers of European armies. Not all railroads operated with blinding speed; men often jumped out of their rail cars and enjoyed a leisurely walk alongside the tracks for several miles to get some exercise, fresh air, and fresh fruit before hopping back inside the slow-moving trains. Rail cars could also be cramped, stuffy, and terribly uncomfortable. Most of them had only the most rudimentary sanitary facilities and some rail cars alternatively transported soldiers and horses without being cleaned before making the conversion. Rail travel, of course, depended on where the rails went. Men therefore still had to march from the nearest railhead to their ultimate destinations. Still, to most men, moving by rail represented a major improvement when compared to walking in all weather while encumbered by weapons and supplies.

Already exhausted from marching or riding the rails, men had to find lodgings along their route of march at the end of the day. Soldiers often slept in open fields during the period of mobilization and campaigning. During pleasant weather most soldiers, especially men from rural communities, had little problem with bivouacking in the open. In poor weather or when men expected to stay in a given area for more than a few days, bivouacking became less appealing and soldiers often billeted with local families. As with the provision of food, armies could make this process less arduous on local communities by paying for their soldiers' lodgings and ensuring that their men behaved with some propriety toward the landlords and their daughters.

Despite long-standing Anglo-American antipathies toward the involuntary billeting of troops in private homes, the process was not always confrontational. Jakob Walter wrote fondly of entering the town of Fürstenwalde in Brandenburg during the 1812 campaign, a place where his unit had stayed for eleven weeks in 1807. Men quickly sought out their former landlords and went back to worship in the churches they had worshiped in five years earlier, although "several men were hiding for good reason and did not wish to be found for fear they would be called a father." Walter himself was pleased to learn that his new landlord was a brewer by profession.[12]

Lengthy campaigns were often accompanied by fears and anxieties about where the unit was headed and when it might see combat. One can only imagine the side conversations in the ranks of Napoleon's Imperial Guard as its soldiers marched toward Austerlitz. The unit covered 1,000 miles in three months without ever hearing a shot fired in anger. Yet the men had to know that their inexorable march east had to have a purpose behind it somewhere. They must also have known that not all of them would survive to make the 1,000-mile journey back to France. Life on the road, however, offered relative freedom from the constant gaze of officers and sergeants and provided changes of scenery "especially when compared to the boredom and discipline of garrison duty or peacetime soldiering."[13]

As soldiers approached battle areas, the atmosphere changed, sometimes quite rapidly. Not all battles were the result of careful planning by one or both sides. Encounter battles might begin at almost any moment if patrols of two forces clashed and called for reinforcements. The largest battle in North American history, at Gettysburg in July 1863, began almost by accident when elements of a Union cavalry unit encountered Confederates who had moved into the town, notably, to look for boots. Both sides quickly rushed reinforcements to the area, leading to a massive clash that neither side had fully intended to fight.

In other cases, men entered areas that they knew to be contested between two forces. Sutlers and camp followers, closely tuned in to the informal network of peasants and other locals from whom they purchased food and supplies, often provided the first glimpses of what lay ahead. Locals usually knew better than soldiers approximately how many soldiers had been through the area in recent weeks and which nation's uniforms they were wearing. Official information rarely filtered down to privates, but soldiers occasionally pasted together bits of intelligence they had overheard from their officers and sergeants. Soldiers might also notice a change in the behavior of those same officers and sergeants that indicated that something serious was afoot. Rumor mixed with exaggeration and reality, but veterans usually had sufficient experience and a keen enough sixth sense to determine what information was plausible and what was not.

More concrete indications of the imminence of battle soon followed. Despoiled land and burned out farms gave evidence of the passage of large numbers of men. The detritus of an army going into combat included unnecessary items that men discarded before a battle. These items included playing cards (men did not want to die with the cards on their bodies for fear that their families might find out that they had been gambling), blankets, and excess items of clothing. Large plumes of smoke off in the distance indicated the presence of camps and armies. The gruesome sight of makeshift military hospitals confirmed not just the presence of armies, but of active combat.

Soldiers entered a battle area with a range of emotions. It is important to keep in mind how young the soldiers were; in both American Civil War armies, 18-year-olds constituted the single largest age group in 1861.[14] Most soldiers, still growing into their bodies and their personalities, tried to hide their fears, but all men felt afraid. They were afraid of death, of course, but they were equally afraid of mutilation, of failure, and in many cases, of killing. Men asked themselves if they would be able to meet the trial of battle, a clear litmus test of nineteenth century masculinity. When the time came, they wondered, would they be able to stand in line and take the enemy's fire? Would they remember their training or would they panic and run away? Would they be able to pull the trigger or drive a bayonet into another human being? Most importantly, would they survive?

COMBAT AND LEADERSHIP

Several historians have tried to capture the experience of battle on paper as part of an attempt to write a military history that focuses on soldiers as well as their commanders. Alistair Horne's classic study of the 1916 Battle of Verdun, published in 1962, relied on the words of the men who fought the battle, many of whom Horne interviewed. Horne combined their experiences with the events that occurred inside the French and German high commands to create a picture of the battle that was both "top-down" and "bottom-up." Similarly, John Keegan's 1976 book *The Face of Battle* used three case studies, Agincourt (1415), Waterloo (1812), and the Somme (1916), to compare across time what a battle looked like from the ranks. These two books were part of a generation of scholarship that reinvigorated attempts by military historians to relate how men have reacted to war on an individual level.[15]

In the years since their publication, other historians have followed Horne's and Keegan's leads, moving military history away from an exclusive focus on senior leadership.[16] Today most military historians understand the need to move beyond technology and senior command as the primary forces driving success and defeat on the battlefield. Such studies have contributed tremendously to our understanding of war as common soldiers fought it. Nevertheless, trying to recreate the feelings, sights, sounds, and smells of battle remains one of the most difficult tasks that military historians face.

Combat

As we have seen, deadly combat was a rare event for most soldiers in the nineteenth century. The rarity of combat, however, stands in stark contrast to the centrality of combat to larger patterns of European and American history. The acts of killing and facing death on a monumental scale inherent to combat, moreover, cut to the very core of human nature. Trying to get inside the minds of men to analyze why they behaved as they did is always a complex process. When this process involves an activity as intense and deadly as warfare the complexities multiply.

Reconstructing the events of the battlefield years later presents several challenges to historians. These challenges, more than any presumed "deficiency" in the character of

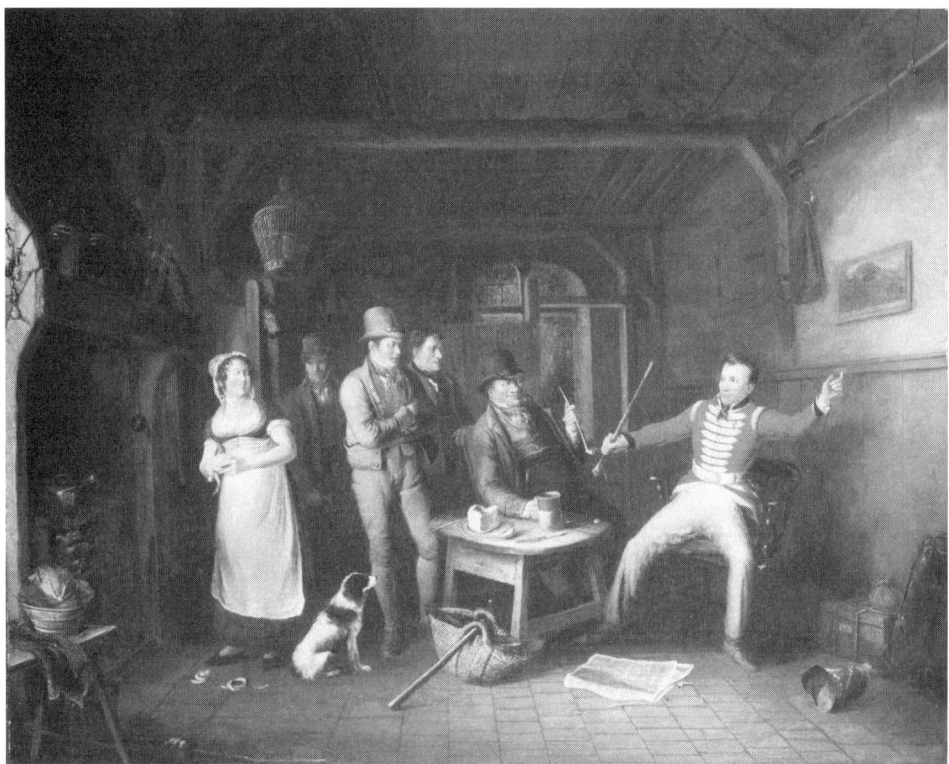

A veteran spins a yard in a tavern. He is wearing a medal from Waterloo and pointing at a Waterloo painting, trying to convince his listeners of his exploits there. From the looks of his fellow drinkers, they are not buying his story. Courtesy of the Council, National Army Museum.

military history, explain why historians have only recently turned their focus toward soldiers.[17] Because of the intensity of what they experienced, many veterans preferred not to talk about what they had done and seen for many years. Sometimes their silence was a function of a need to repress their own actions or to bury the painful memories of losing comrades. In other cases, men remained silent to protect their loved ones from the true horror of what they had seen and experienced. Discussions about the intimate world of combat, they presumed, could only be shared between men who had seen it firsthand. Sometimes the limits of language itself intervened. Many men simply could not find the words to describe combat as it really was. As veterans grew older and more detached from the events themselves, they sometimes became more willing to talk, but by then the vagaries of human memory had intervened. Some men intentionally distorted their own roles in combat, but others had simply forgotten what happened or had succumbed to a natural psychological process of reshaping history in their own minds.

Furthermore, most soldiers from the French revolutionary and Napoleonic periods were illiterate and we therefore have few memoirs, diaries, and letters to tell us how men saw their part in combat. When men did set their memories down on paper or consented to be interviewed, their stories were often of the heroism or of the suffering they witnessed. We have few primary sources from men who deserted, panicked, or fled from the battlefield, although we know that such behaviors were far from rare. Extant sources therefore do not always lend themselves to providing answers to the most fundamental of questions regarding men and how they behaved in combat.

Perhaps most importantly, few soldiers saw much more of the battlefield than the few yards to their left and their right. Many veterans of Gettysburg did not learn about the dramatic events on the Little Round Top or even about Pickett's Charge until after the battle was over. The larger the battlefield, of course, the less an individual could normally see of it. At Leipzig in 1813 more than 500,000 men fought over the course of four days in a battle so large that it became known as the Battle of the Nations. The battle area at Leipzig encompassed nearly sixteen square miles. What one man saw on one part of such a large battle area might not necessarily reflect what happened on others.

These challenges notwithstanding, military historians cannot ignore the experiences of soldiers. The much more numerous diaries, memoirs, and official papers of officers provide tremendous insights into warfare, but they come from a small and unrepresentative group. Relying exclusively on the recollections and experiences of commanders distorts our picture of war in all of its manifestations. We must therefore try to develop as complete a picture as possible from the sources we have at hand, even if we accept the limitations that necessarily accompany them. Studies like Keegan's and others demonstrate that the experiences of soldiers from different time periods share many important features in common. It is therefore possible to extrapolate somewhat from other time periods to explain the behaviors of soldiers from the nineteenth century or from earlier time periods where extant records are even more scarce.[18]

Combat in the nineteenth century also admitted to a wide variety. Large battles involving hundreds of thousands of men such as Gettysburg, Waterloo, and Austerlitz were comparatively rare. Much more common were smaller engagements that were easier for officers to control and for men to grasp. Nor did all battles occur on relatively open fields. Urban combat was a particularly terrifying experience, both because of the number of places from which enemy soldiers could open fire and because soldiers often had little training in fighting in towns and cities. Soldiers also fought in swamps, on beaches, and in forests. The 1864 campaign in the thick Virginia forest known as the Wilderness stood out in the minds of many survivors because the fighting there sparked numerous fires, adding to the danger and fear of the battle area. Soldiers from nations with colonial empires fought in even more varied areas than their continental comrades, from the tropical regions of Burma to the savannahs of Africa. Combat in Asia and Africa was every bit as deadly as it was in Europe, although the tremendous technological advantages of European armies normally gave them a distinct edge. The risks of death in battle were therefore usually lower, even if the rates of death from disease often far exceeded those seen in Europe.

Nor did soldiers always fight other soldiers from armies organized and equipped like their own. Soldiers also faced the unpleasant task of fighting civilians or irregulars. The brutal fighting between French soldiers and Spanish guerrillas during the Peninsular Campaign of 1809–1814 stood out for its savagery. Both sides committed acts of atrocity; the behavior of Spanish irregulars so shocked Wellington that he sometimes refused to work with them, even though they were his nominal allies. Prussian behavior in 1870–1871 toward French irregulars called *franc-tireurs* (free shooters) often shared some of that brutality both because of the randomness inherent in irregular warfare and because of the general disdain in which the Prussians held guerrillas. For most soldiers, fighting irregulars carried with it the extremely unsettling problem of separating innocent civilians from guerrillas and *franc-tireurs*.

Combat therefore had many faces. In all circumstances, men entered battle with a wide range of emotions. For many soldiers, fear mingled with excitement because for all of its dangers, battle represented the "culmination of the campaign, and the chance to prove the man, the unit, and the army."[19] Combat represented the ultimate culmination of the months or even years spent sharpening skills. Unpleasant though it was, combat represented the chance to demonstrate how well a unit had mastered those skills. It also admitted of no middle ground. The abilities of men in combat would reveal themselves in victory or defeat. The prospect was both terrifying and strangely alluring.

Some men succumbed to their fears and tried to desert, but the overwhelming majority of men stayed and faced the danger out of a combination of factors that included the presence of military police, the desire not to let one's comrades down, and the risks of desertion hundreds of miles from home. Deserters normally faced death by firing squad and most men therefore concluded that they would rather face battle and risk a hero's death than desert and risk a coward's death. Peer pressure undoubtedly played the most important role of all. Failure to fight brought with it an immediate and certain stain on a man's masculinity among a his closest comrades.

Battle and the experience of war also bring with them time-honored appeals to men. Several veterans have written about these strange, elemental appeals as a part of human nature that many people would like to pretend does not exist but that combat brings out. They include the sheer spectacle of combat with its almost surreal accumulation of weapons and manpower, the intensity of the experience, and the way that war brings comrades together in a manner unlike any other human relationship. Others have spoken of how the presence of so much death led soldiers to feel life more powerfully just as the ugliness of the battlefield heightened by contrast the beauty of nature. War, moreover, empowered men to release (at least temporarily) their full destructive capacity far from the restrictions and limitations of "normal" civilized life.[20]

Leadership

Alongside soldiers' questions about their own performance came questions about the performance of their comrades and their leaders. Perception, not necessarily reality, mattered most. Confident units stood at a tremendous advantage over units that had not yet developed the task cohesion necessary to ensure the proper functioning of their small unit dynamics. The presence of large numbers of combat veterans in a unit might contribute both morally and materially to such dynamics, especially if the old hands took the time to mentor younger soldiers and reassure them about their doubts. Units that believed they had poor leadership, on the other hand, went into battle with an extra level of uncertainty.

The presence of trusted and well-respected senior officers could add tremendously to a unit's confidence. The sight of a Napoleon or a Duke of Wellington on the field of battle could provide an important source of inspiration. On the night before the

Battle of Austerlitz in 1805, Napoleon and his staff rode among the French lines in the middle of a dark and cold December night. Then at the height of his military prowess, Napoleon was on the eve of one of his great masterpieces, but he and his officers had made difficult progress back to their bivouacs owing to a moonless night and a thick fog. As their commander approached, the men of the French army spontaneously lit the very straw on which they slept in order to light Napoleon's way. As he moved through the army, his men shouted "Vive l'Empereur!" leading Napoleon to refer to that night as "the finest evening of my life."[21] The next day, the French overwhelmed their enemies in one of the century's most lopsided engagements. The psychological impact on Napoleon's Austrian and Russian foes caused by the thousands of small fires and the chanting from the enemy lines played no small role in the French victory.

Service under a trusted general like Napoleon, Wellington, or Robert E. Lee could give men a genuine sense of confidence that their leaders would not sell their lives cheaply or pointlessly. A general like William Tecumseh Sherman, who led his men triumphantly through the South during the 1864 March to the Sea with few casualties, could easily gain the trust of his men. Sherman's soldiers soon gained a faith and a personal feeling of connection to "Uncle Billy" that led them to follow his orders with confidence and with energy. Sherman's swift movements exuded an air of competence and dealt clear material blows to the Confederate cause while liberating slaves along the way. Service in such a unit led one of Sherman's men to note that "to be connected with such a campaign as this is well worth risking one's life for."[22]

The events of the night before Austerlitz or during the March to the Sea were exceptions, as, of course, were Napoleon and Sherman themselves. Few senior commanders inspired that kind of loyalty. Such legendary commanders aside, few soldiers thought much about their senior officers as combat approached. Generals had little contact with their men and regimental colonels normally appeared only at parades and inspections. In societies with clear and distinct class divisions, attempts by more junior officers to mingle among the men came off as phony and unwelcome. To most men, the role of officers was largely negative. Officers became easy lightning rods for all that went wrong in a battle or for orders that seemed to the men manifestly unnecessary or of questionable validity. Soldiers in combat had more important concerns on their minds than what was going on at headquarters or in the minds of the "old man."

Leadership on the field of battle came from sergeants, not officers. Officers might lead a heroic charge, but it was to the sergeants that men most commonly looked for guidance. Unlike the vast majority of officers, sergeants came from the ranks and had therefore "been there" themselves. Many sergeants acquired their stripes after distinguished service in a previous war and therefore had the experience to go alongside their rank. In some armies, sergeants were elected by the men, demonstrating the faith of the men they would be expected to lead. Good sergeants were worth their weight in gold to an army in battle, drawing the best out of their units and alleviating the concerns of the men.

Foremost among those concerns was the need to control one's panic and coolly and professionally execute the steps that the unit had practiced in peacetime. The tendency of drill and weapons training to instill automatonic behavior in soldiers sometimes took over as men capably went through the steps of firing their weapons. Focusing on the tasks at hand had the additional virtue of helping men set their panic aside.

Sergeants and corporals tried to remind men of their individual jobs within the unit and to keep soldiers' attentions squarely on the enemy rather than on the men's own fears and anxieties.

Facing the Battlefield: Fighting and Death

No amount of peacetime training, however, could prepare men for the sights and sounds of a battlefield where chaos and confusion reigned. Hundreds or thousands of guns belching noise and black powder turned an otherwise peaceful field into a loud, smoky, and disorderly place. Although combat tended to heighten one's senses and sharpen one's resolve, physical circumstances often overcame men. Soldiers often arrived on a battlefield tired from marching and several days removed from their last hot meal. Thirst became a natural by-product of long marches and fear. Soldiers' small canteens soon emptied and fresh water frequently became impossible to find or deliver into battle areas. Some men resorted to drinking water "out of ditches in which were lying dead horses and dead men."[23] Others turned to alcohol, often with negative effects, especially on men with empty stomachs unaccustomed to the crude distillates purchased by parsimonious quartermasters. The Austrian army distributed so much brandy to its men at the 1859 Battle of Solferino, in order to calm the soldiers' nerves, that when the enemy finally attacked, "a significant number of Austrian infantrymen were sufficiently impaired that their best chance of hitting anything with their new rifles involved guessing which of the blurred multiple images they saw was the real target."[24]

The most vivid feature of the battlefield, of course, was death. Even peasants whose rural lifestyles accustomed them to an interaction with death and viscera as an almost daily occurrence were shocked by the scale and scope of the carnage of war. Nothing in civilian life could have prepared men for the ability of modern weaponry to tear open human bodies. Keegan identified seven "sorts of encounter" at Waterloo: single combat; cavalry versus cavalry; cavalry versus artillery; cavalry versus infantry; infantry versus infantry; missile-firing infantry versus missile-firing infantry; and artillery versus artillery.[25] Each of these types of combat brought with it a specific type of threat to the human body and spirit. Cannon balls could literally tear a man's head off his body, sometimes leaving the torso intact as it did so. Cavalry sabers could sever limbs or cut a man in two pieces. Bullets could hit a body with so much force that its blood, bone, and tissue splattered the men on either side. Rounds from the French chassepots left exit wounds four times greater than their entry wounds. Bullets from the chassepot and other rifles caused special agony as they tumbled through the body breaking bones.

Because a culminating charge was a central feature of tactics in the nineteenth century, several battles ended with hand-to-hand combat. Hand-to-hand combat often represented the fiercest and most urgent type of fighting. Packed densely into confined spaces, soldiers who engaged in hand-to-hand combat had nowhere to retreat to and thus fought desperately for their own survival. The mêlée and confusion of battle reached their heights in hand-to-hand situations. Bayonets were the most obvious weapon to use in such circumstances, but often rifles took on a new role when used as clubs. Men also fought with knives, their bare hands, and even rocks.

The presence of death weighed heavily on soldiers, but in many ways the presence of the wounded was a greater psychological burden. The sight of comrades suffering from grotesque disfiguring wounds often scared men more than death. Many men hoped for a quick and painless death rather than face a life of agony and physical handicap. The cries of wounded men for medical attention or water tormented soldiers who were powerless to help their dying comrades. During long battles the screams of the wounded called out during the night, haunting men as they prepared for another day of fighting.

Combat and the experience of battle underscored how little control a man had over his own fate. Death on the battlefield struck many soldiers as entirely random and impersonal. Shell bursts often left soldiers wondering why they had escaped entirely unharmed while the men on either side of them fell dead. Given the long ranges of most weapons, soldiers rarely saw the men trying to kill them or the enemy soldiers they were trying to kill. As a result, combat did not fit in with the ideals of personal courage in which so many men had previously believed. Indeed, courage could be counterproductive as soldiers who exposed themselves to danger were often the first men killed.

The chaotic battlefield seemed to lack any overarching logic at all. Religious soldiers soon realized that the pious died just as often as did the nonbelievers. Neither competence nor bravery nor the quality of one's comrades necessarily improved a soldier's individual chances of survival. Chance played the greatest role as the soldier realized that he had "become less an actor in war than an object caught in a process moving forward in ways that would inexorably encompass his own disaster."[26] For many men, the realization that they had no control over their own fate was quite painful and led to intense disillusion.

The full recognition of war's dangers and impersonality led men to fight in ways they had not envisioned. Men who had days before spoken to their comrades of charging the enemy in a death or glory fashion soon found themselves seeking cover, building defenses, and digging trenches. This kind of passive courage was not how men had anticipated fighting the enemy, but in the crucible of combat they reflected no shame. Neither was heroism easy to predict. Men who in peacetime had seemed to hold all of the amorphous qualities of leadership often broke down first, while a unit's worst peacetime drunkards and malcontents often emerged as natural battlefield leaders.

Combat, in short, upturned virtually all of a soldier's preconceived notions. Some men turned to religion to explain this transformation. Stories of bibles and religious talismans stopping or redirecting bullets confirmed the importance of faith to many soldiers. For others combat weakened or destroyed their belief in a just and loving God. For many combat veterans "chaplains no longer wielded the influence that could vigorously demand religious observance."[27] Battle was for all soldiers a transformative experience in the lives of men who experienced it. For almost all veterans, memories of the battlefield stayed with them for the remainder of their lives.

AFTEREFFECTS: WOUNDED PRISONERS, VETERANS

Even if men emerged from the experience of combat with their lives and their souls intact, they still had to face a number of unpleasant aftereffects of combat. Lack of proper medical attention featured prominently in the minds of survivors. Indeed, the fear of being wounded or struck by disease often preyed upon men's minds more than the fear of dying.

Medicine and Treatment of Wounded

Military hospitals in the nineteenth century were petrifying places that men avoided whenever possible. Military doctors, like their civilian counterparts, operated under false assumptions about the nature of disease and the causes of its transmission. Doctors "attributed diseases to noxious vapors or sudden changes in temperature" because their knowledge was so incomplete. One study of doctors in Napoleon's *Grande Armée* concluded that:

> The best of them knew little about the interior of the human body aside from its bones, muscles, principal nerves, and the most obvious functions of its major organs. The idea that the diseases they treated were actually caused by microscopic organisms, and that those organisms could be carried from man to man by biting insects, was beyond the comprehension of their times.[28]

Most doctors learned their trade through an apprentice system that left little room for research or innovation. In the worst cases, barbers or country veterinarians performed operations on wounded soldiers. Lacking an understanding of the body's chemistry, most physicians used ineffective homeopathic treatments or components that turned out to be toxic. Nursing was left largely to volunteers (like poet and Union nurse Walt Whitman) who had a strong stomach and a desire to help the wounded. Still, in the contexts of their times, nineteenth-century military doctors were not manifest incompetents nor were they unaware of their problems:

> They were men who battled constantly with the invisible, unknown enemies. They did the best they could with the knowledge, instruments, and medicines the early nineteenth century furnished them. And they took what skills they had "into the fire" wherever a wounded comrade might have need of them.[29]

The limitations of nineteenth-century medicine caused men more agony than did enemy bullets. During the American Civil War ten men died of disease for every man who died of wounds. The ratios from other wars of the period were even worse. Death from disease, moreover, could be long, drawn out, and terribly painful.

Nor was the inadequacy of military medicine a problem restricted to wartime. Cramped in close quarters, often lacking access to clean water, and wholly ignorant of the methods of disease transmission, soldiers suffered terribly from diseases that in later years became easily preventable. Cooks prepared food under far less than safe conditions; few of them understood the importance of washing hands and properly storing meat. Men suffering from diarrhea, dysentery, and cholera often got little relief from a visit to the doctor. Jakob Walter reported to a hospital during one of his campaigns, believing that the constant fog had made him ill. What he saw revolted him so deeply that he feigned recovery and left:

> Here twelve to fifteen of the men died every day, which made me sick at my stomach and would have caused my death in the end if I and four comrades had not reported ourselves as being well even on the second day and *escaped* (emphasis added). This hospital and three others, according to rumor, had six thousand sick people; and that was the reason also why everyone with an appetite had to suffer great hunger, which was one of the things that moved me to leave.[30]

Thousands of men preferred to suffer in silence rather than risk entering such facilities "for to come under a doctor's care tested fate," sometimes even more than serving in combat.³¹

Several armies recognized the limitations of their medical corps and did what they could to improve the organization, if not the science, of their medical professionals. The Jacobins nationalized military medicine by placing all physicians, surgeons, and apothecaries at the disposal of the Ministry of War. In 1794, the French established a *Service de Santé* complete with military medical schools, an organizational system that accounted for specialized medical knowledge (such as it was), and, after 1806, a routine for regularly inspecting and administering military hospitals. Napoleon developed a network of 28 military hospitals and introduced a method for funding civilian hospitals, provided those hospital reserved bed space for military casualties in time of war. In 1818, the United States formed its own medical service, attracting doctors by offering them officers' pay and, after 1847, officers' ranks as well.

In wartime, overwhelmed hospitals often failed to keep pace with the numbers of wounded soldiers battles created. Few armies developed methods for properly estimating casualties and clearing the needed hospital space for them. French medical inspectors in Spain found that in some cases barbers performed surgeries and that the largest Spanish hospital for French wounded had 3,000 beds but no latrines and no clean water conduits. In other cases, French wounded were cared for by local volunteers, who provided heroic service in the face of great adversity and trauma, but who had no medical training at all.³² Open-air field hospitals were a commonly improvised answer to the lack of bed space, but they were dangerously susceptible to spreading infections from dirt, water, and animals.

A wounded man's chances of survival improved dramatically if his comrades could get him safely off the field of battle as quickly as possible. In the heat of combat, of course, it was not always possible to get to wounded men. Thousands died of exposure or loss of blood because they had fallen in an area that was still unsafe for men to enter or because they had fallen unconscious into an area far away from the main fighting. Men often went to great lengths to find and rescue their comrades, but often they could do little. As a result, many soldiers died alone and anonymously. Most soldiers refused to fire on stretcher bearers or on men trying to rescue fallen comrades, but entering a battle area to pull a man out was always an intensely dangerous task. In some cases, armies called truces in the middle of battles or campaigns in order to care for the wounded and bury the dead, but these cases were comparatively rare.

Whether a soldier managed to walk off the battlefield of his own accord, was rescued during battle, or pulled off the field after a battle, he faced a painful ordeal. Transporting wounded men to hospitals by rickety, horse-driven ambulances over rough roads was agonizing for men with bullet or bayonet wounds; they then went through the triage procedure wherein surgeons decided who would receive medical care first. Those men who appeared to have little chance at survival were normally left to die in as much comfort as doctors could quickly provide. Over time, the now common practice of first treating those men most badly wounded won general favor, but many generals and regimental colonels pressed their doctors to treat the lightly wounded first in order to prepare them for a return to their units as quickly as possible.

Military Hospitals

Because of the fears of gangrenous infections and the sheer number of men who required treatment, surgeons often resorted to amputation. Amputations became so common that one sardonic joke from the Napoleonic period said that surgeons would cure dandruff by amputating a man's head. Commonly using little more than strong brandy as an anesthetic and with very primitive surgical tools, amputations were among the most painful experiences a soldier could have. The introduction of chloroform to the British army in 1854 helped dull the pain of those men who could get it, but supplies were limited. "Good" surgeons therefore learned to amputate quickly (three minutes or less if possible) and cauterize wounds to prevent their becoming infected.[33] Surgeons also learned to amputate legs in a fashion that would facilitate the later adaptation of wooden legs. The sight of piles of amputated limbs was normally enough to keep most officers and many battle-hardened veterans as far away from military hospitals as they could get.

By the middle of the century, the horrors of military hospitals had begun to inspire efforts at reform. British journalist William Howard Russell used the new invention of the telegraph to report on the thousands of British soldiers who died after having received little or no medical care during the first winter of the Crimean War (1854–1856). The resulting scandal caused the resignation of several cabinet officials, including the prime minister, Lord Aberdeen. The subsequent government sent Florence Nightingale, a nurse with experience in the latest European methods, to the Crimea to establish medical facilities that met basic contemporary standards. She and her staff of thirty-eight trained nurses arrived in time to assist the wounded from the Battle of Inkerman and put their theories to the test.

Nightingale was shocked by what she saw in the Crimea. She later wrote that "war has been conducted in more or less forgetfulness, sometimes in total oblivion of the fact that the soldier is a mortal man, subject to all of the ills following on wet and cold, want of shelter, bad food, exercise, fatigue, bad water, intemperate habits, and foul air." Historian Richard Blanco observed that before Nightingale publicized the horrors of the British medical system, most officers took little notice of the conditions of war and their impacts on soldiers. "If troops died due to an arrogant neglect of food, equipment, and medical supplies, there was little official concern."[34] With support from reform-minded War Minister Sidney Herbert, Nightingale set out to make long-lasting changes to the British military medical system.

Appalled by statistics that showed that British soldiers died seven times more often from disease than from battle wounds, Nightingale introduced reforms such as basic notions of sanitation to military hospitals and convinced skeptical British surgeons of the value of maintaining cleanliness in hospitals. As a result, mortality rates fell sharply. She and her nurses also helped wounded men to write letters home, kept their money safe, and ensured that they received the best post-operative care available. Female nurses became a common feature in almost all armies by the end of the century. Although they could do little about the ignorance of contemporary military medical practices, nurses ameliorated as much suffering as possible and featured positively and prominently in the memories of thousands of veterans.

Like William Howard Russell, Switzerland's Jean Henri Dunant used the media to publicize the horrors of the modern battlefield. Dunant's 1862 book *Memory of*

Solferino graphically discussed the plight of thousands of wounded men from the 1859 battle that gave the book its title. His book, combined with the experiences of the Crimean War, led to the formation of the International Committee for Relief to the Wounded in 1863. Later known as the International Red Cross, the organization rapidly received international acclaim and support from numerous governments. One of the most important treaties supported by the organization established the red cross as a neutral symbol, theoretically guaranteeing that soldiers would not fire upon medical personnel wearing the cross.

American medical practices owed much to the woman who organized the American branch of the Red Cross, Clara Barton. Using unofficial channels and private fund-raising, she delivered medical supplies to Union hospitals and brought the issue of care for the wounded to the attention of Union politicians and generals. Her exemplary service as a nurse on numerous Civil War battlefields earned her the nickname "Angel of the Battlefield." Social activist Dorothea Dix organized nurses for the Union in a manner akin to that of Florence Nightingale, although Dix established biased and restrictive criteria, not accepting Catholics or women under the age of thirty.

Nursing allowed women to participate in the otherwise overwhelmingly male environment of war. More than 20,000 women participated in some form of nursing or medical relief work during the American Civil War. Most female nurses were from middle-class backgrounds; their service fit into a long tradition of middle-class female voluntary assistance. These women had no official military rank and received no army benefits. Dix paid for her own lodging and for a nationwide campaign of publicity to raise awareness of the nursing program. Most soldiers welcomed the presence of female nurses, both for the care they provided and because the entrance of women into their world restored a notion of domesticity to their often brutal existences. Dix's desire to recruit only older nurses underscored the importance of that role. Nurses therefore added a female presence to men's lives that was usually more maternal or sororal than sexual.

The hard work of nurses and doctors notwithstanding, medical providers could do little to assist men until the science of medicine made significant advances. In the 1860s, Louis Pasteur advanced his theory of germs, greatly assisting in the prevention of disease and lending scientific credibility to the experiential beliefs on the importance of sanitation advanced by Nightingale and others. Shortly after Pasteur's breakthrough, Joseph Lister developed the process of antiseptic surgery, which greatly reduced the level of post-operative infection. In 1870, using Lister's innovations, just 1.5 percent of Prussian soldiers died from amputations. These advances influenced major reform movements in military medicine that reached fruition at the end of the nineteenth century.

Among the European nations, Prussia made the most important advances in military medicine and the most systematic use of the innovations of Pasteur and Lister. As with many other features of war, the Prussian General Staff planned and prepared for the medical needs of its armies more regularly and efficiently than did most armies. Prussian units in 1870 mobilized one doctor for every 270 men. The Prussian army also vaccinated its men for smallpox and placed special emphasis on field sanitation. Each soldier went to war with a first aid kit containing sterile lint to stop bleeding until he could reach a hospital. Each Prussian corps went to war with 21 doctors and 450 stretcher bearers, with the latter being trained in first aid techniques such as the application of tourniquets.

These images present women as agents of caring and domesticity. The women depicted here are performing a number of services, including laundering clothes and writing a letter home. The appearance of women was a rare treat for many soldiers and often provided a semblance of normalcy. Courtesy of the Library of Congress.

French forces, by contrast, went to war with a highly bureaucratized system that even dictated the treatments doctors could apply in the field. The French system did not include Lister's antiseptic advances among its approved treatments with the tragic result that 10,000 out of 13,000 French soldiers who had amputations in the Franco-Prussian War died of infections. The French system treated its animals better than its people, with the French providing one doctor for every 740 men, but one veterinarian for every 250 horses. This circumstance led to the unusual paradox that "a [wounded] Frenchman's best chance involved being left for the Germans."[35]

Prisoners of War

The desire to get out from under the French medical system notwithstanding, being left to the enemy was not normally a welcome prospect. Becoming a prisoner of war at least had the advantage of removing a man from the immediate dangers of combat. As such, some men often voluntarily gave themselves up, especially if they were fighting in a unit that they believed to be incompetently led or one that they believed had no chance of winning the battle. Surrendering was often a more attractive option than dying for a losing army. Soldiers who had not eaten a decent meal were also more likely to surrender on the hopes that their captors would provide them with some food. Surrendering also carried with it the possibility of a prisoner exchange that might return a man to his home rather than sent him back to the ranks of the army.

Voluntarily giving oneself up did not always guarantee that the other side would honor the surrender. In the heat of combat emotion often overrode logic. In particularly hard-fought battles, units might take it upon themselves to give no quarter, especially if the other side was believed to have committed atrocities. During the *Grande Armée*'s retreat from Russia, the Russian army assigned Cossacks the job of hunting down stragglers from the French forces and killing them, not capturing them. Fewer than one in ten of the French soldiers captured in Spain in 1808 survived.[36] The courtesies (such as they were) afforded to prisoners, moreover, only applied to men in clearly identifiable uniforms. Irregulars and partisans normally could not expect enemy combatants to treat them as prisoners. Most were summarily shot.

Soldiers had good reasons to treat prisoners of war with as much leniency as they could. The more fairly an army treated its captives, the more leniency men could reasonably expect if they themselves were captured. Officers especially had a long-standing tradition of affording courtesies, even luxuries, to one another. Some armies offered paroles that allowed officers to return to their homes if they gave their word that they would not reenter the army. Other officer prisoners of war ate dinner in their captor's mess and had permission to walk around towns during the day as long as they returned to camp at night. Such behavior was a product of a society of officers and gentlemen that transcended nationality.

Common soldiers rarely expected or received such courtesies. They could expect only minimal health care and extremely limited freedom of movement. If their captors had limited food stocks (and sometimes even if they did not) prisoners of war could expect to subsist on minimal rations at best. Starvation and disease killed untold thousands of men unfortunate enough to become prisoners of war. Other prisoners became laborers, some under conditions barely distinguishable from slavery. Austrian prisoners of war in 1800 and 1801 were sent to Corsica to build roads on Napoleon's home island. Some armies, Napoleon's included, offered men a chance to escape captivity by switching sides and enlisting in their captor's army.

Prisoners of war also faced the additional trauma of being separated from their units and comrades; thus they became psychologically separated from the other men in the camp. Unlike military units that trained together and worked together, the conditions of prisoner of war camps usually encouraged selfish, individual behaviors such as the hoarding of food. The emotional and physical isolation of the prisoner of war experience was among its worst ordeals. Attempts by outside organizations such as the Red Cross to inspect camps, deliver mail, and provide food and medicine were inconsistently successful.

Generally speaking, the more ideologically based the war, the more brutal the treatment of prisoners. The French revolutionary armies had standing orders to execute émigrés found among enemy armies, although many soldiers refused those orders. American Civil War prisoner of war camps became notorious for their intentionally cruel abuse. The Confederacy's infamous Andersonville prison at Camp Sumter, Georgia, held 52,000 Union prisoners, of whom 13,200 died in captivity. The Union's Elmira prison saw the deaths of more than one-fourth of the prisoners of war interned there.

Veterans

Survivors of these harrowing experiences frequently faced difficult readjustments to civilian life. Returning to home communities did not guarantee a smooth transition back to civilian life, especially if a soldier had had a long career or seen much combat. Jobs could be hard to find because many men saw themselves as being too old to begin anew. Several business and factory owners disliked hiring military men because of their generally low opinion of soldiers. If a man had managed to save money during his service or had been successful looting on the battlefield, he might buy a plot of land and turn to farming.

Few states provided adequate and regular financial support to veterans, leaving many veterans with few resources with which to cope with lifelong emotional and physical problems. Some states at least tried to establish systems of regular care. Some gave veterans land to farm while others found the money to create pension systems. Pensions had many purposes, however, and not all of them were altruistic. British pensions before 1833 were designed to give a veteran subsistence-level support until he could find a civilian job. The system therefore intentionally paid a man a minimal amount of money lest he become comfortable living off his pension alone.

Pensions also served to reward men for long-term service or participation in important campaigns. Peacetime pensions in the British army did not provide full benefits until a man had reached twenty-one years of service. The system aimed to keep veteran soldiers in uniform until they reached an age believed to be too old for campaigning. Men who stayed in for the twenty-one-year duration often found that they had to live on their

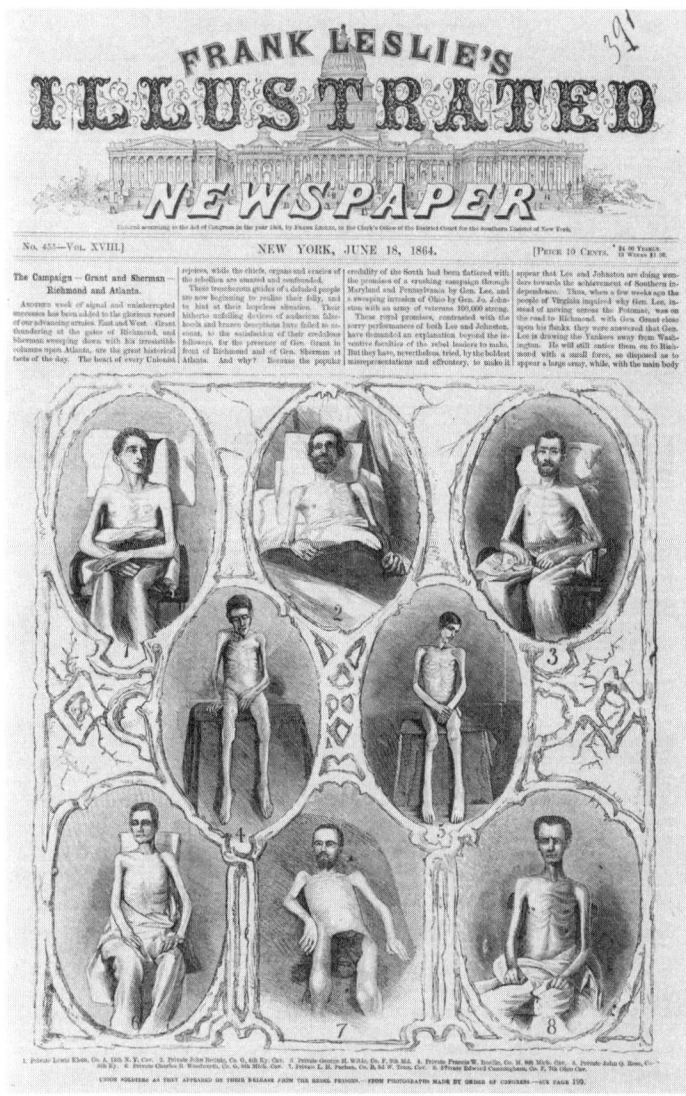

Prisoners of war, like these Union prisoners from the American Civil War, suffered terribly. Controversy continues to rage over whether these prisoners were victims of intentional starvation by their Confederate captors or whether the South lacked the resources to care for them. Courtesy of the Library of Congress.

meager pensions because, then in their forties, they were too old to begin a career in the crafts. British veterans of Waterloo gained an extra year of credit toward their twenty-one years, much to the chagrin of British soldiers who had served in Spain.

Even if they qualified for a pension, the British government often put many obstacles in the way of its veterans. Soldiers often had to appear in person to "pass the board" in London in order to claim a pension. Some pensions required men to prove an injury or war-related disability. For many men the trip to London proved to be a burden that they could not meet due to injury or poverty. Even if approved, veterans frequently waited several years to gain official approval and see any money from the system. In some cases, the testimonial of an officer or local minister might suffice in lieu of a trip to London, but these testimonials provided no sure guarantee of receiving assistance.

As one might expect, Jacobin France introduced some of the earliest methods to reward its soldiers commensurate with their service to the nation. In 1793, France began a pension system to veterans, widows, and orphans, but the state's commitment to provide the money often fell short of the system's promises. Many veterans were left to beg on the streets or seek assistance from local ecclesiastical officials. The French tried to compensate in large cities by opening military hospitals, including Paris's relatively luxurious *Les Invalides*, to men of all ranks, although Napoleon later reinstated the restriction that it be limited to officers only. Today it houses Napoleon's sarcophagus.

Veterans in the United States fared somewhat better. In 1862 the federal government promised to provide wounded Union soldiers with a pension commensurate with rank and severity of injury. Reforms to this system in 1890 provided all soldiers with pensions if they had received an honorable discharge and could not find work as a result of war-related conditions. Beginning in 1906 all Union veterans could claim benefits based on old age and pensions soon became the federal government's single largest expense. Southern soldiers had to rely on the normally less generous systems provided by their individual state governments.

The end of the Franco-Prussian War closed one era of military history and opened another. Most careful observers of continental affairs understood that the extraordinarily harsh finish of that war, which included the bloody civil war known as the Paris Commune, irregular warfare, and a vindictive peace settlement, would create a dangerous Franco–German rivalry. It took more than forty years for that rivalry to reignite as part of a larger and more deadly continental conflict. The soldiers of that war, still known to many simply as the Great War, endured horrors that still have no equal in the entire history of armed conflict.

NOTES

1. Jakob Walter, *The Diary of a Napoleonic Foot Soldier* (ed. Marc Raeff) (London: Penguin, 1991), 54.

2. Although the book has some important flaws, see John Keegan, *A History of Warfare* (New York: Knopf, 1993) for an analysis of the close connection between warfare and culture.

3. Clausewitz and his complicated theories on war are more often discussed than read. A good introduction is Peter Paret, "Clausewitz" in *Makers of Modern Strategy from Machiavelli to the Nuclear Age*, ed (Princeton, NJ: Princeton University Press, 1986), 186–213. The definitive translation of Clausewitz's best-known works is Michael Howard and Peter Paret, eds, *Carl von Clausewitz: On War* (Princeton, NJ: Princeton University Press, 1989).

4. Rory Muir, *Tactics and the Experience of Battle in the Age of Napoleon* (New Have CT: Yale University Press, 1998), 8.

5. Alan Forrest, *Conscripts and Deserters: The Army and French Society During the Revolution and Empire* (Oxford: Oxford University Press, 1989), 3.

6. James M. McPherson, *For Cause and Comrades: Why Men Fought in the Civil War* (Oxford: Oxford University Press, 1997), 21.

7. See McPherson, *For Cause and Comrades*, chapter nine, "Slavery Must Be Cleansed Out," and Victor Davis Hanson, *The Soul of Battle: From Ancient Times to the Present Day, How Three Great Liberators Vanquished Tyranny* (New York: Free Press, 1999), part two.

8. Forrest, *Conscripts and Deserters*, 19. The *corvée* was an especially unpopular tax of the ancien régime period wherein men were required to surrender a given number of days a month or year to their lords as manual laborers.

9. Walter, *The Diary of a Napoleonic Foot Soldier*, 33. Although it covers a much later war, Paul Fussell, *Wartime: Understanding and Behavior in the Second World War* (Oxford: Oxford University Press, 1989) contains an insightful and original discussion of the role of rumor in wartime.

10. Walter, *The Diary of a Napoleonic Foot Soldier*, 33.

11. The standard treatment of this subject is Dennis Showalter, *Railroads and Rifles: Soldiers, Technology, and the Unification of Germany* (Hamden, CT: Archon Books, 1975).

12. Walter, *The Diary of a Napoleonic Foot Soldier*, 36.

13. Muir, *Tactics* 6.

14. See Gerald Linderman, *Embattled Courage: The Experience of Combat in the American Civil War* (New York: Free Press, 1987).

15. Alistair Horne, *The Price of Glory: Verdun 1916* (London: Penguin, 1962); John Keegan, *The Face of Battle* (London: Penguin, 1976).

16. See among others, Victor Davis Hanson, *The Western Way of War: Infantry Battle in Classical Greece* (Berkeley: University of California Press, 1989); Denis Winter, *Death's Men: Soldiers of the Great War* (London: Penguin, 1978); and Linderman, *Embattled Courage*.

17. The phrase is from Keegan, *The Face of Battle*, 25–35.

18. See the introduction of Peter Kindsvatter, *American Soldiers* (Lawrence: University Press of Kansas, 2004).

19. Muir, *Tactics*, 6.

20. Although they are studies of warfare in later periods, see William Broyles, "Why Men Love War," *Esquire* (November 1984): 55–65; and J. Glenn Gray, *The Warriors: Reflections on Men in Combat* (New York: Harper and Row, 1959), chapter two.

21. Muir, *Tactics*, 3.

22. Quoted in McPherson, *For Cause and Comrades*, 160.

23. Walter, *The Diary of a Napoleonic Foot Soldier*, 44.

24. Dennis Showalter, *The Wars of German Unification* (London: Edward Arnold, 2004), 57.

25. Keegan, *The Face of Battle*, 144.

26. Linderman, *Embattled Courage*, 244–245.

27. Linderman, *Embattled Courage*, 253.

28. John R. Elting, *Swords Around a Throne: Napoleon's Grande Armée* (New York: Free Press, 1988), 281.

29. Ibid, 281.
30. Walter, *The Diary of a Napoleonic Foot Soldier*, 10.
31. David S. Heidler and Jeanne T. Heidler, "Medicine," in *Encyclopedia of the American Civil War: A Political, Social, and Military History*, Vol. III, ed. David S. Heidler and Janne T. Heidler (Santa Barbara, CA: ABC-CLIO, 2000), 1303.
32. Elting, *Swords Around a Throne*, 286–287.
33. Elting, *Swords Around a Throne*, 291.
34. Richard Blanco, "Reform and Wellington's Post Waterloo Army," *Military Affairs* 29, no. 3 (1965), 123–132. Both quotations come from p. 123.
35. Showalter, *The Wars of German Unification*, 293–294.
36. Elting, *Swords Around a Throne*, 618.

PART II

✯ ✯ ✯

The Age of Machines: From 1871 to 1918

Five

RECRUITMENT, EVASION, AND DESERTION

> We're marching off in the company with death.
> I only wish my girl would hold her breath.
> There is nothing wrong with me.
> I'm glad to leave. Now mother's crying too.
> There's no reprieve. And now look how the sun's begun to set.
> A nice mass grave is all that I shall get.
> Once more the good old sunset's glowing red
> In thirteen days I'll probably be dead.
> —*"Leaving for the Front" by Alfred Lichtenstein, written in August 1914. Lichtenstein, a German volunteer, was killed in action in October.*[1]

CONSCRIPTION

The experience of warfare from the Crimean War (1854–1856) to the dramatic Wars of German Unification (1864–1871) demonstrated to observant Europeans the need for sustained and intelligent reform of armies. With the exception of the Prussian, none of the European armies in this period had demonstrated any special competence in military affairs. The Crimean War had particularly exposed the weaknesses of European military systems as the immense difficulties of fighting modern war over large distances became manifest. The victorious French and British, no less than the defeated Russians, concluded from the war that they could not afford a repeat performance. Their armies would have to get better or they would risk their state's falling to second-class power status.

In stark contrast to the performances of the belligerents in the Crimean War, Prussia's dynamism during the Wars of German Unification stunned many Europeans

Europe on the eve of war in 1914.

and led to a desire to reform out of fear of falling further behind. The French and Austrians, whom Prussia had humiliated, had obvious needs to reform, but the British, too, quickly realized that their army was in no position to influence the events of the Wars of German Unification even if the government had chosen to do so. These wars, and to a much lesser extent European understandings of the American Civil War (1861–1865), pointed toward massive change in warfare in the coming years. To meet these challenges, European states and the generals who led their armies knew that they would need new military systems and new types of soldiers.

In particular, the developing industrialization of warfare and the growing populations of Europe suggested a future very different from the recent past. Conscription figured prominently in the plans of European leaders to provide manpower for armies that could now grow larger than ever before. As previous chapters have shown, conscription had been a primary means of accessing men into military service since the time of the French Revolution. Although usually unpopular, especially among the men who drew the responsibility for service, conscription offered the armies of Europe a reliable means to get the number of men that they believed they needed.

Moreover, as the power of the state to monitor the whereabouts of its citizens grew, so too did the state's abilities to compel military service more effectively and to track down draft evaders. Conscription thus became an ever more important part of the military accession plans for the continental powers of Europe after 1871. Indeed, it took on a renewed importance as the power of European states grew and the linkages between states and soldiers also grew. Conscription also had value for states beyond the primary one of bringing large numbers of men into the army. It became a critical means to unify the diverse social and political groups inside states and to focus national energy on common goals.

Conscription was most popular among European nobles and other conservatives. Many of them defended conscription on the basis of its ability to "provide buttresses for the status quo" during an era of dynamic and rapid economic and social change.[2] With the specters of the revolutions of 1830 and 1848 still fully in the minds of European elites, many of them saw conscription as a means to socialize young and potentially revolutionary men. The army, they hoped, could channel the restless energies of young men away from disruptive activities and into national service. Thus, Europe could avoid a repeat of the revolutionary fervor that had so deeply threatened the place of conservatives within society.

The army was uniquely suited to fulfill this role as it provided a means for the state to monitor young men closely. Conscription took young men at their most emotionally and intellectually malleable stage and put them through what was essentially a lengthy course in nationalism. In so doing, it ideally cemented the identification of an individual with the state using the army as a vehicle. In the hopes of one French general, conscription and military service would lead to the ultimate unification of state and society. "It is the military family living side by side with the civilian family; it is more than the juxtaposition, it is the blending, in their normal existence of two parts of the same family."[3] Such a "blending" had the twin advantages of making France powerful in the international arena and securing the nation from revolutionaries in the domestic arena.

According to the adherents to this view, men would return to their homes after their period of service with deeper practical and emotional ties to their state. A soldier who had served the state, conservatives rationalized, would be less likely to rise in revolt against it. In addition to these positive national and moral connections, conscription turned male citizens into lifelong military assets to the state. After completing their mandatory period of military service, men then took their military skills into the Reserves, thereby extending the links between citizen and state over decades. By blending Reserve units with active-duty units in the army organization tables, the two forces helped to maintain a man's lifelong commitment to the army and the state it served.

These ideas were far from unique to France. Upon the creation of the new federated German Empire in 1871, all of the German states accepted the extensive Prussian model for conscription. Under this system, all physically fit males were liable for three years of active service followed by four years in the Reserves and five more years in the territorial force known as the *Landwehr*. The *Landwehr* had initially served as a popular militia designed, in part, to counterbalance the influences and power of a large standing army. Like its rough American counterpart, the National Guard, it became increasingly connected to the regular army in the late nineteenth century. Conscription in France, Germany, and elsewhere was thus the beginning of a long-term relationship between the state and its male citizens.

Russia, too, used conscription both to fill the ranks and to create long-term linkages between citizens and the state. The reform of the Russian system was a part of a much larger package of changes introduced into Russia in the wake of its defeat in the Crimean War. The emancipation of Russia's serfs, although more limited in practice than in design, came with a reduction in the period of military service to a shorter, but still astonishingly burdensome, fifteen years. In 1874 the period of service was reduced again to six years, although wealthy Russians served for much shorter terms. Over time, conscription in Russia came to be less onerous and resembled more closely its European counterparts.

Nevertheless, the unpopularity of the Russian state and its army militated against the army becoming a school of the nation in the German or French model. The enormous gulf that separated soldiers from their officers in Russia was far too great for any system of conscription to change. Most officers came from a nobility that greatly disdained traditional Russian society; many noble officers much preferred to speak French or German over Russian, a language that many were uncomfortable using. Few officers expressed even the minimal standards of paternal care for their men that had become commonplace in the German, British, and French systems. The Russian practice of disproportionately conscripting the sons of soldiers underscored the popular image of the army as an institution apart from society and military service as little better than an inherited term in prison.

The Russian exception notwithstanding, the environment of post-1870 Europe added new arguments to the use of conscription as a means to bring men into the army. In an industrializing and increasingly competitive continent, conscription did more than give men a minimal understanding of military life. It also, some contended, prepared men for life in a factory because military service "accustomed [men] to minimal pay, regimentation, and unquestioning obedience to orders."[4] Some conservatives also argued that military service was good for men's health, getting them out of the extremely unhealthy conditions of urban industrial slums and into open-air military camps. In the army many men from poorer backgrounds lived in better housing and ate better food than they had known in civilian life. Men could therefore return to their industrial jobs in better health, prepared for a longer and more productive life in the economic and military service of the state.

Not all Europeans agreed. Middle-class liberals, most notably urban landlords, artisans, and industrialists, objected to the state removing occupational choices from young men. By taking such men out of the labor market, conscription removed workers in their most important and productive years. This system sometimes led to higher labor costs as workers became more scarce. Many urban workers agreed but for different reasons. Once out of the army, they contended, veterans were often at a competitive disadvantage when compared to men who had served an apprenticeship instead of completing military service. Liberals and trade unionists both argued that conscription, and large militaries more generally, were economically counter productive.

Economic concerns merged with social concerns. Even many conservatives often objected to conscription because larger armies obviously required larger officer corps. An expansion of the officer corps, many feared, would lead to an unacceptable influx of middle-class men into leadership positions at a time when many members of the middle class were already coming to dominate the more technical branches such as artillery. Placing large numbers of non-noble officers into the elite branches of the infantry and the cavalry would undermine the very principles of conservatives who argued that lineage, not education, was the best determinant of leadership ability. In an era when the wealth of the middle classes increasingly marginalized the traditional hegemony of the land-based aristocracy, nobles (most notably poorer nobles in Germany and Russia) held on to the military as a base of power and a justification for their continuing social and political dominance.

At the opposite end of the political spectrum, Marxists and socialists objected to conscription because of the nationalizing tendencies of military service and the power that it gave to armies. International in their political orientation Marxists and socialists argued that conscription reinforced the false consciousness of nationalism through the equally dangerous medium of militarism. Many socialists, most notably the charismatic French socialist leader Jean Jaurès, advocated a popular militia constituted of nonprofessionals. A militia, they contended, would serve the state's defensive needs without posing a threat to its neighbors. An army of citizen-soldiers would also be inefficient for the purposes of imperialism, which socialists generally opposed.

To most European workers, the army remained an employer of last resort as conscription gave armies scant incentive to pay soldiers a competitive salary. Moreover, the reputation of the barracks among the working classes remained as low as it had been when Stendhal described it in his famous novels of the 1820s and 1830s. Subjecting the youth of France to such influences and to the presumably conservative, clerical, and antirepublican influences of the army and its officer corps continued to arouse intense suspicions. The outbreak of the titanic scandal known as the Dreyfus Affair in the 1890s only underscored these fears, leading to an extension of the popular perception of the army as insular, furtive, and conspiratorial.[5]

These varied reservations notwithstanding, conscription became a critical component to military service on the continent. Conscription fit into larger fin de siècle patterns in Europe that included compulsory education and so-called womb-to-tomb social services. Military service was therefore a natural adjunct of a much larger pattern in European social and political movements. Many Europeans connected military service to these social patterns in an abstract general fashion. Military service, they concluded, was the price that a society's males paid in exchange for the social services the state provided in return to all citizens.

Conscription held the most emotive power in France. As the nation that had developed modern systems of conscription, culminating in the *levée en Masse* and the Jourdan Law, France was most clearly poised to build on past traditions. The emerging egalitarianism of the French Third Republic (established in the aftermath of the French Second Empire's defeat in the Franco-Prussian War) argued for military service to be shared, or at least distributed, as evenly across society as possible. Even many French socialists, generally opposed to conscription in principle, saw virtue in a system of military manpower acquisition that accessed men from all social classes and all regions.

Following this logic, the French Third Republic abolished the traditional practice of substitution in 1873. The elimination of substitution was designed to underscore the *levée en Masse*'s principle that all citizens owed service to the state regardless of financial means or social status. The logic itself might have been powerful, but it ran counter to the state's actual need for soldiers, which was often so low as to make any system of conscription look patently unrepresentative. In the era of general peace (albeit amid periodic tensions) that characterized the period from 1871 to 1889, the French often called as few as 10 percent of its eligible young men to the colors. The 1873 conscription legislation recognized this reality and also revealed the Third Republic's desires not to force military service on the middle class. The law therefore exempted from military service several middle-class professions that included priests, students, teachers, and seminarians. In place of substitution, the state introduced a dispensation fee payable to the state in lieu of individual military service.

With the army still in general disrepute, even those men that the state expected to serve in the military often sought evasion. They used the usual techniques, including inducing or falsifying medical conditions, running away (a problem most pronounced in *départements* close to the mountainous borders with Spain, Switzerland, and Italy), or convincing local officials to rig the system of choosing lots. Some communities banded together to pay the dispensation fees of men selected for service. Doing so often made financial sense because an absence of young men from a rural community could lead to the need to hire expensive outside labor. The loss of many young men also disrupted local marriage and family patterns. Paying the dispensation fee therefore kept labor costs down and young men at home. Other communities simply continued a time-tested method of registering all new births as girls, although this method became less effective as the power of the central government grew stronger.[6]

Even the French system with its *levée en Masse* traditions was therefore far from fulfilling the egalitarianism that its proponents proclaimed. Many Frenchmen saw the dispensation fee as a class-based exemption little different in practice from substitution. With so few men being called to serve, conscription remained "a heavy tribute exacted by an oppressive and alien state" rather than the duty of the loyal citizen that so many conservatives had envisioned and idealized.[7]

Conscription also carried with it the potential disadvantage of creating a standing army that might threaten the same republic it was designed to serve. The small number of men who experienced military service risked becoming a group of soldiers who identified with the army or its officers, not the larger society as a whole. These men, republicans feared, could become susceptible to the creation of client armies like those that Gaius Marius created in the late Roman Republic.[8] These armies, loyal only to their officers, became an alternate locus for men's loyalties outside the state and an instrument for social discord rather than the stability that armies ideally provided.

Evidence for these fears came in the late 1880s when General Georges Boulanger appeared to threaten a coup using the very army raised via conscription. The charismatic French general used anti-German ideology and the occasion of an economic downturn to rally both the extreme left and the extreme right against the republic. The Boulanger affair ended with the general's exile into Belgium in 1889 and his death two years later, but it demonstrated how easily the soldiers of a republic could turn to a man on horseback during a crisis. The fear of a republican system being used to create a small, distinct army loyal to its officers rather than to the state prompted changes.

An 1889 law in France recognized these risks and made major reforms in the system of conscription. It eased the burden on local communities and on young men by reducing the term of service from five years to three years. The reduction in the time of service would have greatly reduced the number of soldiers available to France and would thus have been unacceptable to the army's senior leadership. The law compensated for this problem by requiring all physically fit males to serve. Thus, despite keeping men for two fewer years, the law actually increased the number of men in the army by more than one-third.[9] The new system also eliminated the much reviled use of dispensation fees and required men in professions previously exempted from military service to serve at least one year.

The system proved to be popular among all social classes because it eliminated the gross inequities of previous conscription legislations. Rather than requiring a relatively small percentage of men to serve for five years, now all physically fit men served for three years. Historian Eugen Weber argues that this change led Frenchmen to see conscription as a more truly national program and, consequently, to see the army as a more truly national institution. Rather than being a hated institution that drew unlucky men away from their land and family, the army became a shared rite of passage for nearly all Frenchmen, giving them an experience in common and, for many, a source of personal pride.

The new law had other consequences as well. As promotion in the new army became increasingly tied to literacy and basic education, the barracks became an extension of the system of national schools. Thus, Frenchmen had sustained contact with the state from their first days of school through the end of their reserve status. While not all men welcomed these close connections, Weber and others argue that on the whole such linkages created a stronger and deeper sense of nationalism among Frenchmen, especially the previously more isolated peasants. Furthermore, by distributing the burden of military service more equally across French society, the 1889 law put veterans on a much more equal footing with their peers when competing for civilian jobs. Thus, Weber concludes, by the 1890s "there is persuasive evidence that the army was no longer 'theirs' but 'ours.'"[10]

What Weber observed for France held true across Europe. Generally speaking, conscription met the least resistance when the obligation of military service was most evenly spread across society. The more universal the nature of the system the more easily the state could make claims about the importance of conscription to larger societal goals. Furthermore, in periods when the international context became more threatening, conscription became a more important national institution. Conscription was simply too intrusive in men's personal lives to be a popular institution in a liberal Europe, but under the right conditions men accepted it and sometimes even took pride in completing it. For the French, another reduction in the term of service, from three years' service to two, completed in 1905, reduced the disruption that military service imposed on men's lives.

Perhaps most importantly, the mass conscription of young men for shorter durations changed public images of the military itself. With a larger and relatively more representative segment of European populations serving in the military, the army came to be less of an institution of the unwilling. Old images of soldiers as criminals, vagabonds, and the unlucky came perforce to be replaced by images of the army as a much more national force. As more and more people in France came to have sons, brothers, and cousins in the army, soldiers became extensions of society rather than exceptions to its general patterns. Desertion rates fell sharply after 1889 and, perhaps more importantly, French soldiers received much more positive receptions in garrison towns.

Although conscripts in all European nations might expect to be better received in the century's final decades than they had been in the Napoleonic era, the image of the army as an institution outside civil society had not completely changed. The many scandals that involved the army, most notably in France, periodically tarnished the idea of the army as a national, unifying force. The repeated uses of troops as strikebreakers in all European nations undermined the army's image among the very constituency (urban workers) presumed to derive the most benefits from military service. When soldiers followed orders and broke strikes and demonstrations, they seemingly confirmed the theory that military service made men more reliable and loyal to the state. When they did not, conservatives saw shadows of 1848 or, worse still, 1789. In 1907, soldiers in France, most of them conscripts, refused orders to fire on striking wine growers, although they also refused the calls from the crowd for the soldiers to revolt. Crises such as this one revealed the enduring tensions between army and society as well as conscription's limited ability to fill in the gap. The development of professional, more powerful police departments separated soldiers from the role of strike breakers except in cases where civil authority collapsed. This change improved the popular image of soldiers and the army more generally by removing it from a particularly odious task.

The 1889 conscription law was largely a product of a changing domestic environment as successive Third Republic governments attempted both to make military service more equitable and to repair the fissures that had opened between France and its army. Shortly after the law's passage, international events increasingly assumed center stage. The two Moroccan crises of 1905 and 1911 and the two Balkan Wars (1912–1913) were symptomatic of a general rise in international tensions. Parallel to these events came vast increases in military expenditures by the great powers. German military expenses rose 142 percent between the first Moroccan crisis and the outbreak of World War I. British and Russian expenditures rose sharply as well as the former attempted to match increased German naval construction and the latter continued to rebuild after Russia's disastrous losses in the Russo-Japanese War (1904–1905).

As expenditures and international tensions rose, so did the size of armies. In 1913, Germany decided to call more conscripts with the ultimate goal of increasing the size of its standing army by 200,000 men. France saw the decision as a clear threat to its security and began to debate extending its term of service from two years to three. The controversial measure met strenuous opposition from the French left but passed amid fears that without it the French army would fail to meet " the standard of its German rival" at a time when the dark clouds of war were clearly gathering.[11]

Conscription therefore became an integral institution in the lives of young European men. It provided the continent with a mass of men trained in military service and the use of the weapons and ancillary systems needed to conduct large-scale military operations. It also provided men with a tangible link to their nation and state that, for many, had been missing before. Military service became a nationalizing force that helped to overcome differences of religion, regional culture, and language. In states like Germany and France this process developed more fully than in the much more heterogeneous states of Austria-Hungary and Russia. Not all men welcomed their years under conscription, but as long as the system distributed the burden equitably it met with more acquiescence than resistance.

ALTERNATIVES TO CONSCRIPTION

By 1914 all of the major (and almost all of the lesser) powers of Europe except Great Britain had systems of conscription in place. Britain remained an important exception to the general pattern. British politicians felt secure in rejecting conscription and a large standing army because the protective power of the Royal Navy made such measures unnecessary to defend the home islands. Even the massive and expanding British Empire needed relatively few British troops owing to the success of the British in recruiting soldiers among local populations in Africa and Asia. Conscription remained much less popular as a political issue in Britain than it was on the continent both because of the manifest lack of a military need for it and because with such a small army the British could never hope to call enough men to the colors to make any system of conscription seem even remotely equitable.

Britain and Conscription

Nevertheless, even Britain had its pro-conscription advocates. Among the most popular was the legendary Victorian soldier, Field Marshal Frederick Sleigh Roberts, known to all by his nickname "Bobs." If any man in Britain could have convinced his countrymen to support conscription, it was Roberts. Winner of the Victoria Cross for his bravery during the Sepoy Rebellion in India in 1858, Roberts became a household name in Britain when he marched a column of 10,000 men 313 miles from Kabul to Kandahar in 22 days in order to relieve a beleaguered British garrison during the Second Afghan War in 1880. The British then sent him to South Africa following the disasters of "Black Week" in December 1899 during the Boer War. Roberts reorganized British forces and began to reverse British fortunes in the war. Immensely popular, Roberts dedicated his life after retirement to the cause of introducing conscription to Great Britain.

Roberts had several powerful supporters. Robert Baden-Powell, also a hero of the colonial wars, was among them. Declaring that every young British male should "learn how to shoot and obey orders, else he is no more good when war breaks out than an old woman," Baden-Powell, like Roberts, argued for compulsory military service.[12] When it became obvious to him that Britain would not embrace his vision, he decided to create a voluntary organization to teach boys survival skills and self-reliance. Baden-Powell's Boy Scouts, formed in 1908, was one of a number of military-related youth organizations that grew in popularity in Britain in the years before World War I. By one recent estimate, 41 percent of all British male adolescents were involved with at least one of these organizations. This spirit carried through to the nation's universities, where one in three Oxford undergraduates had joined the voluntary Officers Training Corps.[13]

The dominant forms and patterns of service in Britain, therefore, remained voluntary. The reluctance of the British state to compel military service from its citizens interacted with the low esteem in which most Britons continued to hold the army and soldiers in general. Soldiers were still mostly men who could not find even minimally rewarding industrial jobs or men who had to get out of town in a hurry. In 1877, William Robertson, looking to escape from the prospect of a life as a domestic servant, told his mother that he planned to join the army. She tried to convince him otherwise, telling him that the army was "a refuge for all Idle people" and warning him that "I would rather Bury you than see you in a red coat." He went against his mother's wishes, enlisting below the minimum age (he was large for his age and was able to convince a willing recruiting sergeant that he was of age), and later becoming the first man in the history of the British army to rise from private to field marshal.[14]

Robertson's mother probably spoke for many more Britons than did Baden-Powell. But the army's low public image was far from its only problem. Both Liberal and Conservative politicians sought to keep taxation low and expenditures on the military to a bare minimum. The enormous costs involved in keeping the Royal Navy the strongest and most sophisticated military force in the world cut deeply into defense budgets. So, too, did the needs of empire, leaving little money for improving conditions inside the army or for raising the pay of the common soldier. After Napoleon, few Britons worried that any continental power could land an opposing force in Britain and thus Parliament felt safe in leaving the army small, poorly funded, and generally neglected.

Victorian ideology also had a difficult time fitting the army into its general ideology of "industrial progress and social improvement."[15] The army (but not the navy) was either incidental to progress and improvement or, in the eyes of many Victorians, an outright hindrance to it. Attracting men into military service, moreover, took them away from industry. Offering them high pay to attract them into enlisting might in turn raise the wages paid to industrial workers, making industry and the army competitors for skilled manpower. Such competition between the state and private businesses was anathema to most British liberals.

British assumptions about military service thus differed significantly from the notions current on the continent where, as we have seen, military service came to be understood as the responsibility of everyone. In Britain, on the other hand, soldiering was to be the realm of those men who had little to offer to industry. The British soldier was to be "redundant and unskilled; and, like the unemployed of the workhouse, he should … be offered only the minimum of pay and the barest of necessities in living conditions."[16] Little wonder, then, that Mrs. Robertson tried to steer her son away from a lifetime of wearing the red coat.

The British therefore had to recruit soldiers in a social and political environment generally indifferent to the army and without the financial means needed to compensate for that indifference through improved pay and conditions. In this environment came the appointment of Edward Cardwell as Secretary of State for War in 1868. A veteran of several ministerial posts, but unfamiliar with the army, Cardwell recognized the need to reform the army within the severe restraints imposed by parliamentary parsimony. Cardwell embarked on a series of fundamental changes that touched virtually all aspects of the Victorian-era army, many of which were strongly resisted by Conservatives and senior military officers.

As regards soldiers, Cardwell knew that he could not expect Parliament to change its long-standing tradition of running the army on a shoestring. Soldiers in the 1870s earned one shilling a day, giving rise to the phrase "The Queen's Shilling" as a synonym for military service. Out of that pay, a soldier had to pay a series of charges or "stoppages" for laundry service, replacement of lost or broken equipment, and repairs to barracks. If a soldier wanted more or better food than was available to him in his mess he faced more stoppages. Lord Roberts estimated that an average soldier lost almost half of his salary to stoppages, leaving him with little chance to save money during his years in service.[17]

Although Cardwell was able to end stoppages for food by providing each man with one pound of bread and three-quarters of a pound of meat per day in addition to the shilling, he knew that no major increase in spending was forthcoming. He therefore sought to induce men to join the army by changing the conditions of service in ways that would not cost the British taxpayer; some of his changes might even save the government money. Cardwell began with changes that cost the government nothing. He reformed the notorious British disciplinary system, banning branding and flogging. He also reduced the size of imperial garrisons, thus also reducing the amount of time men had to spend overseas to a maximum of four years. Reducing the size of the garrisons, of course, also reduced their cost.

Most important, Cardwell sought to replace the traditional long-service British soldier with a relatively short-term recruit who would serve for six or seven years followed by six more years in the Reserves. Cardwell hoped that a shorter term of service would "induce a better class of men to enlist" because military service would be a temporary job rather than a lifelong calling.[18] Reformers also hoped that a shorter term of service would make recently discharged veterans more competitive in the civilian job market because they would have a greater chance at learning a civilian trade. Retiring men at seven years' service rather than twenty also made the men of the army younger and more fit, increased the size of the Reserves, and, significantly, sharply reduced pension costs.

The changes of the Cardwell period also reformed the officer corps, abolishing the system of purchase of commissions in 1871. These changes, although vigorously opposed by Conservatives such as the commander-in-chief, the Duke of Cambridge, did little to change the social composition of the officer corps. Indeed, Cardwell had never intended to open the officer corps up by social class, merely to open it to talent among those who were already wealthy and/or privileged. Parliament was no more willing to increase the salaries of officers than it was to increase the salaries of soldiers. Being an officer, however, came with significant social expectations and was therefore quite an expensive proposition. By one estimate, a cavalry officer needed £600 to £700 per year from private sources, usually from family money, in order to augment his relatively meager salary of £120.[19] Officers continued to come from the elite of British society notwithstanding the odd exception like Robertson.

Cardwell's changes thus improved some of the conditions of the British soldier's daily life, most notably in ameliorating punishments, but the reforms often fell short of expectations. Recruiters often failed to meet goals, leading them to lower age and physical and mental standards to meet even the bare minimum levels. Recruitment was easiest in times of economic downturn as the members of the urban underclass remained those most likely to join. The army would have preferred agricultural workers, "widely regarded as stronger, healthier, and more obedient than their slum-bred counterparts," but they were unable to get them in large numbers. In 1870, 64.7 percent of recruits to the British army were laborers and 19.5 percent were mechanics. The percentage of laborers continued to hover around 60 percent into the twentieth century, indicating the importance of the urban working classes to military recruitment.[20] More than one in four veterans could not find jobs in the civilian world after their service, suggesting both their humble origins and the failure of the army to prepare them for a post-service career.

As the British army recruited heavily among indigenous peoples to police its empire, so too did it rely on thousands of non-English men to fill the ranks. Although it may seem counterintuitive in light of later events, the British army had traditionally relied heavily on recruitment from Ireland. A region of habitual poverty and frequent downturns in the agricultural cycle, Ireland had produced large numbers of soldiers willing to serve the British Empire almost anywhere except against their fellow Irishmen. In 1870, 27.9 percent of men in the ranks of the British army were from Ireland. Over time, however, the British army lost this source of manpower owing to the migration of men out of Ireland, the urbanization of many of those who remained, and increasing tensions between England and Ireland. By 1899 only 13.2 percent of the army was from Ireland. Recruiters thus had to recruit more heavily from the already thin pool of men interested in military service from England and Wales, whose proportion of the army rose from 60.3 percent in 1870 to 76.7 percent in 1899.[21]

These cumbersome problems notwithstanding, the British army had several advantages over its continental counterparts. Most obviously, because Britain had no conscription, all of its army's soldiers were volunteers. Although many had joined out of financial desperation, all had signed up more or less willingly. The British army therefore had a relatively higher proportion of men for whom soldiering held an appeal. These men formed the cores of companies and regiments motivated by a genuine, if sometimes grumbling, desire to serve.

The army also benefited from its close association to imperialism, with all of its appeals of romance, danger, and exoticism. The army became the instrument of imperialism and, by extension, of civilization itself. It was the army that, in the view of many Victorians and Edwardians, represented "civilizing influences" on the indigenous peoples of Africa and Asia. The army, in their eyes, was responsible for "'opening' dark, barbarous sections of the globe to modern civilization."[22] The army, once it became identified as a civilized institution, reflected civilization back on the urban poor who had donned the red coat.

The British army also represented a martial force that served to demonstrate to Britons that their society's material success and luxury had not made them over refined. Soldiers were representatives of the martial values of British society, proving that luxury did not equate to decadence. Victorian notions that certain races were naturally "martial" (Scots, Gurkhas, and Sikhs, among others) led to concerns about the English losing favor in a global racial contest with evident Social Darwinian implications. The "regulated and orderly" British soldier, carrying "the torch of culture and progress" to the far corners of the world, stood as visible evidence that those concerns were without merit.[23]

The Boer War (1899–1902) revealed both the strengths and the weaknesses of the British system. On the whole the British soldier fought well in unfamiliar terrain and endured difficult fighting conditions thousands of miles from home. Despite the repeated frustrations of the war, British units retained both their discipline and their fighting effectiveness. Perhaps more importantly, the Cardwell system of short-term enlistments buttressed by Reserves functioned as intended. Ninety-eight percent of Reservists were successfully recalled to the colors when needed.

But the main lesson of the Boer War was the need for even more reform. Fighting against what was essentially a small enemy proved overwhelming for the army. Chasing down intractable Boer commandos who rarely numbered more than 50,000 men at any one time required 448,435 British soldiers. Of these, 256,340 came from the regulars and the Reserves. The remainder had to be hastily raised from local militias, British volunteers, and troops transferred from other parts of the empire. The war was thus a reminder of how small the British army truly was and how limited its rapid deployment over large distances could be. The highly mobile Boers, moreover, could concentrate their firepower more easily than the cumbersome columns of British regulars and could disappear quickly into the South African *Velt*.

Although the British eventually triumphed in the war, the army's performance brought sharp criticism from both the Liberals and the Conservatives. The war's unexpectedly high cost of £201,000,000 added to these criticisms. More than 5,774 British and

This image from the Boer War contrasts the professional European soldier on the left and the native Boer commando on the right. The professionals came to learn a great deal from the Boers. Australian War Memorial Negative Number ART19683.

Imperial troops died in battle and a further 16,168 died of disease or wounds. These figures pointed to a stark failure of the British officer corps to plan properly for the war and all of the needs of an army engaged in near-constant combat. Also criticized were the "aspects of peacetime planning and tactical assumptions" as well as the ability to rapidly expand the army in the event of a future crisis in the empire or on the European continent.[24]

Soldiers, too, responded to the dissatisfaction of the Boer War. Frustrated by its inability to find and destroy Boer guerrillas, the army turned to a policy of rounding Boer families into camps. The idea was to force the guerrillas out of the *Velt* and into the open field where the British army could fight them on more equal terms. The British eventually built 100 segregated camps that held 116,000 whites and 115,000 blacks. Unprepared to care for or feed the civilian internees, the British system led to deaths of tens of thousands of women and children. The camp system led to international condemnation of the British and stinging criticism in the British press that alienated the reluctant soldiers who carried out the policy from their larger society.

This sense of alienation had important consequences for soldiers and their willingness to remain in uniform. The British army had introduced the concept of the three-year enlistment in order to fill recruiting shortfalls. The War Office had estimated that three-quarters of the men who signed up under the plan would reenlist for another three years, thus bringing them to Cardwell's ideal of a six-year service career. By May 1904, however, the army's links to the Boer War had so tarnished its reputation that only 12 percent of British soldiers had reenlisted.[25] The government's benign neglect of the army would need to end if the army were to recover from the crisis of the Boer War and be ready to serve the nation in a time of need.

The reforms of the British system that came in the wake of the Boer War did not involve soldiers' lives as directly as had the Cardwell reforms of the 1860s and 1870s. Rather, they were aimed at higher-level issues of coordination between senior agencies. The British created a Committee of Imperial Defense and a general staff to bring its organization more in line with those in existence on the continent. In 1907 the British introduced the British Expeditionary Force (BEF), designed to facilitate the rapid deployment of large numbers of British soldiers to the European continent in the event of a major crisis.

These changes did not attempt to address the social composition of British soldiers nor did it make major changes to pay or living conditions. The reforms did, however, indicate the increasing seriousness with which the British government took the army and matters of defense more generally. Thus, while there was little real change in the kinds of men who joined the army between the Boer War and World War I, there were dramatic improvements in the ways in which they were trained and prepared for war. By 1914 the BEF was the most professional and most effective small military force in the world.

United States, Canada, and Conscription

The United States and Canada generally followed the British pattern. Largely secure from foreign invasion and able to handle internal security with militias and small regular forces, neither nation sought to draft its young men. Both nations shared the

British antipathy for central authority and a suspicion that large armies might serve as the instrument through which a government might infringe on civil liberties. The development and modernization of the American National Guard gave the nation a large pool of minimally trained soldiers and a force that state governors could call out in the event of strikes and other domestic disturbances.

America's lone attempts at conscription in the nineteenth century came during its Civil War. The Confederacy passed a conscription law in April 1862 as the twelve-month terms of the original enlistees began to expire. The act offered numerous occupational exemptions and allowed for a draftee to exempt himself from service by hiring a substitute. The legislation was intentionally weak in enforcement mechanisms; few men ever received punishment for not obeying a draft call. The second Confederate draft law, passed in October 1862, favored the rich by increasing the cost of a substitute and included the infamous "Twenty Negro Law," which exempted planters who owned twenty or more slaves. Attempts to add teeth to the Confederate system ran into continued opposition from states' rights activists who argued that the new Confederacy had no more right to compel individuals to act against their will than did the Union from which the Southern states had seceded.

Northern conscription legislation was broadly similar in that it involved exemptions for many middle-class professions and allowed for the wealthy to hire a substitute. Northern opposition to conscription was only slightly less intense than that in the South. Law enforcement authorities experienced tremendous difficulties in bringing draft evaders into the army. Antidraft protests erupted across the Union, most notably in New York City where five days of rioting killed more than 1,000 people. Only 6 percent of Union troops entered the army via conscription, although many men may have volunteered to receive an enlistment bounty rather than risk being drafted.

The popularity of Theodore Roosevelt's volunteer "Rough Riders" in the Spanish-American War of 1898 seemed to confirm to many Americans that the nation did not need to compel military service from its citizens. Conscription had almost no popular support and few American politicians publicly called for a draft until American entry into the war in 1917. Instead, even as World War I raged in Europe, elite Americans voluntarily joined military "preparedness" camps similar to the Officer Training Corps movement in British universities and public schools.

By the outbreak of World War I, then, conscription was the most important and most common method of accessing men into the military, but not the only one. Conscription gave continental Europe thousands of men under arms, thousands more trained men in the Reserves and Territorial/*Landwehr* units, and a system for training many thousands more in the event of war. Only with the outbreak of war did the European and American systems for accessing men show their fault lines. The crucible of World War I forced greater changes and reforms as well as the introduction of entirely new systems to feed the massive personnel needs of armies.

MILITARY RECRUITMENT DURING WORLD WAR I

One of the most enduring images from the early days of World War I is that of eager young men lined up to volunteer for military service. These images have come down to us over the years as a symbol of the innocence of the young men, thousands of

Soldiering did have its appeal for those seeking to see new places. These Americans, sent to China in the wake of the Boxer Rebellion, are sightseeing near the Great Wall. Courtesy of the National Archives.

whom did not survive even the first year of the war. It is, however, a serious mistake to read in the faces of those photographs naïveté or blissful ignorance. While some hoped for a quick war that would let them return to their farms in time for the fall harvest, most men left with a great deal of uncertainty. Most were anxious to serve their nation, but not all were blindly optimistic about winning a quick war and returning home by Christmas without a scratch.

Neither should the anonymous ranks of faces in these photographs deceive us into thinking that their reactions to the outbreak of the war were uniform. Region of origin, class, and political ideology all informed the ways in which young men responded to the outbreak of the war. In general, middle-class men displayed far more enthusiasm for war than did the farmers or members of Europe's working classes. Most British males felt sympathy for people in the invaded nations of Serbia and Belgium, but few held any deep antipathy toward Germany and many held their Russian allies in deep suspicion. In the end, international events played little role in enticing men to volunteer. When making their personal decisions, men most often responded not to international events like the Austro-Hungarian ultimatum to Serbia, but to the ways that the war threatened their own homeland. In the British case, men of all classes volunteered most often in the wake of national tragedies or military setbacks. The British defeat at the Battle of Mons in early September 1914, produced a national shock and led to the highest single-day enlistment of the war. The German execution of English nurse Edith Cavell on charges of espionage led to another surge in recruitment in order to fight the barbarity of the "Hun."

For most young Europeans, even in the aggressor states of Germany and Austria-Hungary, the war became constructed as a war of defense of the homeland. Thus, even socialists could find their way through the contradiction of volunteering to serve in an international war that most socialists had tried to avoid. In France, which the Germans invaded at the war's outset, fighting a defensive war became a natural and easy way to justify one's military service. In the words of one of the most distinguished historians of France during the war, "most of the men left home in the firm belief that the French government had had no hand in unleashing the conflict and that unprovoked aggression had to be resisted."[26] Defensive patriotism thus united Frenchmen of all classes.

Volunteerism

Nevertheless, as recent historical research has shown quite conclusively, European men often volunteered to join the army with much less enthusiasm than the photographs of cheering young might suggest. In his work on London and Wales, Adrian Gregory concluded that "men did not join the British Army expecting a picnic stroll to Berlin but in the expectation of a desperate fight for national defence."[27] Men volunteered to fight not because they were blind to the dangers of war, but because they felt that the threat to their homes justified the risks.

Similarly, a recent study of Germany in 1914 has concluded that the notion of widespread enthusiasm for the war was more myth than reality.[28] The excitement in the streets that followed the assassination of Austrian Archduke Franz Ferdinand quickly subsided as the mood in Germany became more nervous and tense than enthusiastic. Nevertheless, there had been just enough enthusiasm in the early days, and again following major events such as the delivery of the Austrian ultimatum to Serbia on July 23, or the kaiser's rallying speech to the German people on August 1, to allow the German government to promote a myth of war enthusiasm that suggested a much more unified and supportive German people than had actually been the case. Over the course of the war the myth grew in political power, recalling the support and sacrifice of an earlier cohort of Germans in order to inspire later cohorts.[29]

Young European men, therefore, volunteered more out of a sense of resigned determination than an enthusiasm to give their lives freely on the field of battle. We cannot assume that these men went to war blind or deaf to the dangers that awaited them although their passions may have temporarily taken hold of them. Their motivations were far more complex and individualized. For some men patriotism served as the principal factor in driving their enlistments, but for others, peer pressure, a desire to escape the monotony of farm or factory work, and a desire to witness what many clearly understood would be the most important event of their generation all played critical roles in their decisions to enlist.[30]

If most men went to war with much more reluctance than they may have shown, once decided upon military service they did what they thought was necessary to get into the army rather than risking the sting of rejection. With so many of their peers volunteering, the potential shame at being turned away must have been an awesome and daunting prospect. A. J. Heraty was one such young man. He went to a local recruiting station in order to enlist in the British Royal Field Artillery. When asked by the recruiting sergeant his age, he replied that he was eighteen. The sergeant told him he was too young to volunteer. Sensing the young man's disappointment, the sergeant then told him, "I am very sorry, Mr. Heraty, but I'll tell you what you can do. You can have a walk around the town, but if you come into this room again tonight, you must be 19 years of age." Heraty followed the sergeant's advice, enlisted under false pretenses, and began a career that took him to the western front and later to Italy.[31]

Heraty was one of thousands of young men who volunteered for military service despite the risks involved. Volunteerism was especially important to the British, who, owing to their abhorrence of conscription, lacked a large body of militarily trained men. In May 1914 the British army was 6 percent below its authorized strength and had averaged less than 30,000 recruits per year at a time when the German army numbered 661,000 men in its active-duty regulars alone. The new British Special Reserve created out of the old British local militias was 13,699 men short of its stated goal of 74,166 men. The Territorial Force, created for the purpose of home defense, was also consistently below strength and its men were under no obligation to serve overseas, although most Territorials quickly agreed to go to France. The Territorial Force of "Saturday afternoon soldiers" hardly compensated for the small size of the British regular army nor did its amateurishness inspire much confidence in the minds of generals and politicians as a force capable of standing up to the German army, even if the Territorials could be transported to the continent.[32]

Given its small size and heavy early losses, accessing volunteers proved to be especially important for the British army. Nevertheless, and in contravention of the images of enthusiastic crowds, voluntary recruitment in Britain "got off to a moderately slow start," averaging just 7,020 men per day in the first week. These numbers rose during periods of crisis, producing a total of 761,000 men in the first eight weeks, overwhelming the small British army recruitment system but still just barely enough to construct an army. After the initial crises of August had passed, however, recruitment leveled off, falling to just 4,000 men per day by the end of September.[33]

Fortunately for the British, they had another pool of men to call upon, namely, the men of the empire and the Dominions. Some of these men still identified themselves primarily as British and thus saw the danger to the homeland as personally as any man living in London, Birmingham, or Liverpool. Other men, tied to their lives in South Africa, Australia, or Kenya, understood that a British defeat in the war might mean a transfer of sovereignty for their homeland from democratic Britain to autocratic Germany. The war was therefore far from being a remote event thousands of miles away with little or no connection to the daily lives of the people of the empire. Instead, it came to assume the appearance of a struggle for survival.

Consequently, recruitment from the Dominions complemented that in the British Isles themselves. India contributed what was then the largest volunteer army in world history, over 1,300,000 men who served in Europe, Asia, and Africa, although the motivations of Indian soldiers remain poorly understood. Australia provided 322,000 men, over 280,000 of whom became casualties, the largest percentage of any of the

British Dominions. New Zealand provided 124,000 men, representing an astonishing 10 percent of its prewar population. The Australia and New Zealand troops formed the ANZAC (Australia and New Zealand Army Corps) which became intimately connected to the failed British offensive on the Gallipoli peninsula in 1915. The Canadians produced 600,000 soldiers, over 400,000 of whom served overseas in the highly effective Canadian Corps. Of South Africa's 156,000 soldiers, more than 30,000 served on the western front with most of the remainder supporting British efforts in the German colonies in Africa. The small British colony of Newfoundland (not yet a part of Canada) provided 6,500 soldiers and 2,000 sailors. The Newfoundland regiment suffered 684 casualties on the first day of the Battle of the Somme on July 1, 1916.

The Reserves

The sights of thousands of young men lined up to join the army must have proved enormously comforting to European military leaders, but even more comforting was the response of the men of the Reserves. The numbers of men who failed to report in line with their mobilization notices were considerably smaller than many generals had feared, even in states with unpopular regimes like Russia and Austria-Hungary. The logic of defensive war helped to impel men to obey their mobilization orders as did the general atmosphere of national sacrifice. To the great relief of officers everywhere, the Reserve system functioned as designed, providing troops for critical missions.

The local nature of these Reserve units also contributed to the mass obeisance to orders. Almost all Reserve and Territorial regiments had local ties; the men who served in them had often known one another since childhood. The French 77th Infantry Regiment was comprised of men from the Vendée, the 64th of men from Nantes, the 65th of men from the industrial Parisian suburb of St. Denis, and so on. The men of these units had grown up together, served on active-duty together, and had trained in the Reserves together. This system virtually ensured that men would respond to the enormous peer pressure that operated in close-knit communities.

From a military perspective, Reserves were infinitely preferable to volunteers. Reserves were veterans of conscription who had been through a course in military training and although some of their knowledge was out of date, they had at least a minimal understanding of military technology. They also understood basic military discipline, organization, and methods. Many of them needed refresher training to bring their skills up to the level of the active-duty soldiers, but their previous military backgrounds often allowed that training to occur fairly rapidly.

Volunteers, on the other hand, had to be taught even the most basic military matters. Most volunteers had never even fired a rifle, let alone a machine gun or a crew-served artillery piece. Many officers believed that properly preparing civilians to become soldiers in the modern age was a process that required months or even years to complete. Obviously, the armies of Europe did not have the time to wait, so units of volunteers often went into the line with minimal training. If they were lucky, the new volunteers began their service in a relatively quiet sector behind the lines or in a theater with little fighting. There they could continue training and honing skills.

For most European armies outside of the British and their Dominions, volunteers were a relatively small proportion of soldiers. Most men entered military service through conscription. To replace losses on the battlefield (what the British euphemistically termed "wastage"), European armies called the next cohort year of young men. Ideally, armies waited as long as possible to call the cohorts, allowing the young men to mature emotionally and physically for as long as possible. Calling men at too young an age also had the risk of losing too many men too soon. If a cohort of eighteen-year-old men took heavy casualties, there might be no cohort to replace them for another year. As the war dragged on and manpower crises became more acute, cohorts were called earlier and earlier, causing more men to enter military service at a younger age.

The New Armies

The British army continued to resist conscription even as "wastage" destroyed the pre-war British Expeditionary Force by early 1915. Instead, the British hoped to continue their reliance on volunteerism. As recruitment began to lag, however, the British needed to find new ways to entice men into enlisting. As early as the first month of the war Secretary of State for War Lord Kitchener and Director of Recruiting Major General Sir Henry Rawlinson proposed increasing recruitment by guaranteeing men that they could serve in the same units as their friends throughout the course of the war. The notion was to improve recruitment numbers by offering men an individual incentive and by encouraging local leaders to create entire battalions.

The idea, supported by the enormous charisma and presence of Kitchener, one of Britain's most recognizable soldiers, produced immediate dividends. Officially known as the New Armies, they were more popularly known as the Kitchener Armies or, reflecting their purpose, the Pals Battalions. Their names often revealed the shared professions of many of the volunteers. Thus, the 10th (Service) Battalion of the Royal Fusiliers was more commonly known as the Stockbrokers Battalion. Other Pals Battalions with occupational links included the Miners Battalion (officially the 12th Kings Own Yorkshire Light Infantry) and the Newcastle Commercials (officially the 16th Northumberland Fusiliers). Notably, they were all better known by their nicknames than by their official designations. Other units took their names from their locales, including the Sheffield City Battalion, the Leeds Pals, and the Grimsby Chums.

This system proved to be quantitatively successful, yielding 215 battalions (145 Service and 70 Reserve) between August 1914 and June 1916.[34] This figure represents almost 40 per cent of the total manpower raised by the British in this period. The Pals Battalions were all raised outside the normal War Office system by mayors, local chambers of commerce, and enterprising industrialists. The voluntary and intensely localized nature of the New Armies gave the British army a distinct character as they began to arrive in France, first seeing combat at the bloody and ultimately inconclusive Battle of Loos in September 1915, notable also for being the first use of poison gas by the British.

The eager but untested New Armies suffered terribly at the Battle of the Somme from July to November 1916. The 31st British Infantry Division included Pals Battalions from industrial centers such as Bradford, Leeds, Barnsley, Durham, Halifax, Hull, and Accrington. On the bloody first day of the Somme they attacked at the small town of Serre and were mown down by defending German units that fired 74,000 rounds of ammunition, inflicting a terrible 3,600 casualties. The unit's tragic experience on the Somme was repeated across the front, causing the novelist John Harris to later write that the Pals Battalions were "two years in the making, ten minutes in the destroying."[35]

The destruction of the New Armies forced Britain at long last to accept the notion of conscription. In August 1915, a government survey revealed that more than 5,000,000 men of military age still had not joined the armed forces. Hoping to use the threat of conscription to spur enlistments, the British introduced the Military Service Act in January 1916, requiring all physically fit men between the ages of eighteen and fortyone to serve. The Act still allowed for numerous exemptions, including those for men in many essential industrial occupations and sole supporters of dependents. Later reforms winnowed the exemptions beginning with married men and certain occupations. Eventually, the British army raised the age ceiling to fifty, although few men of that age were conscripted into front-line service in the trenches.

Conscription had the important advantage of keeping some war-essential men out of the army. The rush of volunteers in Britain in 1914 and 1915 had deprived British industry and transportation of many highly skilled workers. The relatively more careful French army had used conscription to keep essential workers out of the army. French industry therefore showed remarkable resiliency despite the loss of its most heavily industrialized regions to German occupation in the early months of the war. Britain's decision to turn to conscription was partly motivated by the need to protect the vital workers who had not yet donned the uniform. Of the 5,000,000 men identified by the British government survey in August 1915, nearly 700,000 were in occupations such as munitions manufacturing, mining, shipbuilding, and railways, all of which took priority over soldiering.

The notion of "channeled manpower" dominated the American conscription system as well. Operating in a society with a historical opposition to conscription no less intense than the British, the Americans nevertheless needed a system that could both access large numbers of men quickly and keep men in key industries out of the army. Conscription seemed the perfect solution, but antidraft sentiment remained strong and volunteerism had a vocal champion in former president Theodore Roosevelt, who offered to lead a movement to raise volunteer regiments to serve the American cause in Europe.

To ease the social anxiety over the draft and to head off Roosevelt's initiative, President Woodrow Wilson and Secretary of War Newton Baker decided to place the burden on local officials. Because the federal government still lacked the power to track its citizens and compel military service from them, the Wilson administration urged local leaders to convince the young men of their towns to voluntarily place their names, addresses, and occupations on rolls for "selective service." On June 5, 1917, hundreds of thousands of young men willingly did so, allowing Wilson to claim that the nation did not in fact compel military service from anyone and that the draft was a "selection from a nation which has volunteered in mass."[36]

Like the European conscription systems, the American system exempted men in key occupations like mining, shipbuilding, and railroads. The United States actually drafted a relatively small percentage of its men owing to the brevity of American participation

118 ❧ *The Nineteenth Century*

War wasn't all killing. Here an American soldier teaches two French boys how to fish. Courtesy of the McDermott Library, Special Collections Branch, United States Air Force Academy.

in the war and the difficulty of training so many men so quickly. Only 25 percent of whites and 36 percent of blacks who answered selective service calls were actually placed into uniform. The overrepresentation of blacks reflected the racism of American society (most blacks served in labor battalions during the war) as well as their underrepresentation in essential industries.

Regardless of whether one volunteered individually in the first days of the war, volunteered subsequently as part of a whole battalion, or entered through conscription, beginning military service in World War I was a rite of passage for an entire generation. Only those European men of military age who were working in a war-essential industry generally avoided service. Sometimes enlisting amid great fanfare and a warm local send-off, many men entered military service unaware of the rigors of military training and service that lay ahead. The training process soon shattered that ignorance as civilians became soldiers in the largest armies Europeans had yet seen.

NOTES

1. See Jon Silkin, *The Penguin Book of First World War Poetry* (London: Penguin, 1996), 244.
2. Brian Bond, *War and Society in Europe, 1870–1970* (London: Sutton, 1984), 65.
3. General Lewal quoted in Douglas Porch, *The March to the Marne: The French Army, 1871–1914* (Cambridge: Cambridge University Press, 1981), 30.
4. Bond, *War and Society*, 66.
5. The Dreyfus Affair is far too complex an event to explore here. For a general introduction to it and its many complexities, see Jean-Denis Bredin, *The Affair: The Case of Alfred Dreyfus* (trans. J. Mehlman) (New York: George Braziller, 1986).
6. Eugen Weber, *Peasants into Frenchmen: The Modernization of Rural France* (Stanford, CA: Stanford University Press, 1976), 296.
7. Weber, *Peasants into Frenchmen*, 295.
8. For more, see William Sinnigen and Arthur Boak, *A History of Rome*, (6th ed.) (New York: MacMillan, 1977), 180.
9. Porch, *The March to the Marne*, 26.
10. Weber, *Peasants into Frenchmen*, 298.
11. Porch, *The March to the Marne*, 212.
12. Quoted in Hew Strachan, *The First World War, To Arms!* (Oxford: Oxford University Press, 2001), 146.
13. Strachan, *The First World War*, 147.

14. Quoted in Glenn Wilkinson, *Depictions and Images of War in Edwardian Newspapers, 1899–1914* (London: Palgrave Macmillan, 2003), 15.

15. Albert Tucker, "Army and Society in England, 1870–1900: A Reassessment of the Cardwell Reforms," *The Journal of British Studies* 2, no. 2 (May 1963): 110–141, quotation at 111.

16. Tucker, "Army and Society in England," 112.

17. Tucker, "Army and Society in England," 135.

18. Edward Spiers, "The Late Victorian Army, 1868–1914," in *The Oxford Illustrated History of the British Army* ed. David Chandler and Ian Beckett (Oxford: Oxford University Press, 1994), 189–214, quotation at 190.

19. Tucker, "Army and Society in England," 128.

20. Spiers, "*The Late Victorian Army*," 130.

21. Spiers, "*The Late Victorian Army*," 131.

22. Wilkinson, *Depictions and Images*, 18.

23. Wilkinson, "*Depictions and Images*," 39.

24. Spiers, "*The Late Victorian Army*," 329.

25. Edward M. Spiers, *The Army and Society, 1815–1914* (London: Longman, 1980), 253–254.

26. Jean-Jacques Becker, *The Great War and the French People* (trans. Arnold Pomerans) (Oxford: Berg, 1985), 3–4.

27. Adrian Gregory, "British 'War Enthusiasm' in 1914: A Reassessment," in *Evidence, History and the Great War: Historians and the Impact of 1914–1918* ed. Gail Braybon (Oxford: Berghahn Books, 2003): 67–85, quotation at 80.

28. Jeffrey Verhey, *The Spirit of 1914: Militarism, Myth, and Mobilization in Germany* (Cambridge: Cambridge University Press, 2000).

29. Ibid.

30. See Michael C. C. Adams, *The Great Adventure: Male Desire and the Coming of World War I* (Bloomington: Indiana University Press, 1990).

31. Diary of A. J. Heraty, Imperial War Museum, London, 81/23/1, p. 3.

32. Peter Simkins, "The Four Armies, 1914–1918" in *The Oxford Illustrated History of the British Army* ed. David Chandler and Ian Beckett (Oxford: Oxford University Press, 1994): 241–262.

33. Simkins, "The Four Armies," 245.

34. Peter Simkins, *Kitchener's Army: The Raising of the New Armies, 1914–1916* (Manchester: Manchester University Press, 1988), chapter 3. Simkins, "The Four Armies," 246–247.

35. Gary Sheffield, *The Somme* (London: Cassell, 2003), 47.

36. Quoted in David Kennedy, *Over Here: The First World War and American Society* (Oxford: Oxford University Press, 1980), 150. For a more specialized treatment, see John Whiteclay Chambers, *To Raise an Army: The Draft Comes to Modern America* (New York: Free Press, 1987).

Six

✹ ✹ ✹

TRAINING, LEADERSHIP, DISCIPLINE, AND MUTINY

> We have had several visits from big pots with brass hats and rows of pretty coloured ribbon. They told one poor chap who lies opposite me with both his legs off, that he would be the hero with all the girls when he got home. As he is a married man, I don't suppose he considers even that is worth the loss of his means of locomotion.
> —British Private M. F. Gower in a letter written from a British field hospital to his sister, July, 1918.[1]

TRAINING AND PREPARATION FOR WAR

Historians know much less about the ways that armies prepared men for war in the years prior to and during World War I than they do about men's actual experiences in combat. For most men, the first taste of combat, not the first day of training, served as the sharp dividing line between their prewar lives and their wartime lives. Training either seemed so mundane or so loosely connected to the war they later fought that most men's memoirs treat training lightly if at all. Three of the most famous memoirs/autobiographical novels of the war written by combat veterans, Frederic Manning's *Her Privates We*, Maurice Genevoix's *Ceux de 14* (*The Men of 1914*), and Erich Maria Remarque's *All Quiet on the Western Front*, begin at or near the front lines with the war already underway.[2] Despite this general neglect, however, understanding methods of training gives us important insights both into the ways that men made the transition from civilian life to a soldier's life and the disillusion many men felt when their experiences of combat stood at marked variance from what they had learned in their training units.

As in the revolutionary and Napoleonic periods, basic training taught elementary skills, but it aimed first and foremost to create small unit dynamics and to instill basic obedience to commands. Virtually all military training sought to subordinate the will of the individual to the will of the group, a problem that the British and the Americans thought was particularly difficult owing to the citizen-army quality of their forces and the local nature of their accession. Men had to learn not to call superior officers by their first names (even if they had known them well in civilian life) and to greet those who outranked them with a salute instead of an extended hand.

Notions of informality were especially acute among the famously egalitarian Australian and New Zealand regiments (ANZAC). Officers in these units had to be careful not to insist too much on the letter of the law lest their men lose respect for them or simply ignore their commands. The Australian "diggers" took tremendous pride in their nonprofessionalism, seeing a virtue in what most professional officers saw as dangerous amateurism. Still, there was no denying the digger spirit and no way to force the ANZACs to behave like their professional French or German counterparts. The British army recognized this difference by naming Lt. Gen. Sir William Birdwood as commander of the ANZAC in 1915. Known as "Birdie" to his men, he was a trained British professional officer, but he rarely pressed his subordinates to insist on a complete obedience to formal army protocol or mannerisms and thus won over the Australians and New Zealanders under his command.

Conscript units and recalled Reserves generally had more professionalism than volunteers, but they also had much less of the spontaneous spirit that motivated the ANZACs and the Americans. Conscription, moreover, led to a tremendous turnover in personnel that impeded any long-term development of unit traditions in peacetime or in war. Conscripts were also much more likely to see their terms of service as a temporary inconvenience and not a rite of passage into the unique and special world of the military. Thus, the training process had first and foremost to instill in such men an identification with their unit.

The problem of preparing Reserves was generally less pronounced in Germany because the German army had carefully planned to use Reserves to augment its active-duty formations in the war's first few weeks. Most armies saw the reserves as best suited for secondary roles like static defense and the protection of supply lines. The Germans, by contrast, had calculated that they could not bring sufficient force to bear in order to win a quick war without the early commitment of the Reserves. German Reserves therefore received much more rigorous and realistic training in the years before World War I than did their European counterparts.

Finding enough men to conduct military training posed a major problem. The rapid rush to war in the weeks immediately following the outbreak of World War I forced armies both to access enormous numbers of men and to send their experienced soldiers into front-line units. Consequently, there were precious few sergeants and junior officers with the requisite skills and experience to train the new men coming into the army by the thousands. The responsibility of training therefore often fell either to veterans too old to serve in combat theaters (and therefore often out of touch with the demands of modern warfare) or to men deemed expendable by their own units. This problem

American soldiers cross a river near Manila around 1900. Note the soldiers on the right-hand side guarding the crossing. Courtesy of the National Archives.

grew less acute over time as the war created men whose light wounds or need for time out of the trenches freed them for training duty.

The amateurish nature of much of military training struck many young men as having a distinct "air of unreality."[3] Trainers, especially in the war's early months, seemed to have little idea of how to prepare men for modern war. They therefore devoted enormous amounts of time to drill and marching, presumably because it instilled discipline and unit cohesion. As their fathers and grandfathers had done, men often spent more time learning to march than learning to fight. In the trainers' defense, it took several months for the lessons of the battlefield to filter back to training units and it took longer still to grasp the realization that linear formations of wars past had little tactical utility on the battlefields of World War I.

A lack of appropriate weapons added to the unreality of military training. With rifles, machine guns, artillery pieces, and ammunition all in short supply, many men, especially in the armies of eastern Europe, trained without functioning weapons. Some recruits drilled with wooden rifles or even broom handles. Time spent with the most modern implements of war was rare as was time spent on crew-served weapons. Many men had to learn how to use these weapons in the heat of battle, having found that their preparation was sorely inadequate to the tasks at hand. Even men who had never served in the military understood the inutility of their military preparation. One Frenchman described his training in 1914 as "stupid when not silly—We walk out three miles to a field and learn East and West, keep step, swing by fours. At times Swedish gymnastics, foolish games such as leap-frog, snap of the whip.... So far all the work was petty beyond imagining."[4] His experiences spoke for thousands of men who wondered what exactly the army was preparing them to do.

This British private shows the mass of equipment a soldier had to carry on campaign. The soldier on the march had to bring cooking utensils, canteens, and tools for making camp. Courtesy of the Library of Congress.

Many men trained without uniforms, normally understood as the key physical differentiation between soldiers and civilians. What uniforms armies did have were normally either worn-out or ill-fitting. Photographs from the period show units in all armies wearing motley collections of uniforms, or even civilian clothes. Kits and equipment were also in short supply, making the first weeks of military training seem more like a camping expedition than a serious effort to prepare men for the challenges of total warfare.

Overwhelmed by the number of men they had to train and the skills they had to impart to them, trainers did what they could with what they had. All armies learned to adapt and improvise. French soldiers soon learned to fall back on what they called their "*Système D*" for the French phrase *se débrouiller*, which, roughly translated, means muddling through somehow when the official system predictably breaks down. One British colonel called the word "improvise" "that blessed word of the British army."[5] Improvisation rapidly became critical to all armies, faced as they were with situations which they could not possibly have foreseen and thus for which they could not possibly have planned.

Added to all of these difficulties was the need to train men as quickly as possible. Some basic training programs were as short as ten weeks, barely enough time to teach men the army's rank structure and the basic functions of military administration. Ten weeks was, however, enough time to teach men that they hated marching and that their superiors cared little for them as individuals. British soldiers learned that "man" had different definitions to different ranks. To a staff officer a man was a chess piece, expendable and sent to do a job from which he might not return. To a quartermaster he was "an envelope of skin consuming food, needing a billet." To a subaltern (the lowest officer rank) he was a "shadowy creature." Finally, to a noncommissioned officer, he was "a being tending constantly toward evil."[6] Small wonder, then, that few men wrote extensive memoirs about their days in basic training.

Once out of basic training, most men were sent to infantry units, but armies also had to prepare men for the dizzying array of jobs needed to fight a modern war. As the importance of artillery to the war became increasingly obvious, more and more men took on highly technical artillery training. Aviation, chemical warfare, and intelligence all required sophisticated advanced training as well. Men with foreign language skills were highly in demand, especially in the British and French armies, because their societies produced relatively few bilingual citizens. Men who could type or operate a telegraph were often sent to training centers to learn the daunting art of military staff work. The importance of supply led many men into special training schools for logistics, railway management, and even field cooking. Throughout the course of the war an increasing proportion of soldiers on the western front were specialists of one kind or another.

As the war dragged on, the process of training replacements benefited both from the battle experiences of the men sent to train the new soldiers and the availability of more plentiful stocks of weapons. Nevertheless, the army's dire need to get new men to the front as quickly as possible made properly training them an extremely difficult endeavor. Col. Sir Geoffrey Christie-Miller, charged with training a Pals Battalion from Aylesbury in 1916, later commented that it was "physically impossible" to train his men for war in the time allotted. He increased the time spent on training to a full seven days per week, dawn to dusk, but still felt his job was incomplete. The first four casualties his battalion suffered were all the result of friendly fire, which the colonel attributed to his soldiers' incomplete training. In their first action, his men botched a trench raid owing to poor preparation which led to more avoidable casualties.[7]

Training also became more difficult as accession standards dropped in 1917 and 1918. Colonel Christie-Miller noted that his Pals Battalion received their replacements in the last two years of the war from men "swept up [by conscription] from many places." Many of them had previously been exempted from service owing to physical defects. Others were either younger or older than his previous soldiers. The colonel found the process of preparing men "not … of robust health" to be "discouraging," but it was a problem faced by trainers in all armies by the end of the war.[8]

The Americans should have been able to improve the quality of their military training by observing actual battlefield conditions for three years before entering the war in 1917. Nevertheless, they failed to do so in any systematic way. Anxious to guard his nation's claims to neutrality, President Wilson refused to permit American officers to observe the war firsthand and he became furious when he learned in 1916 that the American General Staff had begun planning for a possible entry into the war. As a result, the U.S. Army did not significantly adjust its doctrine or its methods of training based on the actual conditions of the western front from 1914 to 1917.

Such isolation struck many Americans as exceedingly foolish. After the sinking of the *Lusitania* by German U-boats killed 128 Americans in May 1915, tensions between the United States and Germany rose sharply. Many Americans began to see their nation turning away from neutrality in the coming months, but they looked aghast at a small army that could not possibly affect events on the battlefield without an enormous effort. With the Wilson administration still adamantly opposed to conscription or preparedness, the army and several private citizens characteristically turned to the spirit of volunteerism.

The army, led by its controversial chief of staff, General Leonard Wood, sought to compensate for the government's benign neglect of military affairs by leaning on voluntary civilian preparedness camps. Wood had started the program with two camps for 200 middle-class college students in 1913 as a "voice to the slumbering people of the country." Wood, supported by his friend and Spanish-American War comrade Theodore Roosevelt, "talked of inspiring patriotic spirit, maintaining national virility, and building up the military establishment."[9] With financial support from many key members of the nation's commercial elite, the movement only needed a spark like the *Lusitania* sinking to lead to a massive expansion.

By the summer of 1916, the preparedness movement, based in Plattsburg, New York, had 16,000 men voluntarily accepting military training at twelve camps. They no longer included just college men passing their summer holidays; they also boasted a former secretary of state and the mayor of New York City. The 1916 National Defense Act also created a voluntary Reserve Officers Training Corps at universities nationwide, a program that eventually trained 28,000 officers and 51,000 enlisted men for wartime service. The same act quadrupled the size of the state-based American National Guard units and regularized the quality of training they were supposed to receive.[10]

But these changes were woefully insufficient to train an army that mushroomed to 4,000,000 men by the end of 1918. As a result, Americans went to Europe with only the most rudimentary infantry training and virtually no specialized training in new weapons systems like tanks, poison gas, and flamethrowers. Instead, like their European counterparts in 1914, American trainees spent countless hours marching. They also listened to endless lectures from Progressive reformers about temperance and sexual diseases and endured the nation's first systematic attempts at intelligence testing.

Much to the U.S. Army leadership's chagrin, the American soldier had to be trained in how to fight by learning on the job from his European allies. Americans quickly learned that their training at home bore little relation to the reality of ground combat in 1918. Although American Expeditionary Forces commander Gen. John J. Pershing stubbornly opposed any attempt to place Americans under foreign commanders, he had no choice but to acceded to Americans training with Allied units, mostly the French.[11] In training, Americans soon learned that Pershing's doctrine of "open warfare" did not reflect the war as fought on the ground, nor did it reflect the war of bayonets and rapid charges that they had trained for in the United States. As a result, the Americans learned from their Allies to fight as they had to, not as they wished to.[12]

Thus, it should come as no surprise that most men disliked their weeks of training. Moreover, as they began to experience the war as it was, they realized how shockingly inaccurate and unhelpful most of their training had been. Most men had to learn how to fight trench warfare from the men who had already done it. Not all of them were willing to share the lessons they had learned with their replacements. Each man and each unit had to go through learning curves that the army's own training programs often lengthened. Many men therefore remembered the training period as one in which they had learned little about fighting but much about the army's inefficiency, the incompetence of many of its officers, and the seemingly capricious and inefficient ways that the army managed its manpower. Some men even looked forward to training being over so they could get to the front lines which, although more dangerous, at least contributed to the ultimate goal of winning the war. As one of the soldiers in Frederic Manning's *Her Privates We* noted to a comrade, "The war might be a damned sight more tolerable if it weren't for the bloody army."[13]

GOTT MIT UNS: NATIONALISM, RELIGION, AND SOLDIERS' MOTIVATIONS FOR FIGHTING

The wars of the French Revolution and the Napoleonic period showed how powerful a force nationalism could be in motivating men to fight. The Wars of German Unification, especially the final stages of the Franco-Prussian War, demonstrated the lengths to which a nationalized people would go before accepting defeat. The soldiers of World War I were the products of an even more highly nationalized Europe. As the events surrounding the outbreak of the war demonstrated, national identity superceded identities based on religion, politics, and class, symbolized by the virtual absence of partisan bickering in the war's early years.

Nationalism as Motivator

For most men, nationalism served as an important means of motivation in the early stages of the war. Soldiers from areas occupied by the enemy had a particular motivation to fight in order to liberate their homelands. Members of ethnic or religious minorities, moreover, often fought to demonstrate their loyalty and reliability to the state. Despite the habitual anti-Semitism of Germany, Russia, and France, Jews served in the armies of all of the great powers in numbers disproportionate to their share of the population. Similarly, many leaders of the American black community saw the war as a "'God-sent blessing,' as one Negro newspaper put it, to earn white regard and advance the standing of the race by valiant wartime service."[14] Few of these groups received the rewards that they had hoped for, making their voluntary service and faith in the unifying power of nationalism appear all the more tragic in retrospect.

As the war dragged on, however, nationalism became a much more important force for unifying people on the home front than it was for motivating soldiers on the fighting fronts. Soldiers of all wars have typically shown an increasing separation from abstract notions the longer they live in a world dominated by the cold, hard realities of warfare. The loss of much of their idealism did not, however, mean that men failed to understand the price of victory and defeat. Although their rhetoric may have become less proud over time, they knew that a loss on the battlefield could have enormous implications for their nation and, by extension, for their families and for them as individuals.

Soldiers in the Allied armies therefore received tremendous motivation from the ways that the Germans treated the nations they conquered. Heavily colored by propaganda and exaggeration (probably unnecessarily in light of the German army's actual atrocities), Germany's brutal occupation of Belgium and Romania, among others, served as a visible reminder that as awful as the war itself was, one had to keep fighting. "Against the Boches taken singly, I have no grudge," wrote home one French soldier, "but I am perfectly determined not to allow my linguistic and idealistic family group to be swallowed up theirs."[15]

As this letter shows, men often felt little hatred for their enemies as people. Indeed, as the Christmas truce of 1914 showed (much to the alarm of many senior commanders), men often identified with soldiers on the other side. Unlike civilians at home, the enemy's soldiers were young men fighting the same war and facing the same hardships. Like themselves, the enemy's soldiers had to deal with the same abysmal weather, malfunctioning equipment, dim-witted officers, and inedible food. Even after all the killing of four years, therefore, as soon as the guns went silent on November 11, soldiers crossed No Man's Land to offer help to one another and to shake hands. This sentiment of shared experiences survived into the German occupation of France during World War II, when German and French veterans of World War I often commiserated quite convivially with one other.

For many men, therefore, the motivations for fighting were based only loosely on nationalism or on hatred of the enemy. Often the motivations were personal, such as to avenge the death of a comrade or to see the war to its end alongside one's comrades. Many men understood that winning the war was the only reliable way to end the suffering and, more importantly, to return home to family. As long as the war continued, the best a man could hope for as a means to get home for more than a few days' leave was to be wounded badly enough to be released from military service, but not badly enough to leave a man paralyzed or disfigured for life.

Religion as Motivator, Deterrent, and Guidance

Religion motivated many soldiers despite the mass killing and inherent contradictions in asking God's help to kill one's fellow man. Several senior commanders were intensely religious and derived much of their ability to lead from a resolutely held conviction in God's blessing. British Expeditionary Forces commander Field Marshal Sir Douglas Haig believed firmly that Providence had chosen him to win the war for Britain. Haig once wrote to his wife, "I *feel* that every step in my plan has been taken with the Divine help—and I ask daily for aid." Haig also comforted his subordinate commanders by telling them "that we shall win 'Not by might, nor by power, but by my spirit,' saith the Lord of hosts."[16] Many of the French generals came from devoutly Catholic backgrounds. Edouard Noël de Castelnau was a lay member of the Capuchin order and was known by the nickname "the fighting friar." France's Ferdinand Foch, who eventually commanded all of the Allied armies was, also powerfully influenced by his faith that God was helping to guide his hand.[17]

Only the most skeptical of officers sought to keep religion out of their units. Most saw it as a way to provide comfort and motivation for their men. American Expeditionary Forces commander Gen. John Pershing was not religious himself, but was always careful to ensure that the spiritual needs of his men were met. As the example of the French generals shows, religion was important even in the army of Europe's most overtly anticlerical state. All armies, including the French, used chaplains extensively in a wide variety of functions. They not only ministered to the religious needs of their men, they also wrote letters home for wounded or illiterate soldiers, looked after men's personal effects, and, occasionally, learned to be stretcher bearers or even field medics.

All of the great powers tried to link their cause to God and religion. German soldiers marched to war with *Gott Mit Uns* (God is with us) inscribed on their belt buckles. Russia tried to justify its war on the basis of fighting for the rights of Serbian co-religionists and used the Orthodox Church (with decreasing success as the war dragged on) as a means to link its soldiers to the Tsarist regime. Attempts to use religion to justify the war did not always produce results. The Ottoman call to jihad found few takers outside Anatolia and any attempt to find religious motivation in the heterogeneous Austro-Hungarian Empire, whose chaplains performed services in all of Europe's religions, proved futile.

European Catholics stood in a particularly difficult position. With countries containing large Catholic populations like France and Italy on one side and Germany and Austria on the other, the Vatican found itself in a difficult position. The pope had largely remained marginal to the events of the July crisis and he grew increasingly paralyzed as the war developed. Unwilling to support either side, but equally unable to demand that Catholics not fight, the Vatican soon found itself losing prestige. The manifest failure of the Papal Peace Initiative, in August 1917, to develop any momentum further isolated the Vatican. Nevertheless, Catholics fought in all armies despite the manifest ambivalence of the pope and the Holy See.

The Catholic Church did, however, work to ameliorate as much human suffering as it could. Not associated with any belligerent force, it could work with relief organizations in all of them. Pope Benedict XV spent church funds and the majority of his personal fortune to help resettle refugees, feed victims of famine, and arrange for medical care in areas impacted by Spanish influenza. He also negotiated two large-scale prisoner exchanges. These activities earned the church respect, but played little role in helping Catholics wrestle with their conflicting loyalties.

The ability of German Catholics to overcome the many barriers they faced shows that religion served to motivate men to fight much more often than it inclined them to peace. German Catholics fought for their nation despite Otto von Bismarck's anti-Catholic *Kulturkampf* movement of the 1880s and the German atrocities committed against Catholic Belgium. The Allies widely publicized German attacks on the magnificent cathedral at Reims and German burnings of numerous churches across France and Belgium, most notably at Louvain. Allegations of the widespread rapes of Belgian nuns by German soldiers had little basis in fact, but were widely believed, and underscored the ways that religion became mobilized for propaganda and motivational purposes.[18]

Many men saw the contradictions of religion and resisted its appeal. A recent study of religion in the British army concluded that the war did not lead to a religious revival either among soldiers or among civilians on the home front because religion proved to be an inadequate mechanism for men to understand the mass slaughter of the war.[19] Many men, however, understood their religious convictions to be inconsistent with military service, leading them to declare themselves conscientious objectors.

President Woodrow Wilson, a man whose faith often guided his policy, infused the latter months of the war with a new sense of idealism. Believing America to be the last idealistic nation on earth, Wilson called for "a war to end all wars" and a war "to make the world safe for democracy." Many Americans left for Europe heeding his calls. North Carolina's Willard Newton wrote, just before storming the Hindenburg Line in 1918: "At last we are at the beginning of a real battle between Prussianism and Democracy! And we are to fight on the side of Democracy that the world may forever be free from the Prussian peril! That never again will we have to leave our peaceful pursuits and cross an ocean to fight barbarians."[20]

In light of later events these words seem strikingly naïve, but they captured the spirit of thousands of young and inexperienced Americans. Europeans, physically and mentally exhausted from years of war, often just shook their heads at the new soldiers and figured that a baptism of fire would quickly change their outlook. Several prescient observers noted that the attitude of the "Yanks" in 1918 resembled that of many Europeans in 1914. American naïveté therefore reminded Europeans both of their own now tarnished idealism and the hundreds of thousands of men who had died fighting for those ideals.

Loss of Motivation

As the war could tarnish ideals, so too could it destroy a man's will to fight. In extreme cases, it could destroy an entire army's will. The ideals and beliefs for which men went to war in 1914 too often gave way to pointless death, inept leadership, and a war that, until its final weeks, seemed to have no end in sight. Unlike soldiers in past wars, the soldiers of World War I had no lengthy periods of peace between periods of war and unlike future soldiers, they did not go home after serving a set period of time. The cumulative effect wore men down just as it wore down their equipment.

In individual cases, men who had had too much might desert, but desertion was a serious crime with equally serious consequences. Some soldiers simply disappeared for a few days or took an extra day or two on their leave, pleading that transportation problems prevented their timely return. As we will see below, these "crimes" varied significantly both in degree and how they were received by the men of a unit. Soldiers might also resist obeying orders they thought to be senseless and encourage others to do so as well. More commonly, men who had experienced more than their psyches could handle began to become increasingly less effective. They made careless mistakes, took unnecessary risks, or began to display the psychological symptoms of dementia.

Units with a critical mass of such men often simply dissolved during an enemy attack. Soldiers ran away, surrendered quickly, or hid. Such a state of demoralization helped the Russians break Austro-Hungarian lines during the Brusilov Offensive of 1916 and the Germans to break Italian lines at Caporetto the following year. Intelligence officers carefully monitored the number of men who gave themselves up as a critical gauge of enemy morale. The mounting number of Germans who surrendered without firing a shot in the late summer and fall of 1918 gave Allied commanders their first sure indicators that they could win the war before the end of the year.

The Russian Revolution of 1917 is the most famous example of large-scale loss of motivation, but there were many others. Almost every army had its incidence from the French mutinies following the failed Chemin des Dames offensive to the mutiny of the German navy at the end of the war. Ethnic minorities in the Austro-Hungarian and Russian armies often simply melted away when attacked, having lost all faith in the larger goals of the empire.

Those men who stayed and saw the war to its end often concluded that only one outcome could justify the bloodletting. The war could only offer humanity a better future if, as Woodrow Wilson rather sanguinely expressed, it was to be the last of its kind. Extreme nationalism, militarism, and irredentism would have to give way to a better future based on more noble ideals; thus the rapturous welcome Europeans gave Wilson and the bitter disappointment they felt when he could not convert his rhetoric into reality. As that welcome demonstrates, the Americans were not the only ones to hold out such hope. Frenchman Robert Pellissier spoke for thousands of soldiers when he wrote, "The only raison d'être of this hideous war is that it is the end of European militarism."[21] That it was not explains so much of the anger that Europeans felt in the 1920s and the 1930s.

OFFICERS AND LEADERSHIP

Few soldiers had sustained contact with officers senior in rank to a major or a lieutenant colonel.[22] The debates between well-known generals at division, corps, and army headquarters were as foreign to most soldiers as the châteaux where many of these discussions took place. A visit from a dignitary to an area near the front line was more often than not an unwelcome prospect for most men, involving as it did parade practices, repair of worn uniforms and equipment, and the universally detested order to "clean up" the filthy trenches lest the dignitary happen by. Robert Pellissier noted that a visit to his field hospital by several officers and France's President Raymond Poincaré served as the cause for the rare sweeping of floors and the even rarer appearance of sheets on the cots. Although Pellissier makes no specific reference to confirm it, one can assume that when the president left, so too did the sheets, probably destined for the next hospital on Poincaré's itinerary. On another occasion Poincaré reviewed the men of Pellissier's unit, sending soldiers on a surreal quest to find yellow flowers to decorate the barracks "in style" for the president.[23]

While most senior officers were physically remote and far from men's minds, some of them nevertheless enjoyed good reputations among their soldiers. Senior officers like France's Marie Emile Fayolle, Russia's Alexei Brusilov, and Britain's Herbert Plumer had well-established reputations for careful preparations and an unwillingness to fight rushed or unnecessary battles. Others, like the Ottoman Empire's Mustapha Kemal and the famous German duo of Erich Ludendorff and Paul von Hindenburg, had legendary reputations based on a long string of success. Men under such commanders could convince themselves that their leaders would not sell or give away their lives cheaply or without purpose.

Other commanders grew popular with their men by taking an active interest in the daily welfare of their men. France's Henri Philippe Pétain and Italy's Armando Diaz both took over senior posts with a willingness to listen to their men's legitimate complaints and, more importantly, to take active measures to solve their problems. Both men increased the amount of leave their soldiers received, improved the quality of their food, and forced their subordinate officers to appear in the trenches more often and talk with their soldiers to better understand how they saw the war. They also ameliorated discipline and reduced the harsh sentences of many men convicted of minor offenses.

Appearing in the trenches with an eye toward learning how the war was really being fought (rather than for the chance to be photographed looking officious with the troops) was another way for a commander to win his men's loyalty. The appearance of several civilians (notably French prime minister Georges Clemenceau, who made weekly appearances at the front, Italian king Victor Emmanuel II, and British statesman Lord Richard Haldane) in the trenches, occasionally exposing themselves to enemy fire, raised their stature in soldiers' eyes and shamed many reluctant officers into coming to the trenches themselves more regularly. The more an officer seemed to be genuinely sympathizing with the men he led, the more popular he was likely to be.

Soldiers understood that they very well might die in war; many veterans had even accepted the inevitability of their own deaths. The prospect of dying therefore bothered men much less than the prospect of dying a futile death unconnected to the larger goal of winning the war. Senior commanders with reputations for incompetence or rash behavior could diminish the morale of the men of their units by increasing the prospect of their dying a meaningless death. This problem became increasingly acute as the war dragged on in the Russian and Austro-Hungarian armies where a long string of failures reinforced in men's minds the image of poor, even criminally poor, leadership. Similarly, men viewed with dread the prospect of serving in units led by the hyper-aggressive French general Charles "The Butcher" Mangin and British general Sir Hubert Gough, whose unprepared Fifth Army took a particularly severe beating in March 1918. After that battle, journalist Philip Gibbs met a group of British soldiers being transferred from Gough's Fifth Army to the sector of the more meticulous Second Army commanded by the widely admired Herbert Plumer. "God be thanked we are leaving the Fifth Army area," one of the men told Gibbs.[24] Men could often face the enemy's guns more easily than the presumed incompetence of their own commanders.

Levels of Leadership

Senior commanders, far away and living in relative comfort, became easy lightning rods for anything and everything that went wrong in an operation. Soldiers, of course, knew little of how the decision-making process functioned at high levels, nor did they see the larger strategic picture at work. Rumors of luxury and safety behind lines at châteaux furthered the suspicions many men held about their leaders. Many senior commanders, of course, did perform poorly during the war, but the circumstances under which they had to make their decisions were often vastly more complex than soldiers had any opportunity to understand or appreciate.

All armies separated their officers into line and staff. The former served in the trenches and provided immediate leadership to combat units. Because they "had to share almost the same privations and miseries" as their soldiers, they often developed close relationships with their men.[25] Perhaps more importantly, junior line officers had about as little say in the orders they received and had to execute as did the men they led. Line officers did not conceive operations nor did they draw up the orders for attacks. Like their men, they did not always understand the higher purpose of an offensive. Officers in smaller military units like companies and platoons thus had a shared equality of misery that often drew them and their men together more tightly.

Line officers were responsible for mastering a wide variety of skills, including working with local populations to acquire food and shelter, tactical preparation, inspections, and the maintenance of morale and discipline. A sense of the wide range of tasks demanded of line officers comes from the number of pamphlets and books written by officers (often anonymously) and sold by private publishers to help men prepare for officership. A sample of the titles written by British officers includes: "Notes on Trench Routine and Discipline"; "Parley Voo for British Soldiers"; "Turkish for Tommy and Tar"; "Notes for Quick Training on Active Service"; "Kit and Equipment for Active Service: What to Take and Where to Carry It"; "Questions and Answers on Tactics"; "Shrapnel Effects"; "Guide to Courts Martial"; and "How to Become a Useful and Efficient Officer." The existence of a large market for privately published works such as these reveals the inadequacy many officers must have felt about the official preparation they had received for their jobs.

A rare photo of German officers in World War I. By this point, all armies had adopted dark, dull-colored uniforms designed to better blend into terrain. The Germans called theirs "field gray." Courtesy of the McDermott Library, Special Collections Branch, United States Air Force Academy.

The line officer's most important job, of course, was to lead attacks. Consequently, the line officer corps of all of the belligerents suffered tremendous casualties in the war's early weeks. France lost an astonishing 4,700 of its 44,500 prewar officers in the Battles of the Frontiers in August 1914. Some estimates put the death rate of Austro-Hungarian officers in 1914 alone as high as 25 percent. A survey of four British regular battalions showed that of their 106 officers on August 23, 1914, thirty-eight had been killed before the end of November, with forty-one more wounded in action and one captured in action by the enemy, amounting to an incredible 75 percent casualty rate.[26] The intense combat of the war's opening months destroyed the armies' prewar leadership and showed that line officers fought and died alongside their men, suffering enormously in the process.

Staff officers were a different matter entirely. Rarely seen in the trenches, their job involved planning the myriad of small details needed to make an army march and an offensive function. The precise level of divisions between line and staff officers varied from army to army. In some armies officers rotated between the line and the staff; in others staff officers remained staff officers for the duration of the war. Staff officers, stereotyped recently in the character of Captain Kevin Darling in the popular BBC miniseries *Blackadder Goes Forth* (1989), often lived lives of relative comfort and safety. In most armies they wore distinct uniforms, with British staff officers wearing on their collars the scarlet tab so widely loathed by line officers and the men in the trenches.

Whether an accurate portrayal or not, most soldiers saw staff officers as men entirely out of touch with the realties of warfare. Worse, they were seen as men who had no desire to understand what soldiers had to endure on a daily basis. Philip Gibbs wrote that the staff officers he observed at Field Marshal Sir Douglas Haig's General Headquarters lived "in a world of [their] own, rose-colored, remote from the ugly things of war. They had heard of the trenches, yes, but as the West End [of London] hears of the East End—a nasty place where the common people lived."[27]

Western front veteran Siegfried Sassoon agreed in a scathing poem called "Base Details" (1918). Note Sassoon's use of "scarlet" in the poem, a reference to the color of the staff officer tabs:

> If I were fierce, and bald, and short of breath,
> I'd live with scarlet Majors at the Base,
> And speed glum heroes up the line to death.
> You'd see me with my puffy petulant face,
> Guzzling and gulping in the best hotel,
> Reading the Roll of Honour. "Poor young chap,"
> I'd say—"I used to know his father well;
> Yes, we've lost heavily in this last scrap."
> And when the war is done and youth stone dead,
> I'd toddle safely home and die—in bed.[28]

Barbusse recalled a comrade flying into a rage upon hearing a staff officer say, "Later, when we go home—if we go home." "Now that was too much," the soldier groused. "To say things like that you have to earn the right: it's like a decoration. I don't mind them swinging the lead, but [imagine] pretending to be in danger when you've taken to your heels before even getting there."[29] Of course, not all staff officers were so callous, but Sassoon and Barbusse encapsulated their general reputation among both line officers and soldiers at the front lines.

Finding the right men to become officers posed a significant problem. The amorphous qualities that define "leadership" have always proved elusive. Most armies preferred to recruit their officers, especially their staff officers, from traditional elite groups whose literacy and presumed reliability made them a predictable choice. The senior ranks of the British, German, Austrian, Italian, and Russian officer corps all contained a disproportionate number of nobles. Even the French army, ostensibly republican, had a large number of men from noble families. In 1878, 102 of the 365 graduates from the French military academy at St. Cyr were nobles.[30] The Third Republic took active measures to discourage the concentration of nobles such as monitoring their political activity and forcing all St. Cyriens to spend a year in the line with a regiment before moving on to specialized training. The former created the notorious "fiches" scandal of 1905 and the latter caused a great deal of resentment, but neither measure eliminated the role of nobles in the officer corps.

As the sizes of World War I armies expanded far beyond the capacity of traditional elites to lead, the officer corps opened significantly. Middle-class men were more likely to become officers than were working-class men, especially in staff positions and in the artillery. The Americans, of course, eschewed aristocrats altogether, as did the Australians and the Canadians, who eventually replaced their British commanders with national ones. Many of these men came from militia origins and stood out from their British peers both in background and in outlook. By the middle of the war, the Australians were led by John Monash, a Jewish engineer, and the Canadians by Arthur Currie, a failed real estate salesman. Both were clear outsiders to the British system, but both proved to be superb organizers, trainers, and field commanders.

All armies turned out of necessity to raising officers by promoting men from the ranks. The Germans did perhaps the best job of promoting from the ranks owing to their close prewar attention to the quality of their noncommissioned officers. Men who showed initiative and innate leadership abilities usually stood the best chance of receiving a promotion. As we have seen, such a promotion was far from a guarantee of safety; new officers clearly understood that casualties rates for lieutenants and captains were often among an army's highest because they often led charges personally. Still, a commission meant more respect, more pay, and better material conditions when at the front, behind the lines, and on leave.

Not all men, however, wanted to become officers. Promotion meant associating with other officers, many of whom the men hated on general principles. More important, it meant accepting a social and military barrier between oneself and one's comrades. A comrade of Frederic Manning's protagonist Corporal Bourne asked him if he would accept the commission rumored to have been offered to him. "It was," Manning writes, "as though the boy had asked him if he were going to surrender to the Hun." Bourne told his comrade that he would accept the commission but he did so "harshly, accepting bitterly all the implications in the question."[31]

British private J. Elliott came to the attention of his officers by raiding a German trench without orders and coming back with a dead German soldier. He was soon ordered to see the brigade commander. Believing that he would be severely punished for acting without orders, he "went down that long road to brigade headquarters in fear and trembling." Rather than facing punishment, he found himself facing the equally daunting offer of a promotion to the officer corps. Elliott later recalled his conversation with the brigade commander:

> BRIGADIER STEWART—"WHY DID YOU BRING IN A DEAD HUN?"
> POOR ME (STUTTERING BADLY)—"I KILLED HIM BETWEEN THE WIRES AND THOUGHT I WOULD SEE IF I COULD GET A SOUVENIR."
> BRIGADIER—"EVER THINK OF TAKING A COMMISSION?"
> POOR ME—"NO, SIR!"
> BRIGADIER—"DO YOU WANT ONE?"
> POOR ME—"NO, SIR!"
> BRIGADIER—"DON'T BE A DAMNED FOOL—HERE'S YOUR PAPERS. GOODBYE!"[32]

Thus did Private Elliott become Lieutenant Elliott.

The Europeans were not the only ones facing a massive expansion of their officer corps. The American army needed 200,000 officers for its expanding units, but at the time of American entry into the war the nation had just 18,000 active-duty and National Guard officers. The Americans promoted 16,000 men from the ranks and gave 70,000 direct commissions to men in specialized fields like medicine and logistics. The remaining men had to be trained quickly in programs that sometimes ran from 5:15 in the morning to 10:00 at night. More than half of the 182,000 men the

Americans commissioned in just nineteen months had served in a voluntary program modeled on the Plattsburg system. Approximately 3,700 men became captains upon finishing the training while the rest accepted lieutenancies.[33]

In addition to the leadership provided by officers, smaller units leaned heavily on their sergeants and corporals. Noncommissioned officers had always occupied a central place in the world of the infantry unit. Close to the men in rank, social origin, and military occupation, they often were the critical links between soldiers and the larger army. They provided the mechanism for teaching men how to fight and how to survive the many pitfalls they faced. In many units they became big brothers or even substitute fathers for soldiers, especially young soldiers.

Elite units such as the German pioneers, the Italian *arditi*, and the French *chasseurs à pied* trained their noncommissioned officers to display initiative in combat and to lead in the absence of officers. Experienced noncommissioned officers often assumed tactical leadership during battles, rallying men and making critical decisions in the midst of combat. Because they were so valuable to units, noncommissioned officers did not receive promotions to the officer corps as often as one might expect. Many units thought their veteran and experienced noncommissioned officers were too valuable to them to lose even by promotion to the commissioned officer corps.

The quality of First World War leadership remains an intensely debated subject. It has not been the purpose of this part of the book to enter into the many debates on "good" versus "bad" leaders, but rather to suggest the many ways that soldiers saw their leaders and the roles that these leaders played in their soldiers' daily lives. One of the most despised of those roles centered on the leaders' charge to administer discipline to men who had violated military codes.

DISCIPLINE AND PUNISHMENT

The plot line of one episode of the popular (if not quite historically accurate) BBC series *Blackadder Goes Forth* centered around the eponymous character shooting and eating a messenger pigeon that was carrying an order to attack. The pigeon, as it turned out, was a childhood pet of the commanding general whose staff placed Captain Blackadder under arrest more for having shot the general's beloved "Speckled Jim" than for having disobeyed a direct order to advance. The heavily rigged court-martial, chaired by the general himself, found Blackadder guilty and sentenced him to be summarily shot the next morning. Only the intervention of the War Office spared his life.

Military Justice

The episode lampoons a military justice system that has come under increased fire in the years since World War I. A Pardons movement in Britain has recently tried to posthumously reverse the convictions of several soldiers found guilty of crimes during the war. The harshness of disciplinary systems during the war look increasingly cruel from modern, and presumably more enlightened, perspectives. As with so many other aspects of the military and its administration, military justice had to improvise and adapt to a scale and scope of problems it had never envisioned. In many ways it failed to do so.

Military justice had three fundamental, and sometimes contradictory, purposes. First, it had to enforce standards of discipline and order within military units. An order or a regulation that men could ignore with impunity was worthless. Second, military justice had to aim for equity. A system that seemed to mete out punishments to men identified as malcontents, but not to the commander's favorites, could quickly lose its legitimacy in the eyes of men or in the eyes of civilians charged with its oversight. Last, military justice had to "maintain intact the fragile balances which, in relations between men and their officers, ensured individual and collective consent to an authority recognized to be legitimate."[34] In other words, the system had to administer punishments reasonably in line with the crimes committed. Officers who punished their men too severely might lose moral capital with them; officers who punished too lightly might risk seeing standards in their unit decline. Achieving a reasonable balance between these three goals proved to be difficult for experienced officers and almost impossible for newly commissioned ones.

All armies faced the problem of administering justice on large scales, often to men unaccustomed to the military. In the years before 1914, military justice systems had become generally more prescribed, removing some of the informal local authority traditionally wielded by regimental officers. In 1906 the French introduced trial by a court-martial consisting of a jury of seven officers, legal reviews, appeals, and observation by civilian officials.[35] The reforms, designed to protect the rights of accused soldiers from their harsh or spiteful commanding officers, was far too cumbersome and slow to deal with the greatly expanded French army of 1914–1918.

Added to these problems was the need to solidify the morale and solidarity of military units. Inexperienced officers often drew facile connections between strict discipline and unit morale. Even minor breaches of regulations, they concluded, would hamper the training and fighting effectiveness of their soldiers. For many officers, their negative views of their men reflected deeply entrenched class, regional, and racial biases. Italy's General Luigi Cadorna, who probably administered more death sentences than any other general of the war, loathed his southern Italian soldiers and believed them to be lazy and insolent by nature. Only the sternest discipline, he believed, could make soldiers out of such rotten human characters.

Eastern European generals often held similar views. Russian officers habitually "supported their authority with verbal and physical abuse" against which Russian soldiers had little recourse. Officers in all armies tended to see their soldiers as more or less impersonal resources that should be taught to act, not to think. As one observer of military justice noted, "The idea of the intelligent and responsible soldier capable of individual initiative and rational corporate action in the main took second place to traditional concepts of mechanical obedience based on punishment and fear."[36] Given such attitudes it is not surprising that officers in all armies more often preferred punishments to rewards as the means to force soldiers to act as they wanted them to.

Because of the large number of men in uniform, court-martial systems like the one the French instituted before the war were quickly overwhelmed. Authority during the war normally devolved to a soldier's immediate chain of command, a method that reduced the workload of the military justice system, but at the same time opened it to tremendous abuses at the hands of spiteful or inexperienced officers. Commanders had numerous traditional punishment options at their disposal from incarceration to removal of privileges to assignment of unpleasant tasks like night patrols and cleaning of dishes and latrines.

Among the most notorious tools at the hands of officers was the British Field Punishment No. 1 in which men were tied to posts in a public place. The purpose of such public humiliation was both to punish the offender and to discourage others from following in his footsteps. Other armies used similar methods, many of which became increasingly controversial over time. The German Reichstag intervened to prohibit German soldiers from being tied when under arrest and the practice gradually became less common in the British army as well. Commanders, however, could usually be much more creative in the punishments they ordered than reformers could be in monitoring them.

British Field Punishment No. 1 and other punishments like it were generally used for men guilty (or merely believed to be guilty) of relatively minor offenses. More serious offenses brought with them more serious punishments, including, in the gravest cases, the death penalty. All of the World War I armies used the death penalty, usually for crimes like cowardice in the face of the enemy, failure to follow orders in battle, and, later in the war, inciting others to disobey commanders. Of the armies that kept reliable records, Italy handed down the most capital convictions, 4,028, followed by Britain at 3,080, France at 2,000, and Germany at 150. Eventually, governments in all of these states except Italy began to take a greater interest in the issuance of capital convictions, commuting many death sentences and thereby reducing the number of men actually executed. Even in Italy, however, only a fraction of the men condemned to death saw a firing squad. Italy executed 750 men, Austria-Hungary 740, France 700, Britain 346, and Germany just 48. The Russian army did not keep detailed records, but we can assume that its numbers were much closer to those of Italy than those of Germany.

Capital Punishment

The severity and capriciousness of capital punishment drew considerable attention from the public and from civilian officials. One of the most notorious events occurred in March 1915, and later became the focal point of Stanley Kubrick's powerful movie *Paths of Glory* (1957). A French general, frustrated with the failure of his men to break German lines, ordered an already exhausted company to attack again. They left their trenches, but quickly returned when a storm of German fire made their advance impossible. Furious, the general ordered his own artillery to fire on the French trenches in order to motivate the men to attack again. The artillery commander refused to comply with an order he knew to be both immoral and illegal unless the general put the order in writing. Because doing so would leave evidence of an illegal order, the general refused and rescinded his order.

Angered even further by the refusal of his artillery, the general then ordered four corporals and sixteen privates into No Man's Land in broad daylight to cut the enemy's barbed wire. The men, recognizing a suicide mission when they saw one, left their trenches, but hid in shell holes until nightfall when they crawled back to their trenches, many of them having suffered wounds. The general convened a court-martial that quickly found the corporals guilty of failure to carry out legal orders and condemned them to death. The men of their regiment threatened to revolt if the sentences were carried out so the general ordered troops of another unit brought in for security. A shaky firing squad killed two of the corporals, but only wounded the other two, who had to be executed with pistols at close range.[37] The case became a national scandal in France, but did not end the practice of summary executions of men largely innocent of any crime worthy of the ultimate punishment. Over time, however, the military's power to order harsh punishments came under much more careful scrutiny. In France, President Raymond Poincaré reasserted his constitutional right to review all capital cases in 1917.

The sympathy that soldiers displayed toward the accused or the condemned varied widely, depending not only on the offense but against whom soldiers perceived the offense to have been directed. All soldiers understood that some men, like the unfortunate four corporals executed in the example above, were simply victims of being in the wrong unit at the wrong time. They also understood that the same fate might one day befall them. Other crimes, if deemed justifiable by one's comrades, brought a great deal of empathy. A man who left his unit during a calm period to visit a sick relative was technically absent without leave, but few men saw this transgression as a crime worthy of anything more than a slap on the wrist. Officers who could deal with such cases fairly and judiciously often received a great deal of loyalty from their men in return. Officers who could keep such minor punishments "in house" and out of the formal judicial system showed their understanding of their soldiers and the best way to discipline them with compassion.

In contrast, a man who had committed a crime perceived as weakening the unit in a time of crisis was unlikely to get a sympathetic hearing, even from his own comrades. Frederic Manning describes a Lance-Corporal Miller, already marked in his unit as a poor comrade, who had deserted just before the July 1916 Somme offensive, but was soon located in Rouen and captured. Manning noted that the man's colleagues were unanimous in their judgment that he should meet a firing squad, but not for the official reasons:

> The fact that he had deserted his commanding officer, which would be the phrase used to describe his offence on the charge-sheet, was as nothing compared to the fact that he had deserted them. They were to go through it while he saved his skin. It was about as bad as it could be, and if one were to ask any man who had been through that spell of fighting what ought to be done in the case of Miller, there could only have been one answer. Shoot the bugger.[38]

Manning also noted, however, that no man in the unit wanted to be selected for the gruesome duty of actually serving on the firing squad and thereby having to kill one of their own, however despicable they may have found his behavior.

Serving on a firing squad could be a punishment in itself. In most cases men drew lots to determine who would constitute a firing squad. However, if a soldier had fallen asleep on watch or been drunk and disorderly, but an officer did not want to raise the charge to a formal complaint, making the man serve on a firing squad could serve as a punishment that left no official paperwork behind it. Indeed, the man might receive an official commendation from higher headquarters for performing an unpleasant but necessary task. His comrades, however, would know the truth.

Dangerous Missions and Other Punishments

To punish men for more severe crimes, commanders could order them to conduct extremely dangerous missions. Sébastien Japrisot's widely acclaimed novel *A Very*

Long Engagement follows the efforts of a woman to find her fiancé, whom the army had officially listed as missing and presumed killed in action. As she soon learned, however, he and several comrades had been ordered into No Man's Land in broad daylight by a commander who singled them out at random in order to motivate the unit.[39] Such forms of discipline were officially discouraged, but were nevertheless common practice in many units.

Informal forms of discipline were often much more effective than official ones. The example of Lance-Corporal Miller demonstrates the value of a unit policing its members by self-discipline. More than the fear of punishment from officers, some men were disciplined by their desires not to let their comrades down. These sentiments built upon the close links men formed in their training and reinforced during their combat experiences. In the same way that soldiers fell on grenades to save the lives of their comrades, men stayed with their units and obeyed orders in order to ensure that they did their part to secure the survival of their comrades. To many men, the fear of letting down their comrades was even greater than the fear of dying.

Commanders sometimes reflected this sentiment by resorting to collective punishments. Entire units, or men selected at random from units, might be punished for the actions of an individual, as happened to the characters in Japrisot's novel. Collective punishments encouraged members of a unit to keep close tabs on the behavior of the men in their unit. This practice was most common in the Italian army, which used decimation, the punishment of a random 10 percent of a unit, as a method to encourage discipline in a unit or to punish a group when an individual perpetrator could not be identified.

The unfairness of the military justice system reflected both the limited awareness of armies and the preconceptions of their officers. Unknown thousands of soldiers received punishments while suffering from what doctors today would recognize as post-traumatic stress disorder. While some officers made efforts to understand the ways that what was then called "shell shock" could place enormous psychological stresses on soldiers, armies as a whole were slow to make allowances for such traumas in their judicial systems. Many officers, including many doctors, simply refused to believe that shell shock was anything more than an attempt by cowardly men to evade their military responsibilities.

Prewar stereotypes and images interacted with the justice system as well. Luigi Cadorna's suspicion of southern Italians undoubtedly placed them in the hands of courts martial more often than their northern comrades. The United States executed just ten soldiers serving in Europe during the war, but hanged thirteen black soldiers in Houston following an outbreak of racial tensions in the city that left seventeen civilians dead. The soldiers were tried, convicted, and hanged in just three days with no appeal permitted. Six more were later hanged with the approval of President Woodrow Wilson and Secretary of War Newton Baker. The men of the battalion to which the hanged men had belonged were all disarmed, cashiered out of the army, and transferred to New Mexico for imprisonment. The speed and harshness of the sentences shocked the American black community, which called the sentences "military lynchings," and later led to a formal apology from the United States government.[40]

The German army's military justice system proved to be both the most flexible and the most lenient of World War I, as evidenced by the comparatively low number of death sentences ordered and carried out. German army officials recognized more often than their counterparts the futility of a justice system based on coercion alone. German commanders were expected to deal with disciplinary problems early on and prevent men from becoming repeat offenders. They were also trained to identify potential problems and solve them before they reached the level of a court-martial offense. Special military police companies dealt with violators of military codes at the front, thus alleviating the pressure on the court-martial system.[41]

This flexibility was reflected at higher levels as well. German courts-martial showed more leniency and creativity than those of other armies. The Germans understood physical and psychological trauma as circumstances that could, if not exactly absolve a man of his crimes, at least reduce the charges and ameliorate the punishment meted out. German courts heard from doctors who sometimes testified that accused men lacked the ability to carry out orders given to them. German officials also showed a reluctance to punish men who "had indeed lapsed briefly from their duty, but who otherwise behaved correctly in general," and whose actions "did not undermine the discipline of the group."[42] The Germans thus tried to understand that the pressures of combat sometimes made even good soldiers break down temporarily.

Reflecting all of these beliefs, the Germans introduced a major reform of their disciplinary codes in April 1917. The changes lessened punishments for many offenses, including many of those committed in the field. The reform legislation originated in the Reichstag, but, when consulted, army officials showed a marked inclination to support the changes. Army officials recognized that an overly harsh system did not serve the army's needs and that the justice system itself had to "take into account the specific conditions of recruitment and the structure of the mass army in wartime as well as the violence of modern combat."[43] In other words, as the army brought in more men that it had previously excluded from military service, it came to understand that it could not discipline draftees as it once had professional soldiers.

The Germans had recognized what the Italians seem not to have grasped until it was too late: that the harsher and more capricious the system the less likely it was to achieve its desired ends.[44] Italian soldiers came to despise their officers in part because of the irrational nature of the justice they meted out. These attitudes, reflected in all armies to varying degrees, had important impacts on both the battlefield and in soldiers' remembrances of their time in uniform. The unsympathetic nature of World War I military justice systems demonstrates that the official view of soldiers had changed little from the eighteenth century.

NOTES

1. M. F. Gower to "Flo," July 29, 1918, Imperial War Museum, London, 88/25/2.
2. Frederic Manning, *Her Privates We* (London: Hogarth, 1986), originally published anonymously in 1929 under the title *The Middle Parts of Fortune*; Maurice Genevoix, *Ceux de 14* (Paris: Flammarion, 1950), originally published in 1916; and Erich Maria Remarque, *All Quiet on the Western Front* (New York: Ballantine, 1958), originally published in 1929.
3. Denis Winter, *Death's Men: Soldiers of the Great War* (London: Penguin, 1978), 39.
4. Joshua Brown, ed, *A Good Idea of Hell: Letters from a Chasseur à Pied* (College Station: Texas A & M University Press, 2003), 13. The book is a remarkable collection of the letters

of Robert Pellissier, a native Frenchman who left his job teaching at California's Stanford University to enlist in the French army. He was killed on the Somme in 1916.

5. Memoir of Col. Sir Geoffrey Christie-Miller, Imperial War Museum, London 80/32/1, volume IV, p. 342.

6. Winter, *Death's Men*, 50.

7. Memoir of Christie-Miller, volume II, entries for February to March, 1916, no page number.

8. Memoir of Christie-Miller, volume IV, p. 320.

9. Edward M. Coffman, *The War to End All Wars: The American Military Experience in World War I* (Lexington: University of Kentucky Press, 1968), 14.

10. Michael S. Neiberg, *Making Citizen-Soldiers: ROTC and the Ideology of American Military Service* (Cambridge, MA: Harvard University Press, 2000), 24–25.

11. Robert Bruce, *A Fraternity of Arms: America and France in the Great War* (Lawrence: University Press of Kansas, 2003), chapter four.

12. Mark E. Grotelueschen, *The AEF Way of War: The American Army and Combat in the First World War* (Ph.D. Dissertation, Texas A & M University, 2003).

13. Manning, *Her Privates We*, 95.

14. David Kennedy, *Over Here: The First World War and American Society* (Oxford: Oxford University Press, 1980), 29.

15. Brown, *A Good Idea of Hell*, 158.

16. Quoted in Richard Schweitzer, *The Cross and the Trenches: Religious Faith and Doubt Among British and American Great War Soldiers* (Westport, CT: Praeger, 2003), 83 and 82. Emphasis in original.

17. Michael Neiberg, *Foch: Supreme Allied Commander in the Great War* (Dulles, VA: Brassey's, 2003).

18. John Horne and Alan Kramer, *German Atrocities, 1914: A History of Denial* (New Haven, CT: Yale University Press, 2001).

19. Schweitzer, *The Cross and the Trenches*, chapter eight.

20. Diary of Willard Newton, Imperial War Museum, London, 78/51/1, p. 90, entry for 29 September 1918.

21. Brown, *A Good Idea of Hell*, 128.

22. Field Marshal Sir Bernard Law Montgomery, one of Britain's most effective generals of World War II, remarked that he tried to lead from the front as often as possible specifically because he had never seen an officer higher than a lieutenant colonel during his time in the trenches during World War I. He also complained that he had served under two commanders (John French and Douglas Haig) without ever having seen either of them.

23. Brown, *A Good Idea of Hell*, 70, 163.

24. Philip Gibbs, *Now It Can Be Told* (New York: Harpers, 1920), 477.

25. John Ellis, *Eye Deep in Hell: Trench Warfare in World War I* (Baltimore, MD: Johns Hopkins University Press, 1976), 198.

26. Keith Simpson, "The Officers," in eds *A Nation in Arms: A Social Study of the British Army in the First World War*, Ian F. W. Beckett and Keith Simpson (Manchester: Manchester University Press, 1985), 63–98, 69.

27. Gibbs, *Now It Can Be Told*, 245.

28. Jon Silkin, *The Penguin Book of First World War Poetry* (London: Penguin, 1996), 131.

29. Henri Barbusse, *Under Fire* (trans. by Robin Buss) (London: Penguin, 1916, 2003), 112–113.

30. Paul Marie de la Gorce, *The French Army: A Military-Political History* (trans. Kenneth Douglas) (New York: George Braziller, 1963), 20.

31. Manning, *Her Privates We*, 132.
32. Papers of J. Elliott, Imperial War Museum, London 67/256/1, p. 16.
33. Coffman, *The War to End All Wars*, 55–57.
34. Anne Duménil, "Soldiers' Suffering and Military Justice in the German Army of the Great War," in *Uncovered Fields: Perspective in First World War Studies*, ed. Jenny Macleod and Pierre Purseigle (Amsterdam: Brill Academic Publishers, 2004) 43–60, quotation on 43.
35. Richard M. Watt, *Dare Call It Treason: The True Story of the French Army Mutinies of 1917* (New York: Dorsett, 1969), 98.
36. David Englander, "Mutinies and Morale," in *World War I: A History*, ed. Hew Strachan (Oxford: Oxford University Press, 1988), 191–203, quotations at 192.
37. The incident is recounted in greater detail in Watt, *Dare Call It Treason*, 98–100.
38. Manning, *Her Privates We*, 81.
39. Originally published as Sébastien Japrisot, *Un Long Dimanche de Fiançailles* (Paris: Denoël, 1997).
40. Kennedy, *Over Here*, 160. See also Bernard Nalty, *Strength for the Fight: A History of Black Americans in the Military* (New York: Free Press, 1986), 104–105.
41. I am grateful to Professor Holger Herwig for taking the time to help me clarify these points.
42. Duménil, "Soldiers' Suffering," 51.
43. Duménil, "Soldiers' Suffering," 55.
44. Vanda Wilcox, "Discipline in the Italian Army, 1915–1918," unpublished paper presented at the Second European Conference in First World War Studies, University of Oxford, England, June 23, 2003.

Seven

✶ ✶ ✶

WEAPONS, UNIFORMS, AND DAILY NEEDS

> The Germans, making full use of their artillery, launched infantry attacks in their old manner—close-locked. As formerly, the British and French slaughtered them heavily with machine gun and rifle fire. Then on Thursday the Germans suddenly threw in that attack its asphyxiating bombs, which will doubtless become famous in this war. It succeeded in breaking the line of French near Bixschoote, although not to such an extent as the Germans claim in today's communiqué.
> —*Correspondent Will Irwin describing the first gas attack of the war for the New York Tribune, April 24, 1915.*

A WAR DOMINATED BY MACHINES

Soldiers from 1871 to 1918 had to face a wide variety of weapons that were either new to warfare or had been previously underdeveloped. The cumulative effects of these weapons were two fold. Most obviously, the new weapons introduced another quantum leap in the scale and scope of a military unit's killing power. The range of weapons grew significantly greater and battlefields became correspondingly larger. Secondly, soldiers had to learn to master increasingly complex weapons systems in environments that acted as crucibles for technological innovation, often with soldiers themselves serving as the unfortunate victims of experimentation. As a result, the percentage of soldiers who served as traditional infantrymen declined in the face of an ever-expanding number of specialists.

Rifles and Guns

Infantrymen did, however, remain the single largest category of soldiers. Rifles, whose introduction had radically changed the battlefield of the 1860s and 1870s, remained the most important infantry weapons. The technological development of the rifle continued in the years before World War I; the most significant innovations involved the introduction of smokeless powder, which allowed a rifleman to fire without giving away his position, and a clip or magazine usually holding five rounds that facilitated loading. Rifles of the World War I period could normally fire with reasonable accuracy over distances as long as 2,000 meters, although such extended range rarely proved useful in the close proximity of trench warfare, where the opposing armies were often within 50 yards of one another. Specialized rifles included highly accurate snipers' rifles equipped with telescopic sights and lighter rifles called carbines that were used by pilots, cavalrymen, and sappers.

Although not all military professionals recognized it at the time, the period's most radical and revolutionary technological change occurred in 1884 when American inventor Hiram Maxim introduced his Maxim gun. Originally interested in working on electrical systems, Maxim traveled to Great Britain in 1881 where a friend allegedly told him, "Hang your chemistry and electricity. If you want to make a pile of money, invent something that will enable these Europeans to cut each others' throats with greater facility." A trip to Vienna convinced Maxim of the profits to be made from the ever-expanding European arms market. Reflecting his anticipated customer base, Maxim set up a firm in London to manufacture a method that eventually served as the means by which Europeans did indeed facilitate the process of cutting one anothers' throats.

Maxim's groundbreaking innovation involved making use of a rifle's recoil action. Recoil, the equal and opposite physical reaction to the firing of a projectile, had always posed gunsmiths with an important technological problem. Recoils represented lost energy and caused jerking movements that forced soldiers to re-sight and re-aim their weapons. Using a system of jointed levers, Maxim harnessed the previously unused energy of the recoil to eject a cartridge, load another cartridge, fire it, and begin the cycle anew. He had therefore made a virtue of what had theretofore been wasted, often counterproductive, energy. By using the recoil to eliminate the hand-cranking method of firing used by his competitors, Maxim had made true automatic fire possible. With the addition of a belt feeder made of cloth or steel to supply the ammunition, Maxim's new weapon could fire at the astonishing rate of 600 bullets per minute for almost as long as a gun crew could feed it bullets.

Despite the Maxim gun's favorable results on testing grounds when compared to the hand-cranked mitrailleuse and Gatling gun, European armies were slow to introduce the new system. Despite the tests they had witnessed on firing ranges, some officers doubted that such a rate of fire would be sustainable in the heat of battle. Others questioned whether Maxim guns could keep up with the rapid infantry charges that senior commanders expected would dominate future battlefields as they had dominated past battlefields. Logistics and procurement officers worried about the expense of manufacturing and transporting the millions of rounds of ammunition that the ravenous Maxim guns would require.

Their rapid rates of fire, however, made Maxim guns ideal for small armies needing to control large territories. The British began to take Maxim guns with them on colonial campaigns in 1893 and the weapons soon proved their value. The success of the Maxim guns in colonial campaigns allowed vastly outnumbered European armies to dominate battlefields. The astonishing edge they gave to Europeans over African and Asian opponents led Englishman Hilaire Belloc to write the following poem from the perspective of a European soldier who had just watched Maxim guns annihilate a colonial foe:

> I shall never forget the way
> That Blood stood upon this awful day
> Preserved us all from death.
> He stood upon a little mound
> Cast his lethargic eyes around,
> And said beneath his breath:
> "Whatever else we have got
> The Maxim gun and they have not."[1]

Once the Maxim gun had proved its value in imperial wars, several European manufacturers copied the basic idea and began to innovate. The guns themselves were most commonly known by the name of their manufacturer; the general term "machine gun" came later. Among the most notable manufacturers were Great Britain's Lewis and Vickers (the latter purchased Maxim's patents), France's Hotchkiss, Germany's Bergmann, and the United States' Browning. These firms made improvements to the weapon that rendered it light enough to be mobile on the battlefield or to be mounted on an airplane. A "jacket" around the barrel allowed a machine gun to be cooled by water, allowing it to fire for long periods of time before overheating. Guns mounted on airplanes could normally dispense with the water jacket because at higher altitudes air vents sufficed to cool the barrel.

The Maxim gun and its imitators caused enormous casualties on the battlefields of the Russo-Japanese War of 1904–1905, but many European observers remained convinced that the weapon would not revolutionize warfare. All who witnessed the war understood the incredible power that automatic weapons had in defense, but they were still prone to jamming and even water-cooled guns could sometimes overheat in as little as two minutes in the hands of an inexperienced crew. Nor did machine guns always stop determined infantry charges from seizing even well-defended positions. The Japanese, after all, won the war by attacking. European armies therefore added more automatic weapons to their stockpiles, but did not reorganize their doctrine around them, nor did they anticipate the massive change such weapons would bring to the battlefield.

Ironically, the German army, which planned to begin the war with daring and rapid offensives, most effectively integrated the essentially defensive machine guns into its inventory of weapons. Primarily using Maxim guns, the Germans had 12,500 machine guns in their units in 1914, far more than any other army. Hoping to use their Maxims as an infantry support weapon, the Germans created separate machine gun companies manned by specially trained gunners. Machine gunners worked in crews of four to six men to ensure a smooth and continuous rate of accurate fire. Once the war on the western front settled down into a stalemate, the guns quickly showed their true value in repulsing enemy attacks.

Throughout the war, the machine gun dominated the battlefield as a defensive weapon. The large number of casualties taken by the British Expeditionary Force in Belgium and the French army in the Battles of the Frontiers in 1914 testified to the power of the machine gun. Mounted on a tripod it was stable enough to allow for a high degree of accuracy against targets in the open field, especially large targets like cavalry. The accuracy of the guns actually mattered much less than their ability to sweep a relatively large area with a storm of bullets. Mobile and small enough to conceal behind a protective screen of steel plate or sandbags, machine guns were difficult to locate and destroy. Unless a way could be found to isolate them, machine guns normally rendered offensive infantry charges futile.

Over the course of the war, all armies sought both to increase the number of machine guns they had available and to find ways to increase their tactical mobility. In 1914 the British army only had a few hundred machine guns, preferring to rely on the famed precision of their soldiers' individual marksmanship. By the end of the war, however, the British firm Vickers was manufacturing 5,000 machine guns per month. The French had 2,200 Hotchkiss machine guns in 1914, but purchased nearly 17,000 more during the war. The French also produced 250,000 of the unreliable Chauchat light machine gun, more than 37,000 of which were sold to the Americans to meet their immediate needs. The Americans needed the guns because their own industries had produced just 8,000 machine guns for its forces by the end of 1917, but by the time of the armistice, American industries had manufactured an astonishing 227,000 machine guns of all types.[2]

For the soldier, this massive industrial production meant an intimate familiarity with the machine gun. British infantry battalions, which had just two machine guns each in 1914, had thirty apiece by the middle of 1918.[3] For some men this increase meant learning how to fire and maintain weapons that were coming to be increasingly important tactical tools. For others it meant learning how to dismantle and transport the weapons quickly. All soldiers, however, rapidly learned to fear them and to listen for their characteristic sounds.

For commanders, increasing the number of machine guns per battalion served as a means to increase the firepower of their units in the face of the declining quality and quantity of infantrymen. A single machine gun could compensate for dozens of individual soldiers. Machine guns served as a force multiplier that allowed local commanders to take more men out of the first line of trenches and place them farther back in second and third lines. These elastic defensive systems provided a greater power to absorb and respond to enemy attacks. Front-line soldiers used machine guns to weaken an enemy attack as much as possible while the second line reinforced and the third line prepared counterattacks. Elastic defensive systems, made possible by the defensive power of the machine gun, further doomed offensive attacks.

Soldiers also sought ways to make the machine gun something more than a defensive weapon. Armies had first to increase the mobility of guns if they were to become more effective as an offensive weapon. Lighter guns, like the Lewis and Vickers light machine guns, also served as armament for airplanes. Soon even smaller versions, called submachine guns and weighing as little as nine kilograms, married firepower to mobility. By the end of the war, the Germans had integrated into their infantry units the MG 08/15 machine gun, which was light enough to be carried by a single soldier. In the war's last few months, American inventor J. T. Thompson invented the gun that has carried his name to this day. Originally dubbed the "trench broom," it carried a drum that held fifty .45 rounds and could be fired singly or in bursts.[4] Introduced too late for use in World War I, the "Tommy gun" became famous as the weapon of choice for Chicago gangsters in the 1920s and 1930s, a use that Thompson never envisioned.

Defeating machine guns posed a constant tactical dilemma for soldiers. Attempts to destroy them with artillery fire normally failed owing either to the small size of the guns or the ability of machine gunners to bury their weapons deep underground until the artillery ceased. Soldiers soon learned not to trust the exhortations of commanders who assured them that their preparatory bombardments had cleared the way for their assault. The survival of an unexpectedly large number of German machine guns after a one-week British artillery bombardment on the Somme at the end of June 1916 doomed the British offensive that began on July 1. German machine guns killed or wounded the vast majority of the 60,000 British soldiers who became casualties on that one day, creating what remains the single bloodiest day in the history of the British army.

As the Somme showed, attacking an opponent armed with machine guns was among the most daunting tasks a soldier faced. If the enemy had time to sight, conceal, and protect a machine gun it could hold up an advance and destroy an offensive's timing. On the Somme, the British encountered a German machine gun in a concrete blockhouse protected by four-inch armor plating, and another craftily concealed atop a shaft reached via a tunnel along a railway bank. When a battalion of the Devonshire Pals overran the slopes near the village of Mametz they found "a [German] machine-gun emplacement cleverly sited low down in a bank parallel to the line of advance."[5] Such guns took a terrible toll of advancing infantry. It was not unusual for a single German machine gun to halt the advance of a force as large as three companies.

One German machine gunner recalled how the British attack appeared from the perspective of the defenders:

> When the English started advancing we were very worried; they looked as though they must overrun our trenches. We were very surprised to see them walking, we had never seen that before.... The officers were in front. I noticed one of them walking calmly, carrying a walking stick. When we started firing we just had to load and reload. They went down in their hundreds. You didn't have to aim, we just fired into them.[6]

Grenades and Flamethrowers

Because destroying machine guns was so difficult to do, isolating machine gun nests required either killing the gunners or convincing them to abandon their positions. Hand grenades, first distributed to French soldiers in 1915, proved to be invaluable in this regard. Called "bombs" by the British, a typical grenade was small enough either to be thrown by hand or fitted onto the end of a modified rifle in order to be projected over even greater distances. Utilizing a timed or percussion fuse, grenades carried a shrapnel or an explosive charge. Extremely useful in trench warfare for throwing around a bend or into a blockhouse, they were also an effective means for disabling machine gun crews or clearing out an enemy dugout.

During the course of the war, grenades became a more important weapon in close infantry fighting. The British Mills bomb, introduced in 1916, represented a major technological improvement and soon saw service in all the Allied armies. Utilizing a pin system to make it safer for a soldier to use, it was also more aerodynamic, thus increasing its range. The Germans used a larger grenade nicknamed the "potato masher" because it sat atop a stick to make it easier to throw. The stick also contained a large and powerful fuse. Grenadier units specialized in eliminating concealed or deeply entrenched enemy positions.

The flamethrower served a similar role. First introduced by the Germans late in 1915, flamethrowers used compressed oxygen to propel a burning fuel. Somewhat ironically, the first flamethrower crews were composed of men who had been fire fighters in civilian life. These fearsome weapons could either be hidden mostly underground to help in the defense of a critical static position or mounted on the back of a soldier to provide immediate tactical support to an offensive. The Germans concentrated almost 100 flamethrowers to support their massive offensive in the heavily wooded (and thus readily combustible) area near Verdun in February, 1916. The new weapons terrified the French soldiers who had to stand and face them in large numbers. In one case, a single flamethrower frightened 38 men into surrendering.

Like grenades, flamethrowers provided a means to kill enemy soldiers in protected positions, but they were among the most dangerous weapons for a soldier to use. Not all fuel tanks were self-sealing and the heavy tanks weighed soldiers down, making them inviting targets. British inventor Captain William H. Livens reduced these dangers by replacing the oxygen propellant with a deoxygenated compressed air compound. This change reduced the risks to the flamethrower operator and increased the range of the weapon itself. The Livens system could throw flame seventy yards from a fixed position and thirty yards when used as a portable weapon. The flamethrower could also be used to create large clouds of black smoke to impair the enemy's ability to see and mark targets.

Artillery

Artillery had long served as the decisive arm in modern warfare. Used to disperse large bodies of troops, instill panic into men in open formations, and to destroy standing structures, artillery could deliver the greatest weight of munitions over the longest ranges. Chemical and metallurgical advances in the years prior to the war had vastly increased the ranges and power of artillery guns and their shells. Thus, unlike the artillery of the pre-1914 battlefield, the artillery of World War I sat far back from the front lines and became an unseen killer. Propelled over long distances across a trajectory that increased the speed of the shell as it fell back to earth, the strike force of an artillery projectile had no equal on the battlefields of World War I.

Traditionally, artillery had developed along two interrelated axes. Siege or heavy artillery was designed to reduce the modern fortifications of Europe to rubble or, at the very least, to terrify their garrisons into surrendering. Germany, expecting to have to compel the quick surrender of Belgium's impressive belt of fortified cities, developed some of the most powerful artillery pieces in prewar Europe. They included enormous 305-mm and 420-mm guns that forced the surrender of Belgium's powerful Liège fortifications in just 11 days. The 305-mm Austrian-made Skoda howitzer fired a 385-kg shell as far as 11,800 meters. Nothing in the Allied inventory could neutralize or compensate for a weapon that powerful. The belief that the ability of German

By the middle years of World War I, artillery had grown much larger and more powerful, as exemplified by the heavy British piece shown here. Courtesy of the McDermott Library, Special Collections Branch, United States Air Force Academy.

and Russian siege artillery pieces to reduce fortifications was unassailable shattered many of the key underpinnings of the defensive strategies of nations like Belgium and Austria-Hungary.

Field artillery pieces had the responsibility of supporting the advances of the infantry and cavalry. With a prewar doctrine that emphasized attacking across open country much more than destroying fortifications, the French specialized in field pieces. The heart of the French artillery system therefore revolved around the mobile, accurate, and rapid-firing 75-mm field piece, first introduced into service in 1897. The shell it fired weighed only 7.3kg, a mere fraction of the much larger shells fired by the German siege pieces. The French 75mm, however, weighed just 1,400kg as opposed to the 25,400-kg weight of the Skoda 320mm. The French gun could therefore be mounted on a two-wheeled carriage and, in theory, be used to rush forward with the infantry. France's entire prewar doctrine depended on the 75mm's speed and rapid rate of fire.

The war's early months showed the limited utility of field pieces. The guns were too light to inflict serious damage on well-prepared defensive positions and the low trajectories of their shells proved ill-suited to hitting buried or entrenched targets. Even with the war on the western front stuck in a stalemate, the guns attempted to perform the role for which they had been designed, namely, supporting infantry. Field artillery tried with little success to help ground units break the western front's stalemate, expending enormous quantities of shells in the process. Prewar French calculations had estimated a monthly shell consumption of 100,000 rounds. By late September 1914, the French had fired nearly all of their prewar stocks of shells for the 75-mm gun. The actual usage figures for 1914 approached 900,000 shells per month, rising to 4,500,000 rounds per month by 1916.

As these figures clearly demonstrate, artillery rapidly became a major feature in soldiers' daily lives. Artillerists had to develop systems for commanding and controlling

Officer and men stand with a 12-pound gun from the 1890s. This crew was responsible for bringing heavy firepower up to the battlefield quickly. They were often targets for the enemy's cavalry. Australian War Memorial Negative Number ART19500.

their guns, while simultaneously rendering them more effective for a wide variety of functions. Artillery work was difficult on both the physical and intellectual levels. Even men assigned to units of the British Royal Horse Artillery found themselves moving the heavy guns and ammunition wagons by hand over broken or muddy terrain. Lifting large numbers of 40-, 100-, or 300-kg shells was exhausting work, especially in the heat of battle.

Artillery was also demanding on an intellectual level. Gunners had to correct for climate, the normal wear of gun barrels, and, in many cases, for deficiencies in the quality of shells. Gunnery thus required a high level of both education and training. Artillerists also learned to use their field artillery pieces in new and unprecedented ways. Field artillery became the primary means to destroy the enemy's barbed wire, a difficult task that required a combination of precision, experience, and blind luck. Opening holes in the enemy's wire, however, was a normal prerequisite to any successful offensive.

Gunners enjoyed the luxury of being removed from the trenches, but they were by no means safe from the dangers of war. Even light artillery pieces were cumbersome to move and therefore became targets of enemy artillery pieces in a process known as counter-battery fire. The development of tactical aviation put gunners at considerable risk, both from the fire of airplanes themselves and from the risk of pilots relaying the locations of enemy artillery batteries to their own gunners. These dangers, combined with the long range of their weapons, led artillerists to use sophisticated techniques of indirect fire, wherein they did not actually see their targets. Instead, spotters or pilots would correct the fire of artillery by relaying targeting information via radio, runners, or flags.

Locating the enemy's guns and neutralizing them therefore became a critical task for gunners. The British developed the war's most effective method for doing so in a process known as sound ranging. British gunners used a sophisticated and delicate system of microphones to listen for and triangulate the sound of an enemy gun firing. Gunners also developed a system known as flash spotting, which used similar principles to sound ranging, but looked for the flash of an enemy gun. Once located and properly plotted on an accurate map, British gunners could then fire on the enemy gun and silence it.

The Germans, led by the war's most innovative artillerist, Col. Georg Bruchmüller, developed systems for striking the enemy's communications networks with the goal of eliminating their ability to conduct indirect fire and thus effectively blinding the enemy's gunners. By using his system, German gunners could neutralize their enemy's weapons without actually having to spot and fire on them. Bruchmüller and others also led the way in integrating field artillery with the advances of the infantry. German storm troopers used these tactics with great effect in the spring of 1918.

Siege guns quickly adapted from the role of destroying fortifications to neutralizing the subterranean network of defenses that comprised the western front. To siege gunners, the entire front resembled one gigantic set of defenses to be reduced in order to open passages for the infantry. British and French commanders placed enormous faith in the ability of lengthy artillery bombardments to destroy enemy defenses and open passages for infantry and even cavalry to exploit. French general Ferdinand Foch, himself trained as an artillerist, preached that "the artillery conquers; the infantry occupies." In the most famous case of such operations, the British prepared a one-week bombardment for the Somme offensive in 1916. More than 1,500 guns fired an unprecedented 1,627,824 rounds of artillery in one week over an area approximately 16 miles in length. The barrage grew in intensity, reaching a maximum rate of fire of 3,500 shells per minute. British commanders wrongly expected that such massive shelling would make the success of the infantry advance inevitable; thus the German machine gunner cited above was able to watch a British officer calmly walking toward him in the midst of battle.

Such extended barrages used up tremendous quantities of ammunition and had the important tactical disadvantage of telegraphing the place and timing of a coming offensive, thus giving the enemy time to concentrate reserves and prepare counteroffensives. Gunners therefore developed a "hurricane" barrage technique that struck targets with intense weights of shell without warning. Soldiers then attacked the bombed area with the hope of meeting little resistance and few prepared enemy positions. Hurricane barrages were ideal for armies whose limited industrial capacities reduced the number of shells they could use. The Russians, who lacked the British ability to conduct one-week bombardments, used these techniques to devastating effect during their summer, 1916 offensive, tearing open enormous gaps in the lines of their unsuspecting Austro-Hungarian enemies.

Artillerists also had to learn to perfect means of more directly supporting the infantry. One of the most complex methods involved the "rolling" or "creeping" barrage wherein artillerists fired a curtain of artillery shells that ideally preceded advancing infantry closely enough to suppress the fire of the enemy but not closely enough to risk inflicting friendly casualties. Too far away to see their targets and adjust their fire, artillerists had to rely upon predetermined "lift" periods to allow the infantry to advance while the gunners re-sighted to the next level of targets. Rolling barrages required concentration and meticulous planning. Errors of timing or calculation could cause thousands of casualties. Many British batteries lifted early on the first day of the Somme offensive in order to avoid hitting their own men. The premature lifts inadvertently benefited the Germans by giving them more time to raise and aim their buried machine guns.

Artillery struck most men as an impersonal weapon. Neither the gunners nor their intended targets saw one another. An artillery bombardment was therefore somewhat akin to standing in field during a thunderstorm. Whether one was struck by lightning or not was purely a matter of chance. Neither courage, nor piety, nor élan played any role at all in determining a soldier's death or survival. The concussions from artillery attacks also had the eerie power to kill men without leaving a trace of physical wounds behind.

Perhaps most importantly, artillery obliterated the human body, killing thousands of men so remorselessly that it left no way to identify the victims. Consequently, the battlefields of France and Belgium are filled with memorials to the "missing," the vast majority of whom were literally blown to bits or vaporized by artillery fire.

Artillery also destroyed nature and the physical world the soldier inhabited. Shelling felled trees, obliterated villages, and reduced cathedrals to rubble. Even as large a town as Albert (near the Somme) was so heavily damaged by enemy shelling that the French government considered abandoning it after the war. Countless villages near large battlefields like Verdun, Passchendaele, and the Chemin des Dames were abandoned, leaving only markers to acknowledge that they had ever existed. Shells also tore up water tables and drainage systems, contributing to the muddy morass that so deeply characterized the Passchendaele campaign of 1917.

The damage that artillery did to nature provided some of the most obvious symbols of the destructive power of the war. Forests blew apart as if they were mere collections of matchsticks and entire town squares fell to rubble. Large and famous buildings like Ypres's cloth hall, Arras's hôtel de ville, and Verdun's citadel simply crumbled. Frenchman Henri Barbusse recalled being sent to the town of Souchez, near Arras. Marching through the plains near the town he looked for signs to indicate that they were approaching an urbanized area only to find that the towns themselves were gone. "In point of fact, we have not left the plain, the vast plain, seared and barren—but we are in Souchez! The village has disappeared.... There is not even an end of a wall, fence or porch that remains standing." Similarly, a visitor to the town of Serre on the Somme front in 1917 described an area "skinned, gouged, flayed, and slaughtered, and the villages smashed to powder, so that no man could ever say there had been a village there within the memory of man."[7] Artillery seemingly spared nothing in its destructive quest.

Albert's basilica was home to one of the most evocative symbols of such devastation to soldiers. Atop the basilica stood a golden statue of the Madonna holding the baby Jesus up to the Heavens. Damaged by artillery shelling during fighting at the Somme, the Madonna statue angled down, parallel to the ground but still attached to the basilica. The statue's new position made it appear as if the Madonna were holding Jesus over the ground hundreds of feet below. If she were to let go, the baby would fall and be killed. "No one wanted it to remain what it literally was," notes Paul Fussell, "merely an accidentally damaged third-rate gilded metal statue now so tenuously fixed to its tower that it might fall any moment."[8] Clearly visible to the men of the British, French, and German armies during the Battle of the Somme, the Madonna of Albert led to scores of legends and suppositions from soldiers trying to figure out if the statue's position was a positive or a negative sign from Providence or simply the impact of modern implements of war on old architecture. To many men, the statue became symbolic of the literal and metaphorical assault that the war made on religion and European traditions.[9]

Other Weaponry

Poison Gas

If artillery seemed impersonal to soldiers because it destroyed everything in its path, poison gas seemed to represent the ultimate personification of modern weaponry. Gas created no lasting scars on buildings or on landscape but it killed men in horrid and unendurably painful ways. Heavier than air, poison gases chased men into places that normally provided a modicum of safety, such as dugouts and the basements of forts. It lurked in shell holes and crevices for hours or even days making every corner of a battlefield a potential killer even when there was no active fighting. The novelty of poison gas, its unnatural greenish and yellow colorations, and its use in contravention of international law all lent gas an air of barbarity and savagery that other weapons never had.

Despite the technical illegality of poison gas, all of the great powers had developed stocks of chemical weapons in the years prior to World War I. Nevertheless, most commanders resisted using chemical weapons in the war's early months, less because of their contravention of increasingly irrelevant international law than because the weapons struck professional soldiers as antithetical to the "valued traditions and moral values" of military service.[10] The increasing brutality of the war made a mockery of the legal limits on the use of gas and the stalemate on the western front led commanders to change their minds about its morality as well. As antediluvian notions of honor between gentlemen became replaced by the need to win the war, gas weapons became an increasingly attractive option.

On April 22, 1915, Algerian troops serving in the French army near the strategically important Belgian town of Ypres saw clouds of greenish smoke blowing toward their lines. The smell of the gas and its effect on the men made it obvious that the cloud contained poisonous chemicals. The Germans had released 168 tons of chlorine, a highly toxic asphyxiant, from cylinders into a favorable wind. The troops panicked, choking, coughing, and clutching at their eyes. The attack had opened a four-mile breech in the line, but the attacking German troops were understandably nervous at the prospect of attacking through the gas cloud. By the time the Germans had organized their troops for an attack through the gap, night was falling and a detachment of Canadians had come forward to close the gap. The Germans captured 2,000 prisoners and 51 guns, but the introduction of poison gas had little overall impact on the Second Battle of Ypres.

As the Germans discovered at Ypres, poison gas posed as many risks to an attacker as to a defender. Releasing gas from cylinders, as the Germans had done at Ypres, obviously depended upon the winds remaining predictable and favorable. The British only released gas from cylinders one time because of backwinds that caused large numbers of friendly casualties. All sides therefore began to experiment with ways to deliver poisonous chemicals from greater distances, including placing gas in artillery shells and in glass jars. Special pioneers crossed No Man's Land with the jars in the dead of night and placed them on the enemy's parapets. At dawn snipers broke the jars with rifle fire. This system proved to be as inconsistent as the cylinders. William Livens, the same man who solved the problem of flamethrowers for the British, invented an electrically powered projector that soon took his name. The Livens projector could fire a shell containing thrity pounds of chemicals almost a mile. One version of the Livens system fired twenty-five shells simultaneously.

These new methods led to increasing use of gas weapons, which all soldiers quickly learned to dread. One of the war's most famous poems, Wilfred Owen's *"Dulce et Decorum Est"*(1918) vividly described the effect of a gas attack:

> Gas! GAS! Quick, boys! An ecstasy of fumbling,
> Fitting the clumsy helmets just in time;

> But someone still was yelling out and stumbling,
> And flound'ring like a man in fire or lime …
> Dim, through the misty panes and thick green light,
> As under a green sea, I saw him drowning.
> In all my dreams, before my helpless sight,
> He plunges at me, guttering, choking, drowning.[11]

In the next stanza, Owen described the victim's "froth-corrupted lungs" (asphyxiants killed men by causing the lungs to overproduce liquid) and, in the poem's most evocative image, characterized his agonized face as being "like a devil's sick of sin." Once dead, Owen recalls the man's body being flung anonymously into a wagon.

The terror that gas inspired thus came both from the deaths that it caused and the tortuous ways that men suffered before dying. Many gases left permanent damage including blindness caused by lachrymator agents such as the easy to manufacture xylyl bromide. Images of blinded men soon became a leitmotif of the war and the sufferings of the soldiers who fought it. One of the most famous wartime paintings by American artist John Singer Sargent depicts a file of soldiers with bandages over their eyes walking through a corpse-strewn battlefield, each man with an arm on the shoulder of the man directly in front of him. The painting carries the simple title *Gassed*.

After the German use of gas at Ypres in 1915, all armies rushed to develop newer types and larger quantities of gas. The British used gas for the first time that fall at the Battle of Loos and the French soon followed suit. By September 1918, the British were manufacturing 122,000 shells containing chemical weapons per week.[12] Chemists also worked to develop new gases which were both more powerful and capable of passing through existing respirators. In 1917 the Germans introduced the gas that soldiers came to fear most, dichloroethyl sulfide, better known as yellow cross or mustard gas. Usually delivered by artillery shells, mustard gas vaporized when the shell exploded, then concentrated as a liquid that attached itself to any part of the human body it found. It then caused painful blisters from both above and below the skin surface that burst and became infected. Mustard gas could remain in an area for long periods of time virtually undetected and often men did not show symptoms for days.

The effort to develop more powerful gases was matched by the effort to find ways to protect men from their effects. Soldiers soon learned to take any available cloth (often a handkerchief or even a sock) and soak it in liquid, including urine which contained enough ammonium to counteract some of the effects of gas. Cloth masks soaked in more effective chemicals soon replaced these improvised defenses. The British took a major technological step forward with the introduction of the Small Box Respirator. The SBR protected the eyes with goggles and the nose with a clip. Men breathed through their mouths using a tube that filtered air with a mixture of soda lime and charcoal. Like all masks, the SBR was cumbersome, hot in summertime, and limited a soldier's range of motion. More importantly, masks offered no protection from mustard gas and were normally one generational step behind the gases themselves. German chemical warfare specialists learned to fire irritants like mustard gas first, causing men to remove their masks, then fire asphyxiants against the now unprotected men.

Gas killed far fewer men than machine guns or artillery, but it held a nightmarish hold over men's imaginations. Soldiers in the Italian, Russian, and Austro-Hungarian armies had cause to fear it the most because they received gas masks with the least regularity. Still, the inaccuracy of gas limited its use. Commanders came to see gas more as a means to temporarily incapacitate men than to kill them. Nevertheless, soldiers saw gas as a skulking demon that stalked men, even in their sleep. Men learned almost by second nature to reach for their masks upon hearing a warning bell or the chilling scream "Gas!" Even if soldiers were able to get their masks on in time, they never knew if the mask would operate properly or if the enemy had introduced a new gas that their existing masks could not neutralize.

Aircraft

The soldiers of World War I were also the first to face war in three dimensions. Aviation originally served as a means to observe and photograph the battlefield, but it soon developed into a weapons platform of its own. Images of aces and aerial dogfights have passed down a halcyon view of at least one part of the war as a series of jousts between knights of the air. Such romantic images helped propaganda efforts and made for excellent news coverage, but they were not the dominant image most front-line soldiers had of airplanes or of their pilots.[13] To them, airplanes were simply another means the enemy had of dispensing death from a distance.

Attempts to use aviation to strike men on the ground began rather primitively with pilots dropping winged metal darts called *fléchettes* on the men below them. During the 1916 Battle of the Somme, the British made a major improvement to this system by

A massive German bomber from World War I. Germany's strategic bombing campaign over England in 1917 and 1918 dropped more than 100,000 kg of bombs, killed 1,400 civilians and injured 4,800 more. Courtesy of the McDermott Library, Special Collections Branch, United States Air Force Academy.

equipping fighters with explosives to bomb German trenches and rear areas. The high losses pilots suffered in conducting these missions played a key role in the development of metal airplanes in order to protect airplanes from ground fire. The following April, the Germans launched their first *Schlachtstaffen:* squadrons dedicated to attacking ground targets. Flying parallel to and above the trenches, custom designed German aircraft used machine guns angled toward the ground to strafe the soldiers below.

Strafing aircraft formed a major component of the plans for the German spring offensive of 1918. Thirty-eight *Schlachtstaffen* assisted advancing infantry by striking front-line enemy positions and flying deep behind enemy lines to interdict the movement of the enemy's reinforcing men and supplies. American air warfare mastermind Brig. Gen. William "Billy" Mitchell developed and executed an aerial battle plan that used seventy-five tons of explosives aimed at ground targets.[14] With the numerous ways that pilots had developed to kill soldiers on the ground, it is little wonder that few soldiers saw pilots in the same heroic light as did newspaper reporters.

Mines

When soldiers weren't looking up to see what was trying to kill them, they were often looking down. Unable to effect a decision at or above the ground, some armies tried to do so from below ground. At the end of 1914 a German unit tunneled under British lines near Festubert and dug out ten mines that they filled with TNT. The explosions struck Indian soldiers, killing many, burying others, and sending an entire brigade into headlong retreat. The British responded by creating a unit of Royal Engineers dedicated to tunneling. Its commander recruited volunteers from traditional coal mining regions such as Wales and paid them as much as six times the salary of an average soldier. They soon developed tactics that placed Britain at the forefront of tunnel warfare.

As armies learned to mine, so too did soldiers on the surface learn to listen for the sounds of tunneling going on below. Using custom-designed geophones, tanks of water into which men dipped their ears, and other listening devices, soldiers tried to pinpoint the sound of the enemy working below. Armies then either dug a counter tunnel or moved their troops out of harm's way and attacked the enemy positions with artillery or gas. The British engineers, which grew to 20,000 men assigned to twenty tunneling companies, learned to counteract such methods by developing techniques for digging deeper into the soil of Belgium and France.

Not surprisingly, then, the British had the greatest successes in the war of the mines. As part of the preparations for the Battle of the Somme, the British had dug three large and seven small mines under German lines. The two largest mines each contained twenty-four tons of explosives. One of these two mines sat under a critical German position known as the Hawthorn Ridge redoubt. A Royal Flying Corps observer left a vivid description of what he saw when the two large mines exploded on day one of the offensive:

> [T]he earth heaved and flashed, a tremendous and magnificent column rose up into the sky. There was an ear-splitting roar, drowning all the guns, flinging the machine [i.e., his plane] sideways in the repercussing air. The earthy column rose, higher and higher to almost four thousand feet. There it hung, or seemed to hang, for a moment in the air, like

the silhouette of some great cypress tree, then fell away in a widening cone of dust and debris. A moment later came the second mine. Again the roar, the upflung machine, the strange silhouette invading the sky. Then the dust cleared and we saw the two white eyes of the craters. The barrage had lifted to the second-line trenches, the infantry were over the top, the attack had begun.[15]

One of the mines created the Lochnagar crater, which remains near the town of La Boisselle and serves as an impressive reminder of the power of the mines of the Somme.

The success at the Somme led to even bigger British mining plans. Beginning in 1915, British miners had begun digging under German lines at Messines in Belgium at the rate of ten to fifteen feet per day. By the spring of 1917, the operation had produced five miles of tunnels that held more than 1,000,000 pounds of explosives. On June 7, the British detonated the mine, killing or burying 10,000 German soldiers and inducing a further 7,500 to surrender. The explosion led to reports of earthquakes fifteen miles away and could be heard as far away as the southern suburbs of London. Fear of mines terrorized soldiers, although as the war became more mobile, the threat of being killed by painstaking and time-consuming tunneling operations gradually faded.

Tanks

Mobile warfare, however, brought its own special killing machines. The tank, introduced by the British in September 1916, on the Somme, proved to be both terrifying and, at times, comical. Slow, cumbersome, and extremely unreliable, they often broke down in battle or fell harmlessly into a ditch. When they did function, however, they created a platform to make machine guns and small artillery pieces mobile. The British Mark I tank came in two versions, one of which carried four machine guns and two six-pound artillery guns. The other version carried six machine guns. Tanks were, therefore, a weapon to be taken quite seriously. Largely used by the British and the French, tanks struck German soldiers most often. As the war developed, Allied tank doctrine matured and the tanks themselves became more reliable. The British Whippet tank moved at eight miles per hour and carried four machine guns, making it ideal for pursuit of retreating troops. The smaller, faster tanks were also harder for soldiers to disable with the weapons at their disposal.

With so many weapons possessing so much killing power, it is hardly surprising that soldiers saw World War I as a war of machines in which they had become relatively insignificant. As the next chapter will show, not all soldiers were under the constant threat of death for extended periods of time. Still, the daily lives of World War I soldiers were exposed to a greater lethality from a greater range of weapons at greater distances than had ever been possible before. The net effects on the bodies, souls, and psyches of soldiers remains one of the most unimaginable features of the war.

UNIFORMS AND DAILY NEEDS

Uniforms

The general spirit of reform that marked the British army in the years before World War I paid dividends in many areas, including uniforms. By the 1890s, British regiments had abandoned bright colors like blue and red for khaki, which blended into

Some of the most colorful men in European armies, the Zouaves based their uniforms on those found in North Africa. Often brightly colored, they became easy targets once rifled weapons replaced muskets. Courtesy of the Library of Congress.

terrain more effectively. As they had before the war, British uniforms revealed the tremendous diversity of the empire. British regiments continued to wear individualized insignia or other modifications and Scottish regiments still wore kilts. Experiences of campaigns across a wide empire led to a uniform that was reasonably well-suited to extremes of heat and cold. On the whole, then, British uniforms required little adaptation over the course of the war.

The French uniform sat at the opposite end of the spectrum and stands out as the war's most impractical. The French soldier's pants retained the same style as that introduced in 1867. Colored bright red (ironically the dye came from a German supplier), French uniforms made any attempt at camouflage or blending by the soldiers who wore them impossible. The accompanying bright blue tunic dated to 1878 and provided an unfortunately obvious contrast to the pants. Neither color was often found in nature. The French cap, or képi, had traditionally been red as well, but starting in 1912 some units had been issued with a blue cover that made the cap match the coat. The overall impression was of a soldier whose appearance remained "close to that of his predecessors from the Franco-Prussian War."[16] Even in 1870 this uniform had been impractical; by 1914 it was deadly.

Many French officers understood how dangerously the uniform made French soldiers stand out from their environment. Still, making changes to the uniform meant tackling a series of daunting budgetary issues for such a large army. Discussions had been underway since 1911 to begin changes, but the various governmental and military organizations that oversaw the army could not agree on a single uniform. The bright blue and red uniform, however impractical it may have been, was also popular with French civilians and soldiers alike. Although generals with colonial experience such as Joseph Gallieni had urged changing the uniform to khaki or grey, Minister of War Eugène Etienne dismissed them in 1913 by declaring "red trousers *are* France!"[17] Bright, proud, and dramatic, the uniform fit in with the French image of what an army should be much more than the practical but pedestrian khaki of the British or the field grey of the Germans.

The early weeks of the war proved both how vulnerable the uniform made French soldiers and how important a seemingly prosaic subject like clothing can be to a soldier's survival. North Africans of European descent called Zouaves wore even more conspicuous uniforms, although Senegalese soldiers, attired to fight in Africa, wore khaki. As the casualties mounted, the French army quickly changed its uniform coloring from bright red and blue to a lighter blue-grey known as the "horizon blue." Unable

Uniforms and equipment varied from region to region. The tall fez-like hats of these soldiers mark them as Turkish. Note the X-shaped webbing for their backpacks, a system the Americans and British eventually adopted to the great relief of their men. Courtesy of the Library of Congress.

to effect a rapid change, the French began by introducing horizon blue overcoats in the hope that the coats could cover the red pants, which many men still wore well into 1915.

The more diverse the army, the more varied its uniforms. Beginning in 1908 the Austro-Hungarian Empire began to move to a standard grey that more closely matched the color in service in Germany. Still, the empire marched to war with the least consistency in its uniforms, as ethnic minorities preferred to wear a uniform that reflected their own heritages. In 1916, the Austrians replaced their uniform diversity with a standard uniform that almost completely matched that of their German ally. The uniforms of the Austro-Hungarian Empire thus mirrored the increasing dependence of the empire's army on that of their German ally for equipment and strategic direction.

Head Gear

The most important general changes in clothing and uniforms came in the nature of headgear. Most soldiers marched off to war in 1914 wearing cloth caps. More durable helmets made of steel were normally reserved for dress occasions or for elite units like the cuirassier heavy cavalrymen. The famous German spiked helmet known as the *Pickenlaub* was an exception. Although it became virtually synonymous with the German army, it, too proved to be ill-suited to the needs of combat.

Steel helmets offered only limited protection. No steel helmet could protect a man from a powerful artillery blast nor did helmets stop most bullets. They did, however, protect men from debris such as the shards of rock that artillery shells often sent flying. Helmets became one of the most distinctive elements of a uniform. The French *casque Adrian* helmet, based on a design used by firefighters and introduced to the army in 1915, instantly became a symbol of the French army. Today original helmets from the war still sit on top of the mile stones leading along the famous *Voie Sacrée* from Bar le Duc to Verdun. In 1916 the Germans abandoned the *Pickenlaub* in favor of a more practical helmet, the *Stahlhelm*, known derisively as the coal scuttle helmet. It is unlikely that the switch to steel helmets saved as many lives as manufacturers claimed, but it showed an increasing interest from armies in clothing and equipping their men as completely as possible.

Russian sentry on patrol in the mid-1890s. Russian troops tended to be less well-cared-for than their western European counterparts. This soldier at least has clothing that appears minimally suited to the fierce Russian winters. Courtesy of the Library of Congress.

Boots

Life in the trenches also required good boots. Trenches quickly filled with water following rain or snow and they normally drained very slowly. Failure to keep feet dry could lead to the painful condition that, not surprisingly, became known as trench foot. Symptoms included swelling, numbness, burning, and, eventually, an inability to walk because of the intensity of the pain. Some battalions lost more men to trench foot than they did to combat, although few men actually died of the condition. Supplying men with appropriate footwear was, therefore, no small matter. The French army's boots were among the worst, leading many men to order boots from home or to wear the boots taken from a dead German. The British and Americans were the envy of men from all armies as they wore high vulcanized rubber boots that resembled fisherman's waders. Soldiers in poorer armies like the Russian, Bulgarian, and Austro-Hungarian often went with no footwear at all.

Soldiers' Equipment

As war grew more complex so did the nature and amount of equipment men had to carry. The French soldier's kit in 1914 included the following: a bayonet in a leather case; a leather suspension belt to hold the backpack in place; a belt; a one-liter canteen; 120 8-mm rifle cartridges; three ammunition magazines; the 1893 model Lebel rifle; a satchel for carrying food; and a backpack. The backpack contained: an individual mess tin; a military manual; boot laces; a forage cap; a spare shirt; a spare belt; soap; a sleeping tent or bedroll; a food bag; a sewing kit; a spoon; and two days' worth of food. Typical items in the food ration were: twelve biscuits, two jars of preserved meat; rice; potatoes; salt; sugar; and coffee. Ammunition could be among the heaviest items to carry; thus French soldiers welcomed the introduction of the Lebel, which used 8-mm ammunition as opposed to the 11-mm ammunition of the rifle it had replaced.

To assist their soldiers in carrying this burden, in 1908 the British developed a webbed cotton belt system that more evenly distributed weight and fitted all a soldier's equipment together into one pack. Lacking cross straps, the webbing enabled men to access their pockets and move reasonably freely. The system's greatest feature was undoubtedly the soldier's ability to put it on or take it off like an overcoat. When given the order to take a five-minute rest, men could easily set the entire pack down and then pick it up again. The British made modifications to the system, based on their experiences in the grueling campaigns of August and September 1914, that made it even more efficient. The Americans were so impressed with the British system that they quickly issued it to their own soldiers in 1917.

The responsibility for moving communal items such as cooking pans, signaling flags, and musical instruments had to be shared among the men of a unit. (Soldiers also needed equipment for digging trenches and developing defensive lines.) Soldiers in French infantry companies, for example, had to divide the responsibility for carrying 185 individual tools including 80 spades or entrenching tools, 80 pickaxes, 8 saws, and 4 pairs of shears or wire cutters.[18] As the war settled down into stalemate, many of these items could be discarded, although equipment for repairing damaged wire and replacing broken sandbags and fallen timbers was always in need.

The heavy weight of the soldier's kit limited his movements tremendously. Soldiers leaving their trenches at the Battle of the Somme carried sixty-six pounds of equipment that included: a rifle, ammunition, grenades, rations, a cape, empty sandbags, a helmet, gas masks, goggles, field dressing, shovel or pick, a water bottle, and a mess tin. Moving uphill for most of the first day of the battle, the weight of the pack limited men's movements to a slow walk and virtually prevented them from lying down and getting back up with any agility.[19] British officers, however, believed that the men would not need much speed because the artillery would have cleared the battlefield of immediate opposition. The men would, however, need the equipment to dig in and repulse the anticipated German counterattacks. Because the artillery did not do the job the officers had anticipated, the net result was to slow the British soldiers down and make them even more inviting targets for enemy machine guns. Even in times of relative inaction the kit could be a fatiguing and demoralizing burden. Frederic Manning, a Somme veteran, recalled that carrying such a heavy kit made soldiers "disinclined to take much heed for the morrow."[20]

Efficient armies not only provided needed supplies, but found ways to replace worn-out items. The American army, which proved adept at handling many logistical and administrative problems despite the distances involved, ideally provided each soldier with a new overcoat every 5 months, a new blanket every 2 months, new shoes every 51 days, new underclothes every 34 days, and new socks every 23 days.[21] Of course, these were ideal numbers that even the Americans did not always meet. Many soldiers had to make do with what they could scrounge, trade for, or obtain in other ways. Many soldiers only received new clothes when they had to trade in their old uniforms to be deloused. As the Allies (with the exception of Russia) increasingly won the economic war, they proved generally more reliable in providing needed clothing and equipment than did their Central powers foes.

Food and Drink

Feeding the armies proved to be an even greater challenge than supplying them. The British army, which had needed 3,600,000 pounds of meat and 4,500,000 pounds of bread per month in 1914, needed 67,500,000 pounds of meat and 90,000,000 pounds of bread per month by 1918.[22] These increases had to be met despite the enlistment of thousands of farmers into the armies and despite surface and submarine blockades that prohibited many items from reaching their destinations. Governments, moreover, had to manage a food supply system both for soldiers at the front and for the civilians at home. Few governments had planned for such a food emergency before the war and they therefore had to improvise solutions.

If soldiers understood the challenges their governments faced, they rarely expressed much sympathy given the quality of food they normally received. The three largest armies on the western front each took different approaches to the task of feeding their armies. The Germans were the most efficient, developing mobile field kitchens to deliver hot food to the men at the front. The French were the least efficient, delivering raw food to men who then had to prepare it themselves, with all the attendant risks of allowing too much smoke to billow over one's position. The French, to whom bread remains a food group of its own, defined as "fresh" any bread that had been baked in the last eight days. All bread inevitably reached the men quite stale, often having to be dipped in coffee or tea to be made edible. Even stale bread could be a rarity at the front. Manning recalls bread being in such short supply that thirteen men had to share a single loaf.[23]

The British attempted to deliver food as often as possible in prepackaged containers that men had only to heat. Ideally, British soldiers were to receive 1.25 pounds of meat, 1.25 pounds of bread, .25 pounds of bacon, 3 ounces of cheese, and a half-pound of vegetables, as well as tea, jam, salt, butter, mustard, milk (often condensed), and pickles. The British government boasted that this ration gave the British soldier a daily intake of 4,300 calories, compared to a "passable" caloric intake of 3,400 and an average intake of 3,859 calories for civilians.[24]

The reality, of course, fell quite short of the stated goal. British soldiers rarely receved what the government promised it could deliver. Among the most common foods, especially at the front, were the tinned pork and beans, "the kind," Manning recalled, "in which there was never any pork," and the famous Maconachie stew, named for the government contractor who manufactured it.[25] The stew contained turnips, carrots, beans, gravy, and one pound of unboned, usually fatty meat. Uniformly detested as "a mankiller," especially when it had to be eaten cold, the men of the trenches lampooned it in a satirical advertisement reproduced by John Ellis. It included "testimonials" from men like Corporal Will Bashem that read, "Please forward me the residential address of Mr. Maconachie, as when next on leave I wish to call and pay my compliments" and Private A. Codder who wrote, "During the last advance my pal was mortally wounded, and his dying regret was that he had never met your world-famed proprietor."[26]

The stew came in 22-ounce tins shared by two, three, or even four soldiers.

The nearly unanimous condemnation of army food from men accustomed to austere peasant and working-class diets is its own damnation. Peasants who prior to the war normally ate plenty of fresh vegetables complained of the absence of green vegetables from their diets and bemoaned the ubiquity of potatoes and turnips. The lack of variety in the soldier's diet grew tiresome as well. Day after day of the same food underscored the drudgery of the soldier's daily life and the seeming low esteem in which his army and his government held him.

A primitive meal for some American soldiers since hot food was another rare treat for men on campaign. Courtesy of the National Archives.

Men naturally found ways to supplement these rations. Numerous cafés and estaminets opened behind the lines to sell men food and wine. Ironically, the poorly paid French soldier often had less recourse to the estaminets than did his British and American counterparts. The British army separated (both officially and unofficially) their estaminet system into those for officers and those for the other ranks. The former, of course, had a wider variety of goods for sale. This system caused no end of complaining from British soldiers, whose own estaminets often provided little better than omelets and fried potatoes. Men accustomed to Maconachie gladly ate estaminet food, but rumors of the delicacies available to officers caused tremendous resentment.

All armies supported the relief efforts of groups like the YMCA and the Red Cross to provide food for men in rest areas. Many of these organizations provided hot meals, but often refused on principle to provide alcohol. A cheap or free bowl of soup was therefore a welcome dietary change, but the accompanying cup of hot chocolate proved to be a disappointment. These groups were especially sought after at holiday times because they often provided rarities like game, goose, and turkey. Packages from home were another source of food. Always a welcome sight, they often contained treats like sweets, sausages, and homemade favorites. It went without saying that a soldier was expected to share the contents of his package with his closest comrades.

The French tried to regularize this system by matching soldiers with a *marraine de guerre* (wartime godmother) who wrote them letters and sent them food. The program, known as the *Famille du Soldat* (soldier's family) movement, matched women of all ages, social classes, and regions of origin with soldiers at the front whom the government hoped would develop a "personal reason to fight on." More practically, *marraines* sent hand-knitted gloves, scarves, and socks that were not only more homey than those provided by the army, but warmer as well. The *marraines* also sent food and wine. The program became so wildly successful that the popular journal *Revue de Deux*

Mondes noted in 1916 that the *marraines* were "too well known for us to lay stress on."[27]

All of the systems for delivering food to soldiers were prone to breaking down in combat or during period of crisis. Failure to provide regular food had serious military consequences as hungry armies were rarely dependable armies. Food shortages served as the immediate triggers to many acts of indiscipline, especially on the eastern front. Even in relatively cohesive armies, the lack of food could cause tactical problems. The German storm troop units that advanced so rapidly during the spring offensives of 1918 often broke enemy lines with astonishing ease. To their commanders' dismay, the only factor slowing them down was their own hunger. Thousands of German soldiers stopped their advances to loot from captured Allied stores, which, despite the complaints of British soldiers, were wonderfully abundant in comparison to what the German soldier had been eating. German divisions who came upon the whiskey caches of Scottish units were often held up for days.

As the previous example shows, An army does need both food *and* drink. Finding clean and safe drinking water posed a further challenge to armies. Fresh water came to the front in large tins, many of which had only recently carried gasoline and still tasted like it. Boiling it and brewing tea or coffee with it helped, but not much. Moving large supplies of water forward during the heat of a summer offensive posed a major logistical challenge. Some limited actions were cancelled or postponed as a result.

Armies also tried to provide their soldiers with stimulants like coffee and tea. Drinking the latter beverage continued to be among the most important elements of the British soldier's day. Lucky soldiers could supplement their tea with sugar or, more rarely, milk, making the daily tea both a ritual reminiscent of happier times and a nutritional dietary supplement. Coffee and tea were among the commodities most often denied to German soldiers as a result of the British blockade. A variety of ersatz substitutions appeared in the trenches, made of bark, leaves, and berries.

But no army marches on tea alone. As their fathers and grandfathers in uniform had done, men sought out alcohol. Most armies went to great lengths to provide a daily alcohol ration, both as a boost to morale and as a way to help men pass the down time between operations. British army rum, remembered as "potent stuff" by Manning, came in large, 1.5-gallon earthen jars marked "S. R. D."[28] The letters officially stood for "service ration depot," but the men knew them to stand for "seldom reaches destination" or "soon runs dry." The jar was carried through the trenches "like the ark of the covenant" and the rum inside was always dispensed in the presence of an officer.[29] Medical officers could authorize an extra ration in cold weather, although some teetotalling commanders denied alcohol to their men altogether. Nevertheless, by the end of the war an average British division was drinking 300 gallons of S. R. D. rum per week, or one-third of a pint per man per day.[30]

French and German units received wine or coarse brandy more often than rum. Each army tried to provide approximately one pint per man per day. The quality of the wine rarely approached anything men might have seen in peacetime. The standard French alcohol ration, the indispensable *pinard*, was a rough red wine occasionally diluted with water, both to make it last longer and to ease its sting. Soldiers, of course, found plenty of ways to supplement their official alcohol rations, including purchasing wine or beer from locals and, in some units, brewing their own potent beverages. A presidential executive order prohibited the American army from issuing alcohol to its men, but those who wanted it had little trouble finding it. These comforts were intended to help men deal with the emotional and physical stresses of the modern battlefield. The combat environment of the 1870–1918 period represented one of unprecedented intensity, duration, and danger. The following chapter turns to that environment in all of its diversity.

NOTES

1. Quoted in John Ellis, *The Social History of the Machine Gun* (Baltimore, MD: Johns Hopkins University Press, 1975), 94.

2. Leonard P. Ayres, *The War with Germany: A Statistical Summary* (Washington, DC: U.S. Government Printing Office, 1919), 67.

3. Hew Strachan, "Economic Mobilization," in *World War I: A History* ed. Hew Strachan, (Oxford: Oxford University Press, 1998), 134–148, 145.

4. Ellis, *The Social History of the Machine Gun*, 149.

5. James Edmonds, *Military Operations: France and Belgium 1916*, vol. 1 (London: Imperial War Museum, 1932; 1992), 352–353. Quotation from footnote 1, page 353.

6. Quoted in Ellis, *The Social History of the Machine Gun*, 135.

7. Quoted in James Hannah, *The Great War Reader* (College Station: Texas A & M University Press, 2000), 20.

8. Paul Fussell, *The Great War and Modern Memory* (Oxford: Oxford University Press, 1975), 131.

9. Visitors to Albert today can see the reconstructed church complete with the statue in its original form. The entrance to the city's trench museum is, symbolically, at the foot of the church.

10. Albert Palazzo, *Seeking Victory on the Western Front: The British Army and Chemical Warfare in World War I* (Lincoln: University of Nebraska Press, 2000), 1.

11. Palazzo, *Seeking Victory*, 157.

12. John Silkin, ed. *The Penguin Book of First World War Poetry*. Second Edition (London: Penguin, 1996) p192–193.

13. See Linda R. Robertson, *The Dream of Civilized Warfare: World War I Flying Aces and the American Imagination* (Minneapolis: University of Minnesota Press, 2003).

14. I am grateful to my colleague, Major Michael R. Terry, USAF (ret.), for his help on this subject.

15. Cecil Lewis, *Sagittarius Rising* (London: P. Davies, 1936), 104.

16. Jean-Pierre Verney, "Le Fantassin de la Marne: Équipement et Uniforme," *14–18: Le Magazine de la Grande Guerre* 15 (août-sept. 2003): 20–23, quotation on p. 20.

17. Quoted in Anthony Clayton, *Paths of Glory: The French Army, 1914–1918* (London: Cassell, 2003), 38.

18. Verney, "Le Fantassin de la Marne," 21.

19. Martin Gilbert, *The First World War: A Complete History* (New York: Henry Holt, 1994), 259.

20. Frederic Manning, *Her Privates We* (London: Hogarth, 1986), 41.

21. Ayres, *The War with Germany*, 61.

22. Edmonds, *Military Operations*, 99.

23. Manning, *Her Privates We*, 49.

24. Denis Winter, *Death's Men: Soldiers of the Great War* (London: Penguin, 1978), 147.

25. Manning, *Her Privates We*, 172.

26. John Ellis, *Eye Deep in Hell: Trench Warfare in World War I* (Baltimore, MD, Johns Hopkins University Press, 1976), 129–132.

27. Susan Grayzel, "Mothers, Marraines, and Prostitutes: Morale and Morality in First World War France," *International History Review* 19, no. 1 (February 1997): 66–82, quotation at 70. The article also discusses the sexual roles that many *marraines* served for their soldiers.

28. Manning, *Her Privates We*, 28.

29. Winter, *Death's Men*, 103.

30. Ellis, *Eye Deep in Hell*, 133.

Eight

✷ ✷ ✷

SOLDIERS AND THE MODERN BATTLEFIELD

> [We attacked] as if on parade, the battalions advancing in perfect order with rifles on our shoulders and ready to throw ourselves at the machine-gun laden trenches. It was under a true hail of shells and bullets that the assault lines leapt over a 600-yard-long slope. But even then courage was powerless against material obstacles and the most audacious could do little more than die in the coils of barbed wire. Our losses were heavy: ten officers dead and two-thirds of the regiment lost.
> —*History of the French 171st Infantry Regiment describing an attack in Champagne, September 1915.*[1]

THE UNDERGROUND WAR: TRENCH WARFARE

The final months of the American Civil War witnessed a new kind of fighting. At battlefields such as Spotsylvania Court House, Cold Harbor, and Petersburg, Confederate soldiers had dug deep entrenchments that required repeated bloody charges to take. Cold Harbor was one of the bloodiest Union victories of the war, costing Gen. Ulysses S. Grant's army more than 13,000 casualties to inflict 3,000 enemy casualties; nearly 7,000 of the Union casualties came in the space of just one hour. Soldiers had always constructed defenses to protect their positions. Normally such defenses consisted of above-ground breastworks to discourage the enemy's cavalry from attacking. By the end of the Civil War, however, the opposing sides had come to realize that in modern warfare the real danger came less from horses than from low-trajectory rifle and artillery fire. Modern artillery, moreover, could destroy the wooden breastworks.

Being underground thus provided critical benefits to soldiers needing to protect themselves from enemy fire.

Trench warfare was a key feature of the Russo-Japanese War as well. Observers of the war from all of the great powers saw the strength of well-defended trench systems and many, though by no means all, European officers concluded that the age of Napoleonic infantry and cavalry charges had ended. Nevertheless, in the years prior to World War I, most officers were reluctant to devote much time to training for trench warfare. Few senior commanders believed that the next war would be marked by long periods of stalemate and most thought that practicing for the routine drudgery of trench warfare was bad for their soldiers' morale.

The first few weeks of World War I seemed to confirm these beliefs. The rapid German advance through Belgium and northern France in August and September 1914, seemed to show that a well-prepared and well-led army could fight a war of maneuver even against a modern army equipped with the latest weapons. At the same time, the war in eastern Europe also showed that movement, at times quite rapid movement, could still characterize the battlefield. Many senior leaders therefore concluded, quite reasonably, that the war would be characterized more by movement than by stasis.

The First Battle of the Marne (September 5 to 10, 1914) provided the first indications of the limitations of the war of movement. It also forced the great powers to shelve their meticulous, offensive-minded battle plans. On the western front the war of careful preparation yielded to a war of improvisation, as both sides stretched their forces north in what became known as the "Race to the Sea." German commanders, realizing that their chance to take Paris had (temporarily, they believed) been lost, selected easy-to-defend high ground in front of critical lateral railroad lines. Because they were defending territory that did not belong to them, they could afford to give ground where it made the most operational sense to do so and to be more choosy than their French and Belgian opponents, who were fighting to regain as much of their invaded homeland as possible.

The process of digging in often began informally. In many sectors men began to dig in without waiting for orders from above. The complex system of trenches that so characterized World War I thus began as a rather haphazard series of discrete actions by soldiers who understood better than their commanders how the early weeks of the war had changed the nature of combat. During the final months of 1914, soldiers connected shell holes together or dug trenches often as a means to protect themselves from the autumn rains. Trenches, of course, also protected men from machine gun and field artillery fire, but only the most prescient of soldiers could have anticipated that the slapdash trenches would become their homes for nearly four years.

By the end of 1914, two parallel systems of trenches faced one another from the North Sea to the Swiss border, with only a few small breaks in the rugged terrain of the Vosges mountains. The opposing trench systems were separated by an area known, appropriately, as No Man's Land. On some parts of the western front, No Man's Land was 1,000 yards wide and cows sometimes peacefully grazed therein. In other sectors, the two sides might be separated by as little as a few feet. Often, opposing soldiers were close enough to one another to smell their cigars and overhear their conversations. Men could even shout across No Man's Land in order to communicate with enemy soldiers nearby or exchange newspapers, although officers did what they could to discourage fraternization with the enemy. Most soldiers actually preferred to serve in trenches close to the enemy's line as it reduced the risk of the enemy firing heavy artillery in an area with such risk of friendly fire casualties.

Generally speaking, the more active the sector, the more complex the trench network. A typical trench network consisted of two to five layers of trenches. The front, or main, trench sat closest to the enemy. Trenches tended to zigzag or be built with sharp right angles. This design prevented an infiltrating enemy from employing enfilading fire up and down a trench and it also limited the impact of artillery concussions. A series of saps or carefully concealed observation posts jutted out of the main trench into No Man's Land. Soldiers in these posts kept watch to provide advance warning of enemy activity. Sandbags and wooden beams kept trench walls from falling in and also protected the parapet, or front wall of the trench.

A support trench ran behind and parallel to the main trench. The British and German armies typically had a third, or reserve, line ever farther back. German trenches, intended for a defensive role, often had as many as five trench lines to form a system known as an elastic defense. Communication trenches ran perpendicular to the main trench and connected the three lines, allowing supplies and reserves to come forward. Trench sections often adopted names of streets familiar to men from home. Directional street signs completed the feel of a world moved entirely underground. North of Loos, the British trench system included portions nicknamed Saville Row, Cromwell Road, and Essex Lane.[2] Aerial observation allowed each side to make reliable maps of the other side's trenches.

Some regions allowed for the digging of better trenches than others. The flooded Belgian plain that surrounded the strategic and symbolic town of Ypres was the most difficult area to entrench. Trenches there flooded with regularity, leading men to joke sardonically of having seen U-boats in the trenches. The defenses near Ypres therefore were based upon a system of small above-ground strongpoints to supplement the shallow trenches of the region. These defenses included concrete pillboxes and the reinforced remnants of farm buildings. The chalky region around the Somme River, by contrast, proved to be ideal for digging trenches that went as far as thirty feet underground. In general the Germans dug the most sophisticated and strongest trenches because they knew that the Allies had to attack in order to win the war. The Allies, by contrast, could convince themselves that the trenches were merely a temporary expedient. The next great offensive, they were sure, would move the lines in their favor and open warfare would render elaborate trenches unnecessary.

Life in the Trenches

The German reputation for having relatively comfortable and durable trenches spread to the Allied lines. One British commander enjoyed enticing his men into complaining about the discomfort of their trenches. When they did he would tell them, "The Germans over there have got very good dugouts. You can go and take them as soon as you like."[3] Indeed, when British or French soldiers did take German trenches they usually adapted them to face east instead of west and made them a part of their own defensive lines.

Even on the German side, daily life in a trench offered soldiers few amenities. Paul Fussell described the trenches as a "troglodyte world" that robbed many men of their sense of humanity by reducing them to a bestial existence.[4] Trenches, with their primitive sanitary arrangements and the constant presence of corpses, underscored the animalistic nature of soldiers' daily lives by attracting all kinds of creatures. The most feared were the enormous rats that feasted on exposed rations and the unburied bodies in No Man's Land. The rats quickly found their way into trenches by the thousands; some commanders offered bounties to men who killed them. Many soldiers' memoirs also recall the ubiquitous lice that lived in uniforms and on soldiers' bodies. Lice were such a constant concern that the word "lousy" became a synonym for unpleasant. Lice were also called "chats," bequeathing the English language with another new term, this one to denote the gossiping men did as they sat around picking lice out of their clothes and hair.[5]

In most sectors, men stayed in the trenches for days at a time before being relieved. During that period a man never dared to expose even a portion of himself above the parapet of the trench for fear of being killed by vigilant enemy snipers. Soldiers quickly learned to use trench periscopes to see what the enemy might be doing and to look for any changes in the enemy's front line. Any repairs or improvements to one's own line usually had to be made at night and even then only under ideal conditions. Few men wanted to work on the line during a full moon or when enemy airplanes were operating in the area.

Oddly enough, trench warfare could be a boring enterprise. The near-constant presence of death might suggest otherwise, but for much of a soldier's day, even sometimes on active fronts, there was little to do. During the daily morning "stand to" men checked their positions, loaded their rifles, and prepared to defend against an enemy attack but most days it did not materialize. By midday the risk of an enemy attack had virtually disappeared. In the evening men performed a "stand down" and tried as well as they could to get some rest while sharing the responsibilities for night patrols, sentry duty, wire repair, and other nighttime tasks.

An axiom of warfare states that 95 percent of military service is spent waiting for the other 5 percent to happen. To while away the time in the trenches men wrote voluminously to friends and loved ones, kept diaries (although diaries were technically forbidden for fear that they might get captured and reveal secrets to the enemy), read, played cards, and performed the numerous small jobs associated with trench life. Some sectors were famous for the satirical newspapers that soldiers published on makeshift machines. In the Ypres sector (pronounced Ee-pre, but known to the British as Wipers) soldiers produced the *Wipers Times* whose name hints at another of its many uses. Trench newspapers often derided official propaganda that suggested a much more positive war than the one the soldiers saw firsthand. They also provided a means for offering mild criticism of their officers. Although some commanders failed to appreciate the good humor of trench newspapers, they were so vital to trench morale that they were almost impossible to ban or even to censor.

Soldiers normally rotated in and out of the trenches on a regular pattern that gave them a brief respite from the rats, lice, and mud. When out of the trenches, men usually went to a Reserve area a few miles behind the lines. There they could find indoor sleeping arrangements, entertainment, a drink, and better food. If they were lucky they could also trade their old, lousy uniforms for a shower, a shave, and a new uniform. The quieter the sector, the longer a man's unit could stay out of the trenches. When in Reserve men might also train in a new weapons system or a new tactic.

Although it seems improbable, most men disliked the Reserve areas despite the relative comforts they could enjoy there. Once out of the trenches, many men soon wished to return. In the primitive conditions of the trenches, officers cared little about the condition of a man's uniform or if his kit was in proper order. Few men shaved in the trenches, giving French soldiers the common nickname *poilu* (hairy one). Officers also did not demand salutes from their men in the trenches lest a peering enemy sniper identify them as leaders and thus as inviting targets. Once in the Reserve area, however, soldiers often complained of staff officers upbraiding them for the poor condition of their uniforms or for having a beard. They also insisted upon sharp salutes and the letter, rather than the spirit, of official guidance. Many men therefore found it more pleasant to deal with the rats and lice than the petty harassments of hard-charging officers who had little conception of what the war at the front line was really like.

Leave

In times of relative calm, men might take leave and get away from the front altogether. French and Italian soldiers received relatively fewer leave days than did the men of most armies. French soldiers who lived far from the front often had too little time to get home and back within the allotted leave period. In 1917 the French changed this system by not counting time spent in transit as leave time. Soldiers serving in eastern Europe or distant theaters like the Middle East or Africa had no chance to come home. Ironically, German and British soldiers serving in France often had more opportunity to return home on leave than did the French. The proximity of the British positions to "Blighty" (as the British home front was called) provided chances for men to go home on leave. A British soldier could leave the trenches in Belgium and take a ship across the English Channel in time to have dinner in England served on a white tablecloth with real silverware.

All men looked forward to leave as a time away from the devastation of the war and the chance to see loved ones. But leave also left many men confused when they saw how poorly most civilians understood what the war was really like. Unable to find the words to describe the horrors of the war and their own disillusionment with the higher ideals of the war, men soon found themselves strangers in their own hometowns. They also reacted with unease at the sight of civilians going about their daily business as if there were no war at all. Many men felt that civilians neither understood nor appreciated the sacrifices that soldiers made on their behalf.

Leave thus often proved to be bittersweet and even disorienting. Robert Graves noted that:

> England looked strange to us returned soldiers. We could not understand the war madness that ran wild everywhere, looking for a pseudo-military outlet. The civilians talked a foreign language and it was newspaper language. I found serious conversation with my parents almost impossible.[6]

In the trenches, by contrast, men understood the language their comrades spoke and felt more at home than they might have liked to admit.

Soldiers Writing about War

Leave also gave men time to think and to process their experiences. Because the men who fought World War I were the best-educated cohort of men in European history, they passed much of their time putting those experiences down in writing.

Well-educated soldiers wrote memoirs or poetry, often filled with classical allusions, and elegantly describing the horrors of the war. Some of these works, like Frenchman Henri Barbusse's *Le Feu*, were published during the war, giving readers a sense that the war was not what the national media reported it to be.

Poetry has become intimately linked with the soldier's experience of World War I, especially in the British and French cases. Although the "antiwar" poetry of Wilfred Owen, Guillaume Apollinaire, and Siegfried Sassoon is best known today, not all poets wrote negatively about the war. Rupert Brooke, whose poetry remained popular well into the 1930s, represented a starkly different strand of poetry. Brooke's agonizing death from blood poisoning in 1915 created a sharp contrast to his romantic vision of war, but he remained for many years among the most read World War I poets:

> Now, God be thanked Who has matched us with His hour,
> And caught our youth, and wakened us from sleeping,
> With hand made sure, clear eye, and sharpened power,
> To turn, as swimmers into cleanness leaping,
> Glad from a world grown old and cold and weary,
> Leave the sick hearts that honour could not move,
> And half-men, and their dirty songs and dreary,
> And all the little emptiness of love![7]

As historian Brian Bond notes, "virtually everyone was 'anti-war' in not wishing to see another conflict like that of 1914–1918," but not all writers believed the war to have been a total waste.[8] Even some of the most antiwar writers, like Erich Maria Remarque and Frederic Manning, found in the war a test of character and a source of comradeship missing in peacetime. A rare few, like Ernst Jünger, even saw more good than bad in war. Jünger envisioned a series of total and civil wars as an inevitable part of human development. He even welcomed the prospect as a means of finally settling accounts between nations and creating a new world order. War, he hoped, would "overcome the human experience of impotence in a technological world" and find a nonmaterial mission for those adventurous men willing to embrace it.[9]

But few soldiers sat around writing or reading poetry, most of which was published in literary journals unlikely to find a large audience among soldiers in the trenches. Soldiers had their own kind of poetry in the songs that they sang to pass the time and remind them of better days. Musicians on the home front wrote tunes like "Hang the Kaiser from a Sour Apple Tree," but such songs rarely caught the soldiers' fancy. Instead, the men had their own favorites that expressed their feelings of melancholy and homesickness more directly. A trendy prewar music hall tune, "(It's a Long Way to) Tipperary," became one of the most popular British songs and, with the addition of new lyrics, even spread to the French and German armies despite the language barrier. The song mentioned several London landmarks and its subject matter of an Irishman leaving behind his sweetheart struck a chord with thousands of men. The war gave the lyrics new poignancy, especially for Londoners and Irishmen:

> It's a long way to Tipperary,
> It's a long way to go;
> It's a long way to Tipperary,
> To the sweetest girl I know!

> Good-bye, Piccadilly!
> Farewell Leicester Square!
> It's a long, long way to Tipperary,
> But my heart's right there!

Other songs, like the heartrending "Till We Meet Again," the lively "Over There," and the playful "How Ya Gonna Keep 'Em Down on the Farm After They've Seen Paree," captured the sentiments of many men far from home.

The most popular French song, "Quand Madelon," was about a girl working in an estaminet who empathized with the plight of the soldiers to whom she served wine and food. The song reminded men of the comforts of civilian life and the platonic company of women, who had become almost entirely absent from their daily lives. "Quand Madelon" also spoke of the loved ones that men left behind, including the women they hoped to marry when (or if) they survived the war:

> We all have a country girl at home;
> Who is waiting for us and whom we'll marry.
> But she is far away, much too far away to tell her so;
> That is what we'll do when we return.
> In counting the days we sigh;
> And when the time seems too long to us,
> And there is so much we cannot tell her,
> We'll tell it to Madelon.[10]

Soldiers sang patriotic songs like the German "Wacht Am Rhein," but the most popular piece of music of all was a ribald tune probably written by a British sergeant about a middle-aged French madam. "Mademoiselle from Armentières (Hinky-dinky Parley-Vous?)" had a catchy tune and a limerick-like lilt that made it a huge favorite among the men in the trenches. Over the course of the war it developed literally hundreds of improvised variations among soldiers in every army on the western front. One of the tamer versions ran:

> Oh Mademoiselle from Armentières, Parley-Vous?
> Oh Mademoiselle from Armentières, Parley-Vous?
> You didn't have to know her long,
> To know the reason men go wrong!
> Hinky-dinky Parley-Vous?

Although most versions of the song dealt with love, lust, and sex in one form or another, the tune was so easy to match to simple lyrics that it quickly became a way for men to express all kinds of frustrations:

> The Colonel got the Croix de Guerre, Parley-Vous
> The Colonel got the Croix de Guerre, Parley-Vous
> The Colonel got the Croix de Guerre
> But the son of a gun was never there!
> Hinky-dinky Parley-Vous?

Some men had more time to sing and write than others. The intensity of trench warfare varied tremendously from area to area. Hot or active sectors offered more constant danger and shorter rest times. Quiet sectors, however, were generally safe and, at times, even comfortable. In some sectors, opposing armies developed what Tony Ashworth called a "live and let live" system. In these areas, men worked out truces with their enemies across No Man's Land. Most of these truces "evolved spontaneously, not conspiratorially" and operated as long as neither side fired on the other.[11] In such sectors men could (although still with some risk) pop their heads above the trenches, cook a meal despite the telltale smoke released by the stove fire, grow flowers, and even hang laundry out to dry. Some trenches had paneling, furniture, and electricity. In at least five recorded cases, soldiers had dairy cows living in the trenches with them to provide fresh milk.[12]

Truces

Informal truces also existed during periods of extreme weather or to bury the dead from a recent engagement. The latter type of truce had the positive benefits of removing decaying corpses from the battlefield, allowing at least a few men to have a proper burial, and keeping the rat population down. Other truces involved what Ashworth called "perfunctory" use of weapons. The soldiers of one side, anxious to be able to write truthful reports to their commanders that confirmed that they were fighting the enemy, fired their weapons, but aimed intentionally high. The other side, understanding the meaning of the enemy's inaccuracy, replied in similar fashion.[13] Soldiers were thus complying with the intent of orders to attack the enemy, but the truce kept the sector safe for a while longer.

Officers in all armies officially discouraged the practice of truces, especially if negotiated directly with the enemy. Fraternization, displayed briefly during the Christmas truce of 1914, rarely emerged during the rest of the war. Men stuck together in No Man's Land might converse or trade cigarettes, but nothing on the scale of Christmas 1914 ever occurred again. Officers, of course, took official steps to prevent a recurrence of such large-scale fraternization, but the increasing hatreds of the war and its high stakes convinced most soldiers of the foolishness of any large-scale fraternization. Even when many French divisions refused to attack following the bloody Chemin des Dames fiasco of 1917, they took close care not to reveal the low state of their morale to the Germans serving nearby.

Unlike fraternization, most truces occurred without direct collusion between the two sides and implied no sympathy with the enemy or his cause. Rather, they were designed to keep a given sector as quiet as possible for as long as possible in order to increase soldiers' chances of surviving the war. Senior commanders worried that extended truces could sap the offensive spirit of the soldiers and issued standing orders against passive truces. Still, bans on truces were hard to enforce and, perhaps more importantly, quiet sectors served important roles for all armies. Tired units could be sent to so-called "cure" sectors to rest and refit in relative security. New units often entered the front in a quiet sector to learn about the war firsthand but without having to engage in active combat. The Vosges sector became a frequent starting place for new units precisely because it was normally quiet. Occasionally, commanders ordered attacks in quiet sectors to destroy truces already in place, but the system of truces remained a feature of at least some sectors throughout most of the war.

Raids

Not all sectors were so cushy. Even the absence of large battles was no guarantee of safety. Desultory gas, mortar, or artillery fire was always a possibility. Even in quiet sectors men engaged in periodic deadly nighttime trench raids. These operations involved groups as small as a four-man squad or as large as an entire battalion crossing No Man's Land to attack a dedicated portion of the enemy line. Trench raids served many purposes such as destroying snipers' nests, disrupting the enemy's routine, gathering intelligence about the enemy's defenses, and deceiving the enemy as to the location of a future attack. Men were less convinced by the arguments of many commanders that raids were necessary in order to sustain the offensive spirit of the attacking army.

Raiders often called themselves the "suicide squad," but their job was important. Even if no soldiers operated regularly in No Man's Land, units believed it was necessary to dominate No Man's Land in order to prevent the enemy from mining it or from using it to creep toward one's own lines. A successful raid might reveal the presence of a new type of gas mask in the enemy lines (an indicator of a possible enemy attack with a new form of gas) or even a copy of the enemy's plans. A German trench raid in 1917 brought back a complete set of orders for France's April Chemin des Dames offensive and helped the defenders to plan accordingly.

Raids usually began with men cutting their own wire to create alleys for the raiders to pass through. Artillery fire then tried to isolate a sector of the enemy line and destroy the wire in front of it. Specialized troops with wire cutters advanced through No Man's Land to open passages through wire left undamaged by artillery. Soldiers then attacked the enemy at close hand with grenades, rifles, and bayonets. Trench raids had to be quick and deadly, inflicting as much damage as possible before the enemy recovered and responded in force. At a predetermined signal, such as a whistle or a flare, raiders returned to their own lines with prisoners and whatever they may have found worth taking. Friendly machine gunners covered the return with their fire and ensured that the raiders were not pursued. Normally conducted in the dark, raiding was a complex and delicate operation that eventually became the preserve of dedicated specialists.

Trench life thus varied considerably from place to place and time to time. Few men looked back on the trenches with any nostalgia. Even the best trenches were dirty, lice-ridden, and within view of an enemy who, even on quiet sectors, could send any number of deadly projectiles across No Man's Land without notice. Still, soldiers who served a large portion of the war in a quiet sector like the Vosges were lucky. Those who fought in places like Ypres, the Somme, and Verdun experienced a hell unimaginable to the modern mind.

UNDER FIRE: THE EXPERIENCE OF BATTLE

Although participating in a large-scale battle was a rare event for most men, it was, of course, the most dangerous episode of a soldier's experience. Battles have always been horrific and deadly events, but in two ways the large battles of World War I were unlike any that had come before. First, the sheer scale and scope of battle dwarfed those of all previous military engagements. The main action at Waterloo in 1815 occurred over a space considerably less than four miles long. The Battle of Valmy, with which this book began, was fought over a battlefield small enough for the commanders to see both ends of it by simply turning their heads left and right. The 1916 Battle of Verdun, by contrast, began along an eight-mile span that soon spread to more than twenty miles along a curved front. The Battle of the Somme was fought over an even greater distance and required Allied coordination between the French south of the Somme River and the main British attack north of the river.

There were important consequences that derived from the size of these battles. Generals could not monitor these enormous battlefields in person as they had in previous wars. They therefore had to rely on telephonic reports and the advice of their staff officers. These systems did not always give commanders the accurate information that they needed to make critical decisions. Large battlefields also complicated logistics as widespread areas often had to be supplied via a relatively small number of roads and railways. The entire French garrison at Verdun had to be fed, rearmed, and replaced along one small forty-mile-long road so important that it took on the name "La Voie Sacrée" (the Sacred Way).

The second major difference of World War I battles involved their duration. Valmy ended in less than one day. The 1813 Battle of Leipzig, so large that it became known as the Battle of the Nations, took three days to fight. The titanic Battle of Mukden in the Russo-Japanese War in 1905, then the largest battle ever fought, lasted seventeen days. A three-day engagement in World War I, however, might be too small to merit even a passing mention in the extensive official histories published by the armies after the war. Large battles lasted so long that it is more appropriate to speak of them as campaigns in their own right: Verdun lasted from February 21 to December 18, 1916; the Somme lasted from June 24 to November 13, 1916; and the Third Battle of Ypres (known as Passchendaele) lasted from July 31 to November 10, 1917.

The length of these battles reflects the astonishing ability of modern nations to produce weapons in quantity and supply them over long distances to an army in the field. It also testifies, however, to the determination of men not to quit when they are fighting for a cause they believe in deeply. In his 1933 novel *Tender Is the Night*, the American writer F. Scott Fitzgerald called the Somme "the last love battle" and predicted that "This western-front business couldn't be done again. The young men think they could do it, but they couldn't."[14] Perhaps he was right. Many Frenchmen in 1940 concluded that surrender might actually be better for their nation than enduring another bloodletting like the one in 1916. "Better Vichy than Verdun," many reasoned.

But Vichy lay in the future. For the soldiers of World War I the enormity and length of large battles meant that they had little respite from the war. All of the British divisions on the western front except one fought on the Somme at one point during the mammoth battle that eventually cost 420,000 British casualties. The French rotated divisions through Verdun in order to provide men some time out of the battle, but the system ensured that the vast majority of *poilus* experienced the carnage at the "slaughter house" of Verdun. It was a rare and lucky German soldier indeed who managed to avoid the killing grounds of Verdun (434,000 German casualties), the Somme (650,000 German casualties), and Passchendaele (260,000 German casualties).[15]

In contrast to conventional images of repeated, simplistic, and suicidal charges, no two World War I battles were identical. The strategy of the opposing armies, the nature of the terrain, and the weather all contributed to giving each battle a unique tone. The soldiers of World War I fought in a wide variety of battlefields from the Alps and Vosges mountains to the deserts of the Middle East and Africa to the thick forests of the Ardennes to the swampy marshlands of the Somme. They fought in extreme heat and extreme cold, rain, snow, and sleet. Some unfortunate soldiers, like those who fought at Gallipoli in 1915, experienced all of these conditions in a single campaign. Veterans of Passchendaele forever remembered the mud that ran waist-deep or even higher.

It is therefore difficult to describe one general battlefield experience of World War I because each had its own peculiar character. But for the men who fought the war, all battles were alike in their terrifying killing power and their state of chaos. Soldiers, of course, rarely knew the larger strategic picture behind a battle and usually only saw the immediate portion of the battlefield on which they were engaged. Some men were not even aware of large battles taking place on other sectors of the same front. Robert Pellissier made no mention in his letters of the First Battle of the Marne, which was taking place less than 100 miles away from his position in Burgundy, nor did he mention France's largest battle of the war at Verdun. Possibly he omitted mention of the battles for fear of a censor stopping his letters, but it is more likely that he had too little information about the battles to comment intelligently about them. Many men remained relatively ignorant of the larger picture of battles in which they participated until well after the war.

On the Offensive

Signs of an impending attack were usually obvious to experienced soldiers. If one's own side was preparing to attack, soldiers would normally undergo refresher training in old methods or new training in the methods to be used in the forthcoming attack. Soldiers would see stockpiles of ammunition, notably heavy artillery shells, the accumulation of manpower reserves closer to the front line, and, most ominously, the construction of new field hospitals. The appearance of more senior officers on inspection tours in the trenches was another telltale sign. An increase in aviation in a given sector indicated either the gathering of aerial intelligence or an attempt to gain air supremacy before an action.

Divining the intentions of an enemy was harder, but not impossible. An increase in enemy artillery fire in quiet sectors was normally a dead giveaway. Enemy gunners usually tried to "register" their guns in the weeks and days before an offensive in order to calculate their ranges and improve their accuracy. Increased patrols in No Man's Land or even the mere sound of men working might also yield clues. In some cases, enemy soldiers deserted and surrendered to the enemy rather than fight in an upcoming battle. Interrogations of prisoners and deserters often gave critical information about the enemy's intentions. Sometimes this information produced gold, sometimes pyrite; after all, officers kept their men in the dark specifically to minimize the risks of a deserter or a prisoner giving away secrets.

Nevertheless, soldiers and their officers had to be careful with the information they collected because the clues did not always add up. Attacking armies, moreover, became adept at deception. Prior to the 1918 Battle of Amiens the British flew large numbers of airplanes over the designated attack area to cover the sounds of tanks assembling in the woods nearby. The armor surprised the Germans, who were accustomed to looking for a pre-battle artillery bombardment as an indicator of an upcoming enemy attack. The tanks made the artillery unnecessary and turned the battle into a watershed Allied victory. Shortly thereafter, the Americans concealed their upcoming offensive at St. Mihiel with the so-called Belfort ruse, a sophisticated plan complete with false radio traffic designed to confuse the Germans about the exact location and timing of the anticipated American offensive. Only four American officers knew about the deception plan, which kept the Germans guessing until the day of the attack.

Even when armies had all the information they needed to foresee an enemy attack, they did not always succeed in properly preparing for it. The French high command ignored the repeated pleas of battalion commanders in late 1915 that the Germans were assembling large forces in the woods near Verdun, which had been a quiet sector through much of the year. The devastating German assault therefore caught the French woefully flatfooted. Similarly, although everyone in all armies knew that the Germans would attack the Allies in the spring of 1918, the British Fifth Army had done so little to prepare for an attack that one lieutenant described the night before the main assault as "quiet as a nun's wedding night."[16] British soldiers had inexplicably been given leave and no reserves were ready to repulse an attack. This lack of preparation cost the British dearly in March and April when the Germans struck.

On active sectors of the front surprise was nearly impossible. Even during relative lulls fighting in the Ypres region raged intensely. In 1917, during the third major battle fought there a British officer remarked that "at night it was possible to mark out the Ypres salient by our gun flashes as they were practically continuous."[17] The difference between a battle and the daily carnage of such sectors was often a mere matter of degree.

Regardless of what higher command had decided at division, corps, or army headquarters, battle for most men was experienced at battalion level. Given the secrecy and sophistication of larger battle plans, few soldiers had any deep understanding of the overall goals of an operation. Instead, they fought for a narrow goal alongside men of their units. After being briefed by an officer or a sergeant about their objectives and methods the night before, men tried as well as they could either to rest or to write letters (often their last) to family members.

Soldiers often had an intuitive understanding of their own chances at success in a given mission. Despite the incredible risks of combat, many men nevertheless entered battle with high morale, especially if they believed that their mission might achieve meaningful goals. Even before tragedies like the Somme and the Chemin des Dames, men attacked with a high degree of élan and spirit. In other cases, men understood the foolhardiness of their attacks, believing either that they were to be needlessly sacrificed or that their operation stood no reasonable chance of success. One commander on the Somme tried in vain to convince higher headquarters that the artillery preparation had utterly failed to destroy the enemy barbed wire, meaning that "the sally ports [the precut exits in Britain's own wire] were effectively covered by machine gun fire and progress was impossible." Even after taking heavy losses, including almost all of its noncommissioned officers, his unit was ordered to attack again. "It proved next to impossible to persuade the Authorities that there was nothing left to attack with."[18]

Fighting on the defensive presented less of a dilemma as such battles invariably became matters of sheer survival. Because the weapons of World War I lent a tactical advantage to the defenders, fighting on the defensive normally required precise teamwork and careful use of individual and crew-served weapons. Each man needed to know how to perform his own task and the tasks of the men near him in the event that they fell. Men also had to rely on one another to ensure that no one broke and ran before the order to retire was received as panic had a way of spreading quickly through the ranks.

Whether soldiers were fighting on the offensive or the defensive, most battles began with an artillery barrage. The purposes of artillery were fourfold: first, and most obviously, to kill as many enemy soldiers as possible in order to reduce the enemy's ability to respond to an offensive in force; second, to cut the enemy's barbed wire in order to open passages for one's own soldiers; third, to keep the enemy soldiers who were not killed underground in their dugouts for as long as possible; and fourth, to prevent the enemy from bringing supplies and reinforcements from their reserve trenches to their main trenches. Depending upon the battle plan and the amount of artillery ammunition available, barrages could last just a few hours or as long as several days.

Surviving a barrage was a test of a man's courage and his ability to endure physical and psychological strain. As noted in the last chapter, artillery, "the greatest inducer of fear," blew apart human bodies in unnatural and terrifying ways.[19] The sounds, concussions, and sheer power of shelling drove many men insane. Living for a week under constant bombardment day and night from the enemy's heavy guns proved to be a trial of unimaginable terror. Men dug as deeply as they could, but found that no trench or dugout provided complete security. At the Somme, the intense British shelling kept German soldiers underground for as long as a week, often with no food or water. Many of these German soldiers were unknowingly lucky; lacking large numbers of heavy explosive shells, the British artillerists had relied on shrapnel, which lacked the penetrating power needed to kill men who were heavily entrenched.

At a predetermined time or on a given signal, the artillery barrage either ceased or "lifted" to a set of targets farther behind the enemy lines. A moment of eerie calm preceded the most dramatic moment of most battles, the instant when men climbed out of their trenches and went "over the top" and into No Man's Land. As soldiers advanced, field artillery and mortars normally began to fire at targets of opportunity such as undamaged wire, exposed enemy soldiers, or enemy strongpoints. Machine gunners opened fire on the enemy front line to discourage enemy gunners from setting up positions on their parapets.

Once in No Man's Land, the experience of battle usually began to vary considerably from the plans. No matter how intense the artillery barrage, soldiers had no way of knowing how much enemy resistance they would meet. Inevitably, the artillery barrage designed to protect them had left the ground severely damaged, slowing their advance through the dangerously exposed area between the lines. As officers and noncommissioned officers fell, men had to look for leaders to emerge or had to take charge themselves. Privates often found themselves in command of platoons or even companies.

As command structures broke down and plans fell apart, the "fog and friction" that is an inevitable part of military operations took over. Unable to know what was happening on the smoky, confused, and noisy battlefield, soldiers had to improvise. Instinct took over from training and many men became so focused on the jobs at hand that they were later unable to recall exactly what they had seen or done. The battlefield could thus become an intensely lonely and solitary place where each man had to fight on in relative isolation from his own comrades and the safety of the trenches.

Communicating information and receiving fresh orders presented incredible challenges. Field radios were still primitive and telephones relied on wires which rarely survived even a few minutes of battle intact. Runners might or might not make it to their destinations. Flares or flags might be spotted by the enemy and invite artillery fire. The confusion and incompetence of many brigade and divisional staff officers often revealed themselves fully in the height of battle. One officer recalled a runner entering his dugout during a fierce moment of the Passchendaele campaign. Hoping that he was about to receive guidance about what to do next, the officer "tore open the envelope in full expectation of relief orders. In fact it was a rebuke from the area sanitary officer to the effect that the grease traps in the horse lines some twelve miles back were not in perfect condition."[20]

Some attacks revealed their futility quickly. If the artillery had failed to damage the enemy's lines, then machine gun fire easily tore up an attack, as happened on the Somme, where the British suffered 60,000 casualties in one day. A well-prepared enemy normally had preregistered artillery ready to fire on advancing infantry and, in many cases, had prepared counterattacks with fresh troops in place as soon as the advancing infantry showed signs of fatigue. Such a system was characteristic of the German "elastic" defense.

Assuming that an attack had made its way through No Man's Land, soldiers still faced numerous obstacles. Uncut wire had to be destroyed and the defenders of an enemy trench had to be killed. Here light weapons with medium ranges such as hand grenades and flamethrowers played critical roles. If an enemy's front-line trench fell, soldiers still had either to prepare for the enemy counterattack, await fresh reserves, or advance onto the next set of trenches and resume fighting.

Success therefore depended on chance as much as it did on proper planning and execution. Once engaged in battle men became victims of their circumstances, not masters of it. The post-apocalyptic art of German painter and western-front veteran Otto Dix vividly depicted this loss of control over one's own fate. Machines and chance so dominated the battlefield that men stopped speaking of courage and pitied newly arrived troops who still believed in such antediluvian ideals.

If an attack had obviously failed, men could normally return to their trenches with their honor intact, although, as in the case cited in chapter six, commanders were the ultimate arbiters of whether an attack had failed or not. Unable to witness an attack firsthand, staff officers often looked to casualty reports to determine whether a battalion should have fought on or chose the correct response by retreating. Low casualties indicated to many officers a unit unwilling to advance, while high casualties indicated that the unit had done its best and should not be punished for its ultimate failure to take objectives.

Individuals could honorably get out of battle in several ways, although each one carried risks. Carrying a wounded comrade to safety offered a chance both to help save the life of a fellow soldier and to remove oneself from the heat of battle. Soldiers normally rescued men out of sheer altruism and humanitarian concern, not out of desire to save their own skin. One veteran recalled that altruism as one of the bright spots of his otherwise horrifying wartime experience. "An ordinary, self-centered creature performs acts of dazzling generosity toward fellows he does not even know. He will rescue a man under heavy shelling to whom an hour before he would have refused to lend sixpence."[21] Apparently not all men were motivated solely by humanistic concerns as headquarters usually set down limits on the number of men who could aid wounded comrades to reach safety. Carrying a heavy comrade through open ground, moreover, made a man a large, slow moving target.

Many men sought safety in a shell hole in the midst of a battle. There they hoped to wait out the worst of the fighting then return to their own lines and claim that they had become separated from their units. Officers often looked askance at such men, but unless they could prove that a soldier had intentionally absented himself from the battle, they could not press official charges. Such men might also have to face the wrath of comrades who had advanced while they had sought safety. Seeking shelter while the members of their battalion risked their lives clearly violated the soldiers' unwritten code. Soldiers could also try to obtain wounds serious enough to excuse them from battle but not serious enough to cause long-term damage. The risks of this type of behavior are self-evident.

Most soldiers understood that all men had a breaking point that they would eventually reach if exposed to combat for too long. Men in the trenches probably realized this truth before doctors did. Seeking safety, moreover, conferred no mark of cowardice. But soldiers were expected to suffer through the same miseries as their comrades and, in all circumstances, were to put the lives of their comrades before their own.

Soldiers also developed rituals about killing. Odd though it might seem, men in the trenches developed their own unwritten morality that guided their actions even in the midst of a war that killed millions. Many soldiers refused to shoot unarmed men who were trying to surrender, or men who were engaged in routine housekeeping activities like filling canteens or carrying food back to their mates in the trenches. Soldiers therefore differentiated the act of killing during active combat from what they perceived as cold-blooded murder. To be sure, not all units observed these distinctions, but a large number did.

The failure of so many infantry assaults on prepared positions, even if well designed and executed, led to numerous doctrinal and strategic innovations at higher levels that changed the experience of battle for most men. The German army developed the most highly specialized type of infantry warfare with the introduction of Special Assault Detachment soldiers, better known as storm troops. These men, all volunteers, undertook specialized training for dangerous assignments in exchange for extra rations and excusal from manual labor work details. They quickly became the elite of the German army.

Storm troops learned to fight under a new tactical system, developed in all armies, but made most famous by the Germans in 1918. Using light weapons like grenades and small mortars, storm troops learned to fight independently of high command in order to reduce the fog and friction that so often occurred in the middle of battle. They were therefore able to move quickly and achieve surprise by attacking without the aid of a long artillery bombardment. Storm troops normally attacked weak points in an enemy line, infiltrating through them and moving quickly to reserve and communication nodes in the hopes of denying the enemy's capability to resupply and reinforce. Once isolated, the enemy's front line became more vulnerable to an assault by standard infantry units which now stood a greater chance of success.

Storm troops performed so well in battles in Russia and Italy in 1917 that entire units were trained in the new methods and used to tear open holes in the Allied lines during the German spring offensives of 1918. Artillerists learned to support storm troop operations with gas rather than explosive shells in order to leave the ground intact. Storm troop tactics, however, relied on elite formations, which took severe casualties during their high-risk operations. Once lost, new storm troop units were difficult to raise and train. They therefore achieved spectacular early success, but only rarely sustained that success. By the summer of 1918 the German momentum had petered out and the cream of their infantry units was gone.

The Allies had experimented with similar tactics, but did not develop them to the same extent as the Germans did. Instead, the Allies relied increasingly on a combined arms approach that used armor, aviation, artillery, and infantry in tandem. The newly mechanized way of war returned mobility to the battlefield, but forced soldiers to adapt their training and fighting to the new methods. Soldiers learned to rely on tanks to flatten wire and provide close-range suppression of enemy fire. Generals like the Australian John Monash perfected techniques for air-to-ground communication and experimented with airplanes delivering supplies to men as they advanced. Trucks and armored cars allowed infantry to move faster and along routes that lacked rail lines. The Germans, in the summer of 1918, demoralized and exhausted from the Spring Offensive, had no answer to this type of warfare, forcing them to lose an initiative that they never recovered.

AFTEREFFECTS: CARING FOR PRISONERS AND THE WOUNDED

Expecting a short war, none of the great powers had made any sustained plans for detaining or feeding large numbers of prisoners of war. Nevertheless, the rapid mobility of the war's first six months yielded more than 1,500,000 prisoners. German operations in the east specifically aimed to create prisoners by using *Kesselschlacht* (killing cauldron) tactics wherein the smaller German army looked to surround its larger Russian enemies and cut off their avenues of retreat as well as their lines of communication. Once isolated, the Russians often had little choice but to surrender. In this way the Germans hoped to defeat the Russian army despite their numerical deficiency. The tactic worked beyond the wildest imaginations of German generals at the Battle of Tannenberg (August 26–31, 1914), where almost 100,000 Russians surrendered, and at the First Battle of the Masurian Lakes two weeks later, where 30,000 more Russians surrendered. The total of Russian prisoners of war exceeded the prewar estimates of the German General Staff more than fourfold.[22]

The stasis of trench warfare did not reduce the number of prisoners of war. Many men, dazed by artillery bombardments or terrified by the prospect of an enemy advance, laid down their arms. Prolonged artillery bombardments often forced soldiers to hide deep in subterranean dugouts. By the time they felt it was safe to emerge, the lines had changed sides and they soon found themselves in custody. Soldiers in armies like the

Austro-Hungarian, that had trouble feeding their soldiers, often surrendered out of sheer hunger. In other cases, ethnic minorities in the Russian and Austro-Hungarian armies lost faith in the army in which they served and were often glad to give themselves up. Once an army was beaten and routed in combat, its constituent elements often had little choice but to surrender. In one spectacular case, the Italian army, following its drubbing at Caporetto in October 1917, lost more than 250,000 men who gave up after being surrounded and cut off from any hope of rescue.

Wounded Spaniards during the war with the United States in 1898. For these men the war is over, although their suffering may not have been. Courtesy of the National Archives.

Prisoners of War

The armies of World War I not only lacked an overall infrastructure for handling prisoners of war, they also lacked a legal code for treating the men they had in captivity. The Hague Convention of 1907 had dealt with prisoners of war, but no one at that meeting could have possibly imagined the scenario that had developed by the end of the war's first year. The rules set down in 1907, for example, forbade using prisoners as manual laborers, but given the shortage of labor caused by so many men being under arms, few armies bothered to obey the proscription, even if they had signed the 1907 agreement. Armies used prisoner of war labor in all sorts of war-related work from home front industries to the construction and repair of front-line trenches. The Germans, for example, used Russian prisoners of war to construct an intricate line of defenses in France known as the Hindenburg Line in 1917.

In order to deal with such a rapidly developing problem, a system for the treatment of prisoners of war, like so many other facets of the war, had to be rapidly improvised. Placing prisoners of war in regions far from the front like Siberia or Scotland reduced the chances of escapes and therefore reduced the need to build airtight prisons. In the war's first months, governments often paid locals to care for prisoners detained in their communities. One German town welcomed its first contingent of French prisoners with chocolates and wine.[23] Over time, caring for prisoners of war became more bureaucratized and systematized, symbolized by the creation of offices like the British Directorate of Prisoners of War.

Few prisoners were greeted with wine and chocolates. Some armies took prisoners less willingly than others. The combatants on the eastern front often neither gave nor expected quarter. Unknown numbers of soldiers never made it to prison camps either because they were victims of either summary executions or neglect on their way to camps. The camps themselves were often makeshift, open-air facilities lacking protection from the elements, rudimentary sanitation, or proper medical care. The simplistic conditions of prison architecture allowed many men to escape by cutting wire or digging tunnels. Even the six-foot-five-inch-tall Lt. Charles de Gaulle managed to escape from a German camp and return to French lines to fight again during the Battle of Verdun.

The Vatican and the International Red Cross made attempts to monitor and visit the camps, but the efforts of international nongovernmental organizations to improve the daily lives of prisoners were inconsistent at best. The Red Cross did establish a database of millions of information cards on prisoners of war that tracked prisoners' health status and informed loved ones when a prisoner died. Prisoner exchanges, although encouraged by international humanitarian groups, were a rarity and were usually limited to invalids and men with serious medical conditions.

Most armies on the western front tried to care for prisoners of war as well as they could, if for no other reason than they hoped that the enemy would reciprocate. In 1917, working through diplomats in neutral Holland, both sides agreed that prisoners could not be sentenced to death for trying to escape, but could be sentenced to solitary confinement or given hard labor. All sides allowed prisoners not under special punishment to write (heavily censored) letters that were delivered through Holland, Sweden, or Switzerland to loved ones. Church services, the performance of plays, and study groups also served as means to pass the time.

Despite their best intentions, governments had few resources to spare for the purpose of caring for enemy soldiers. Those same governments were simultaneously struggling to feed, clothe, and care for their own soldiers and millions of suffering civilians. All governments except that of Russia developed voluntary aid societies that encouraged civilians to send food packages to their soldiers held in enemy prisoner of war camps. The British and French governments established a food distribution system in neutral Denmark that warehoused food and organized it for delivery into German camps.

Officially, the governments of Great Britain, France, Germany, and the United States worked as hard as they could within resource limitations to ameliorate the wretched condition of prisoners of war. Conditions in the camps, of course, varied considerably, and sadistic guards undoubtedly made life harder for prisoners than it need have been. By the same token, however, most prison guards behaved as properly as they could both to make their jobs easier and to retain their cushy positions far from the front lines.

At the end of the war more than 6,500,000 prisoners of war sat in camps. The release of Allied prisoners occurred most rapidly because the victors were able to impose their will on the conquered. The vast majority of German prisoners remained in custody until the signing of the Treaty of Versailles in June 1919, as a form of insurance against any German attempts to resume hostilities. Thousands of Russian prisoners literally walked home from Germany, many with great trepidation, unsure of their reception in the new Bolshevik Russia and unwilling to leave a prisoner of war camp only to be dragged into fighting in the Russian Civil War.

The Wounded and Sick

Wounded soldiers could often expect better treatment than that given to soldiers of previous eras. Nevertheless, as was the case with the prisoner of war influx, the nations of Europe had done little to anticipate or prepare for the 21,000,000 men who were wounded in the course of the war and the estimated 42,000,000 men who needed to see a medical specialist to deal with non-combat-related maladies. Doctors, moreover, were not at all trained for treating the hideous types of wounds caused by artillery and gas, nor had they been trained to handle the infections and gangrene that invariably accompanied wounds suffered in the filthy and pestilent atmosphere of the trenches.

Generally speaking, the British and German medical systems performed best during the war. The civilian medical communities in both nations had led the way before the war in the development and dissemination of the most modern medical techniques. Military medicine in both armies had also advanced, with the British incorporating the lessons they had learned in the Boer War. In 1903 the Royal Army Medical Corps opened its own school and three years later opened a second school to teach the principles of sanitation. France, whose civilian medical community generally resisted teaching and practicing antiseptic medicine, and the Russians, who paid little attention to military medicine at all, were among the least prepared.

All sides faced the enormous challenge of expanding their medical systems to meet the exigencies of the war. The British Empire, which had just 18,000 hospital beds in 1914, eventually added 619,000 more beds by 1919. Great Britain also added 16,000 nurses and trained Volunteer Aid Detachment (VAD) workers to perform hospital jobs from sweeping floors to assisting in surgery.[24] Mostly female, the VAD nurses came from all levels of British society and included many daughters of the nobility and the upper middle class. Many conscientious objectors served as nurses, field medics, and stretcher bearers. Foreign volunteers, most famously Ernest Hemingway, also volunteered to drive ambulances, undertake medical training, or serve as forward aid medics.

Retrieving wounded men from the battlefield presented tremendous challenges. Commanders normally gave strict orders that forbade anyone except stretcher bearers to remove wounded men during the height of a battle. With just four stretcher bearers per company (companies contained roughly 200 men each) and with soldiers naturally desirous of helping wounded comrades, these orders sometimes went unheeded. A stretcher, moreover, required at least four men to carry it; in muddy conditions it might require as many as ten men. Still, stretcher bearers performed noble, extremely dangerous work. One British general remarked that if he had 1,000 Victoria Crosses (the army's highest award), he would give them all to stretcher bearers.[25]

Their efforts notwithstanding, a wounded soldier could not expect to be removed quickly. Many sought out shell holes or other relatively safe areas, tried to remain conscious, and attempted to call or moan in order to alert comrades as to their presence. Most soldiers carried a field dressing that, if they had their wits about them, they could apply to stop the bleeding. Stuck in No Man's Land, many men died of recoverable wounds because no one could get to them in time. Soldiers often spent days waiting for an informal truce or brave comrades to rescue them. Some armies even trained dogs to find wounded men and then bark to indicate their location. John Ellis reports the case of one soldier who survived in No Man's Land for eleven days before he was found, treated, and, eventually, recovered from his wounds.[26]

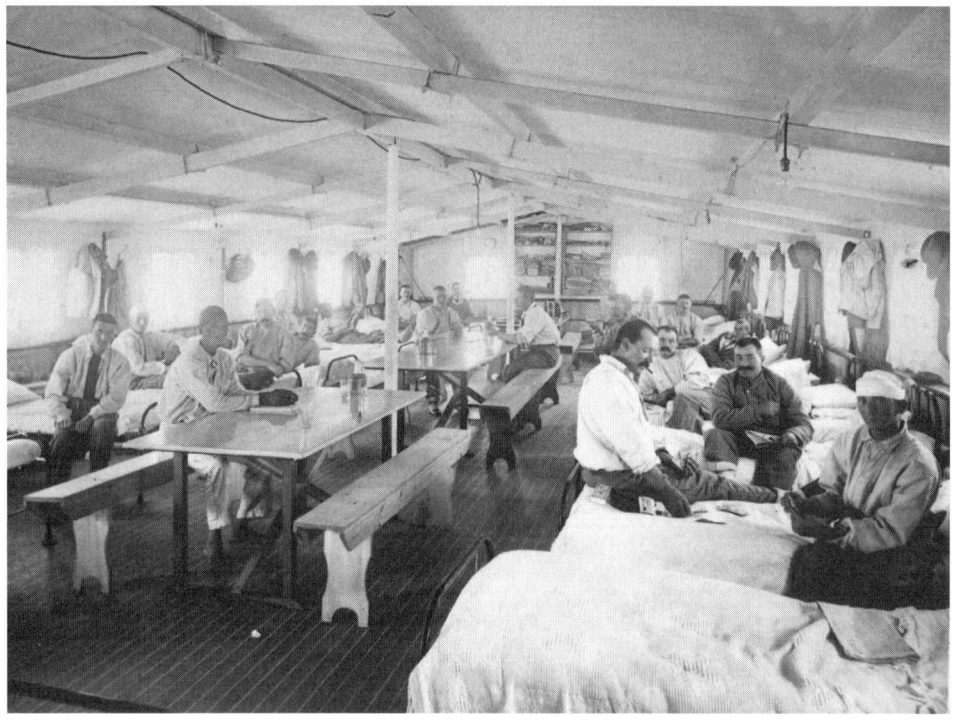

A primitive hospital at Kaalong during the Boer War. Medical care in the field was often rudimentary at best. In most nineteenth-century wars, many more men died from infections and diseases than from battle wounds. Australian War Memorial Negative Number P01855.003.

Soldiers lucky enough to crawl, limp, or be carried off the battlefield first went to a forward aid post in trench dugouts where their field dressings were removed, their wounds cleaned, and, perhaps, they were given a shot of morphia to dull the pain. Not surprisingly, men recalled these stations as places of unendurable agony where badly wounded men were often left to die and painful, though not serious wounds, were left untreated. Robert Graves also noted that to many British soldiers RAMC stood not for Royal Army Medical Corps, but Rob All My Comrades, as he awoke at an aid station to find that he was missing everything he owned except his personal papers and a "ring which was too tight on my finger to be pulled off." His experience contrasts with that of the British general cited above; it is reasonable to assume, however, that men gladly traded their watches and the money in their pockets for the transportation that the RAMC provided from No Man's Land to an aid post.[27]

From the aid station men went to larger, more sophisticated divisional field hospitals behind the lines. Here doctors performed surgeries and amputations on the most serious cases. In this more sterile and less chaotic environment men could get clean drinking water and, if their conditions permitted, a decent meal. Soldiers also had the opportunity to discuss their wounds with doctors and nurses. They thereby were able to learn learned if they had received "une bonne blessure" (a "good" wound) that would end their military service and send them home. Once the immediate crisis had ended, men had the time to write to loved ones and give them the news that they had been wounded, but were still alive.

Once stabilized, men often had the chance to return home or to a hospital near home to convalesce. Men with light wounds returned to their units as soon as a doctor cleared them for service, while men with moderate wounds and infections normally required close monitoring. Seriously wounded men looked forward to a discharge from the army, although they knew they would have to deal with the ramifications of their wounds for the rest of their lives. Blinded men held out little hope of ever regaining their sight (although many gas victims in fact did), and amputees had to learn to live without one or more limbs. A cottage industry soon developed to provide men with prosthetics and masks to cover parts of their face that had been shattered.

The intensity of the war produced new disorders that doctors struggled both to diagnose and to treat. Aviation presented its own special medical challenges as did extended tours of duty in the trenches. Doctors also began to observe soldiers who showed obvious signs of trauma but had not been physically wounded in any way. Doctors and officers argued over whether these men had psychological disorders, unmarked physical disorders (perhaps caused by gas or the concussions of artillery shells), or were cowards trying to shirk military duties. When large numbers of men with excellent military records began to show the signs of trauma, many doctors dismissed the third theory, although senior officers were often harder to convince.

The problem grew much more quickly than the understanding of it by medical professionals. In 1915, 9 percent of all battle casualties were victims of the puzzling malady and only a few showed physical symptoms. Eventually, doctors began to diagnose a syndrome they called "shell shock" caused by extended exposure to the noise, death, and stress of the battlefield. But identifying the problem did not lead to finding cures. Most men diagnosed with shell shock were treated with nothing more complicated than a period of rest in the hopes that they might then be able to return to duty. Britain alone had 30,000 men returned to the home islands for rest owing to shell shock.[28]

Soldiers also had to cope with the wide variety of diseases that occur when men live in proximity to one another without the benefit of modern sanitation. Dysentery, cholera, and a painful kidney disorder called nephritis were all recurring problems. The more primitive the theater of battle and the more questionable the quality of water, the greater the health problem. In warm climates like the Salonica front in Greece and in Africa, malaria was a major health problem. Any time soldiers came in contact with women, venereal diseases also put them out of action.

The most serious disease, in terms of the number of people it killed, developed late in the war. Known as the Spanish Flu (although it almost certainly did not originate in Spain), influenza took advantage of the relatively poor health conditions that the war directly and indirectly fostered. The illness killed as many as 20,000,000 people worldwide, making it one of the worst pandemics in human history. Tens of thousands of soldiers also died from the illness in 1918 and it continued to kill veterans and civilians alike until it disappeared in 1920 as quickly as it had appeared.

These horrors combined to produce a battlefield environment unlike anything that had been seen before. The inability of commanders and soldiers to envision how awful the conditions of war would become in World War I led to a manifest inability to deal with them. Haphazard solutions failed as often as they succeeded, increasing the misery of soldiers' daily lives.

NOTES

1. Histoire du 171ième Régiment d'Infanterie [n. d.], p. 9, Service Historique de l'Armée de Terre, Vincennes, France, 26N1736.

2. Martin Gilbert, *The Routledge Atlas of the First World War* (London: Routledge, 2003), 100.

3. Quoted in Tony Ashworth, *Trench Warfare, 1914–1918: The Live and Let Live System* (New York: Holmes and Meier, 1980), 93.

4. Paul Fussell, *The Great War and Modern Memory* (Oxford: Oxford University Press, 1975), chapter two.

5. Ashworth, *Trench Warfare*, 5. According to the *Oxford English Dictionary*, both terms had existed in the English language before the war, but the war seems to have reinvigorated their use and changed their meaning somewhat.

6. Quoted in Ashworth, *Trench Warfare*, 147.

7. J.M. Dent, ed, *Rupert Brooks and Wilfred Owen: Selected Poems* (New York: Sterling Pubushing, 2003), 47.

8. Brian Bond, *The Unquiet Western Front: Britain's Role in Literature and History* (Cambridge: Cambridge University Press, 2002), 30.

9. Thomas Rohkrämer, "Strangelove, or How Ernst Jünger Learned to Love Total War," in *The Shadows of Total War: Europe, East Asia, and the United States, 1919–1939* ed. Roger Chickering and Stig Förster (Cambridge: Cambridge University Press, 2003), 179–196, quotation at 195.

10. For more on the song and what it meant to French soldiers during the war, see Charles Rearick, "Madelon and the Men—In War and Memory," *French Historical Studies* 17, no. 4 (Autumn 1992), 1001–1034.

11. Ashworth, *Trench Warfare*, 99.

12. Ashworth, *Trench Warfare*, 131.

13. Ashworth, *Trench Warfare*, 102.

14. F. Scott Fitzgerald, *Tender Is the Night* (New York: Scribners, 1933; 1982), 56.

15. Estimates of losses, especially German losses, vary considerably. I have used figures from R. Ernest Dupuy and Trevor Dupuy, *The Encyclopedia of Military History* (2nd. rev. ed.) (New York: Harper and Row, 1986).

16. Lt. Pat Campbell, "Even in the Cannon's Mouth," vol. 25 "The Ebb and Flow of Battle" (privately published, n. d.), 10, located at the Imperial War Museum, London, P. 91.

17. Diary of Private Albert Victor Bullock, Imperial War Museum, London, 02/43/1, 28.

18. Memoir of Col. Sir Geoffrey Christie-Miller, volume two, 1920, Imperial War Museum, London, 8/4/03 185, 188.

19. Denis Winter, *Death's Men: Soldiers of the Great War* (London: Penguin, 1978), 117.

20. Quoted in Winter, *Death's Men*, 184.

21. Quoted in Winter, *Death's Men*, 180.

22. Norman Stone, *The Eastern Front, 1914–1917* (London: Penguin, 1975), 66.

23. Hew Strachan, *The First World War, To Arms!* (Oxford: Oxford University Press, 2001), 105.

24. Ian Beckett, "The Nation in Arms," in *A Nation in Arms*, ed. Ian Beckett and Keith Simpson (Manchester: Manchester University Press, 1985), 14–15.

25. Winter, *Death's Men*, 196.

26. John Ellis, *Eye Deep in Hell: Trench Warfare in World War I* (Baltimore, MD: Johns Hopkins University Press, 1976), 106–107.

27. Robert Graves, *Good-bye to All That: An Autobiography* (New York: Anchor Books, 1929; 1998), 224.

28. Winter, *Death's Men*, 129.

✯ ✯ ✯
CONCLUSION

None of the patterns from the period 1789–1918 made the Second World War inevitable. The history of soldiers' lives from this period did, however, assure that once the war began it was fought with the ferocity of a total war by mass armies tightly connected to the societies and states they served. Over the course of the time period under study here, the power of military forces increased dramatically. Typically, historians attribute this change to the increase in the power of weaponry and the ability of home fronts to mobilize economic and social resources that kept armies in the field for longer periods of time.

The conclusions of this book do not refute these conventional notions, but I hope they add to them. Alongside technological change and economic mobilization as explanations for changes in the nature of warfare in this period must come changes in the nature of soldiers and the daily lives they led. From the time of the Battle of Valmy (which began this book) forward, soldiers became much closer reflections of the societies that produced them. Because of their connections to social and political goals they stayed in the field longer, fought harder, and became more determined not to abandon the cause until all other options had seemingly disappeared.

The military is, of course, a direct extension of the state. Indeed, the military in European history during this time period was one of the most important institutions of governance. The financing of military appropriations often formed the single largest expense item in government budgets. Conscripting or otherwise coercing men into military service also represents the state at its most intrusive, taking men away from their civilian pursuits and placing them into an environment in which they may be asked to give their lives. At the very least, men who left military service entered a civilian economy that had little use for the skills they had learned as soldiers. Military service thus put such men at an economic disadvantage that often dogged them for the rest of their lives.

This study, then, ideally analyzes more than the mundane events of the daily lives of soldiers. Rather, it is an examination of the many ways that human beings interact with their societies and their governments. It addresses at least two long-standing issues in the historical subfield known as social history. First, it examines the ways that historians of society can "bring the state back in" to historical analysis. By examining how governments used the military to influence the daily lives of the young men in its armed service, historians can see better how governments arranged their systems for governance and their large-scale institutions and programs.

Second, looking at soldiers' daily lives allows us to focus on the many ways that men in turn influenced their government and society. In effect, by creating a large group of veterans, governments created a cohort (or several cohorts) of men who saw themselves as having a common experience. Perhaps more important, such men saw their service to the state as bestowing upon them special recognitions and special privileges. The widespread veterans' movements of the 1920s and 1930s influenced not only financial policy but activist politics as well. The Bonus Army in the United States in 1932 drew much sympathy from the American people (though significantly less sympathy from the Hoover administration) because of the especially troubling sight of men who served and fought for their nation being reduced to a state of extreme poverty. Veterans played key political roles as well and were a vital target constituency in the minds of fascists in Germany, France, and Italy.[1]

This book is also a not-too-subtle argument for seeing armies and units of armies as something more than anonymous collections of more or less replaceable men. The nomenclature of the military reinforces this view, as, indeed it intends to do. Thus, the names of armies either take the name of their commander, implying that they "belong" to a single man, or a number, implying that one is interchangeable with another. Thus to most people there is scant difference between, say, the British Third Army and the Fifth Army. The British tried to break this system with its New Armies of World War I such that infantry divisions took on place names in addition to their numbers; thus, for example, the 36th (Ulster) Division and the 47th (2nd London) Division.

This system has military utility but it complicates our understanding of the soldiers within these units. The presumption of anonymity, moreover, reinforces the view of soldiers not only as interchangeable but as essentially passive instruments in their own lives. Ordered and commanded by senior officers and administered by a large bureaucracy indifferent to their welfare, soldiers appear to be so little empowered that their views and mentalities do not need to be studied. But such an approach is a serious mistake. Tony Ashworth, Leonard Smith, and others have shown how soldiers can and do both influence their environments and set limits on what senior commanders can order their men to do.[2] A social history of the military, therefore, has important overlaps with labor history and the history of oppressed groups.

This book, then, is about much more than what soldiers wore, what they ate, and what weapons they fired. Ideally, it is about what their lives said about who they were, what kinds of societies produced them, and how they in turn shaped their societies.

These are, obviously, questions for military historians, but they are not exclusively military problems.

For too long, military history as a subfield has been disconnected from the larger study of history. As I hope this book demonstrates, however, militaries are critical institutions not just on the political and diplomatic levels, but on the social and cultural levels as well. Especially in a time period when military service among young men was such a common shared experience, it is critical to understand it and bring it back into our larger understanding of Western society in the long nineteenth century. The daily lives of soldiers serves as a lens through which to examine these larger patterns.

NOTES

1. See Jennifer Keene, *Doughboys, the Great War, and the Shaping of Modern America* (Baltimore: Johns Hopkins University Press, 2001) for the American case and my *Warfare and Society in Europe, 1898 to the Present* (London: Routledge, 2003) for the European case.

2. Tony Ashworth, *Trench Warfare: The Live and Let Live System* (New York: Holmes and Meier, 1980) and Leonard V. Smith, *Mutiny Amid Obedience: the Case of the French Fifth Infantry Division During World War I* (Princeton, NJ: Princeton University Press, 1994).

BIBLIOGRAPHY

GENERAL RESOURCES

Baker, Chris. *The Long, Long Trail.* www.1914–1918.net. Extensive site for research on the British experience in World War I, including history, discussion forums, personal accounts, book reviews, links to other reputable sites, and the like.

Bertaud, Jean-Paul. *The Army of the French Revolution: From Citizen-Soldier to Instrument of Power.* Princeton, NJ: Princeton University Press, 1988.

———. *Conscripts and Deserters: The Army and French Society During the Revolution and Empire.* Oxford: Oxford University Press, 1989.

Forrest, Alan. *Soldiers of the French Revolution.* Durham, NC: Duke University Press, 1990.

Imperial War Museum. http://www.iwm.org.uk/. Begun in 1920 to collect material related to the Great War (World War I), this museum in London contains a vast selection of posters, paintings, recordings, documents, tanks, aircraft, and other materials related to British involvement in campaigns since World War I. The Web site also provides access to many images and documents.

Strachan, Hew. *European Armies and the Conduct of War.* London: Routledge, 1983; 1993.

CRIME AND PUNISHMENT

Burroughs, Peter. "Crime and Punishment in the British Army, 1815–1870." *The English Historical Review* 100, no. 396 (July 1985): 545–571.

Duménil, Anne. "Soldiers' Suffering and Military Justice in the German Army of the Great War." In *Uncovered Fields: Perspective in First World War Studies* edited by Jenny Macleod and Pierre Purseigle. Amsterdam: Brill Academic Publishers, 2004.

Smith, Leonard V. *Mutiny Amid Obedience: The Case of the French Fifth Infantry Division During World War I*. Princeton, NJ: Princeton University Press, 1994.

Watt, Richard M. *Dare Call It Treason: The True Story of the French Army Mutinies of 1917*. New York: Dorsett, 1969.

MOTIVATIONS FOR SERVING, ENLISTING, AND FIGHTING

Gregory, Adrian. "British 'War Enthusiasm' in 1914: A Reassessment." In *Evidence, History and the Great War: Historians and the Impact of 1914–1918*, edited by Gail Braybon. Oxford: Berghahn Books, 2003, 67–85.

Karsten, Peter. "Irish Soldiers in the British Army, 1792–1922: Suborned or Subordinated?" *Journal of Social History* 17 (1983): 31–64.

Linderman, Gerald. *Embattled Courage: The Experience of Combat in the American Civil War*. New York: Free Press, 1987.

McPherson, James M. *For Cause and Comrades: Why Men Fought in the Civil War*. Oxford: Oxford University Press, 1997.

Verhey, Jeffrey. *The Spirit of 1914: Militarism, Myth, and Mobilization in Germany*. Cambridge: Cambridge University Press, 2000.

Weber, Eugen. *Peasants into Frenchmen: The Modernization of Rural France*. Stanford, CA: Stanford University Press, 1976.

MEMOIRS AND FIRST-PERSON ACCOUNTS

Brown, Joshua ed. *A Good Idea of Hell: Letters from a Chasseur à Pied*. College Station: Texas A & M University Press, 2003.

Graves, Robert. *Good-bye to All That: An Autobiography*. New York: Anchor Books, 1929; 1998.

Manning, Frederic. *Her Privates We*. London: Hogarth, 1986.

Walter, Jakob. *The Diary of a Napoleonic Foot Soldier*, edited by Marc Raeff. London: Penguin, 1991.

WEAPONS AND COMBAT

Ashworth, Tony. *Trench Warfare, 1914–1918: The Live and Let Live System*. New York: Holmes and Meier, 1980.

Ellis, John. *Eye Deep in Hell: Trench Warfare in World War I*. Baltimore, MD: Johns Hopkins University Press, 1976.

———. *The Social History of the Machine Gun*. Baltimore, MD: Johns Hopkins University Press, 1975.

Muir, Rory. *Tactics and the Experience of Battle in the Age of Napoleon*. New Haven, CT: Yale University Press, 1998.

Palazzo, Albert. *Seeking Victory on the Western Front: The British Army and Chemical Warfare in World War I.* Lincoln: University of Nebraska Press, 2000.

Showalter, Dennis. *Railroads and Rifles: Soldiers, Technology, and the Unification of Germany.* Hamden, CT: Archon Books, 1975.

Winter, Denis. *Death's Men: Soldiers of the Great War.* London: Penguin, 1978.

MUSIC, WRITING, AND RELIGION

Fussell, Paul. *The Great War and Modern Memory.* Oxford: Oxford University Press, 1975.

Grayzel, Susan. "Mothers, Marraines, and Prostitutes: Morale and Morality in First World War France." *International History Review* 19, no. 1 (February 1997): 66–82.

Rearick, Charles. "Madelon and the Men—In War and Memory." *French Historical Studies* 17, no. 4 (Autumn 1992): 1001–1034.

Schweitzer, Richard. *The Cross and the Trenches: Religious Faith and Doubt Among British and American Great War Soldiers.* Westport, CT: Praeger, 2003.

OTHER TOPICS

Blanco, Richard. "Reform and Wellington's Post Waterloo Army." *Military Affairs* 29, no. 3 (1965): 123–132.

de Pauw, Linda Grant. *Battle Cries and Lullabies: Women in War from Prehistory to the Present.* Norman: University of Oklahoma Press, 1998.

McNeill, William H. *Keeping Together in Time: Dance and Drill in Human History.* Cambridge, MA.: Harvard University Press, 1995.

Tucker, Albert. "Army and Society in England, 1870–1900: A Reassessment of the Cardwell Reforms." *The Journal of British Studies* 2, no. 2 (May 1963): 110–141.

INDEX

Absolutism, monarchical, 72
Act of Union (Great Britain, 1707), 17
Afghan War (Second), 105
Africa, deadliness of combat in, 79
Aircraft, 157–58
Alcohol: and soldiers, 64; and sutlers, 62
All Quiet on the Western Front (Remarque), 121
Allies, French defeat of, 4
Amiens, Battle of, 179
Amputations: commonness of, 86; Lister's influence on, 87
Anderson, Benedict, 30
Anti-draft protests, of New York City, 111
anti-Semitism, 127
ANZAC. *See* Australia and New Zealand Army Corps
Appert, Nicholas, 61
Aristocrats, political preferences of, 41
Armies: ethnic diversity problems within, 30; food/drink of, 164–67; growth explosion of, 53; need for reformation of, 97; peasant suppliers of food to, 59; reasons for development of, 71; threat of client, 102–3. *See also* New Armies
Army of the Potomac, 75
Artillery, 150–54; development of, 56–57, 150–51; impersonality of, 153–54; intellectual demands of, 152; nature's destruction by, 154; training for, 124; of World War I, 150
Asia, deadliness of combat in, 79
Auerstadt, Battle of, 19
Austerlitz, Battle of (1805), 35; Napoleon's inspiration of soldiers at, 81; size rarity of, 79
Australia, volunteerism of, 114–15
Australia and New Zealand Army Corps (ANZAC), 115, 122
Austro-Hungarian ultimatum, to Serbia, 112
Austro-Prussian War (1866), 55

Baden-Powell, Robert, 105–6
Baker, Newton, 117
Balkan Wars (1912–1913), 104
Baron de Montesquieu, 11
Barton, Clara, as "Angel of the Battlefield," 87
"Base Details" (Sassoon), 134
Battle of Austerlitz (1805), 35, 79, 81
Battle of Jena, 19
Battle of Quebec, 67
Battle of the Nations, 79, 178
Battlefield(s): fighting/death on, 82–83; leadership on, 81; music on, 38

Battle(s): of Amiens, 179; of Auerstadt, 19; of Austerlitz, 35, 79, 81; of Frontiers, 133, 148; of Gettysburg, 46, 76, 79; of Loos, 156; of Marne, 170; of Mukden, 178; of the Nations, 79, 178; of Somme, 116, 153, 157–58, 178; of Tannenberg, 184; of Valmy, 3–8, 12, 19; of Verdun, 77, 154; of Waterloo, 9, 79, 177; of Ypres, 155

Belgium: French victory in, 7; sympathizing with, 112

Bentham, Jeremy, 42

BFE. *See* British Expeditionary Force

Birdwood, William, 122

Bismarck, Otto von, 129

Blackadder Goes Forth (BBC miniseries), 133, 136

Blanco, Richard, 86

Boer War (1899–1902), 109, 110

Bomb(s): aircraft and, 158; British Mills, 150; hand grenades as, 149

Bonaparte, Napoleon. *See* Napoleon

Boulanger, Georges, 103

Bourbon monarchy (France), restoration of, 5, 21

British Expeditionary Force (BFE), 110, 116

British Field Punishment No, 1, 138

British Infantry Division, 116

British Mills bomb, 150

Bruchmüller, Georg, 152–53

Brusilov, Alexei, 131

Brusilov Offensive (1916), 130

Cadorna, Luigi, death sentences of, 137

Canada: and conscription, 110–11; internal security of, 110

Capital punishment, 138–39

Cardwell, Edward, 107–8, 109

Carmagnoles, as volunteers of Valmy, 7

Castelnau, Edouard Noël de ("the fighting friar"), 128

Catholic Church, Napoleon's concordat with, 15

Catholicism: of Europe, 128; of Germany, 129

Ceux de 14 (Genevoix), 121

Chance, as greatest role of soldier, 83

Charles X (King of France), 23

Chauchat machine gun, 148

Chemical warfare, 124

Christie-Miller, Geoffrey, 125

Citizen-soldiers: appeal of, 12; lengthy tenures of, 9; military entrance by, 8–11; revolutionary discipline of, 13; seasonal desertions by, 10

Civil War (U.S./1861–1865), 17; conscription attempts of, 111; death ratio of, 84; death statistics of, 84; European understanding of, 98; and hardtack biscuits, 62; Minié rifles of, 54, 55; nurses of, 87; and prisoner of war camps, 89; railroad's importance to, 74–75; Twenty Negro Law of, 111; Union victories of, 169; weapon inexperience during, 50

Civilians, transition to military life by, 27–32

Clausewitz, Carl von, 71

Clemenceau, Georges, 131

Client armies, threat of, 102–3

Coldstream Guards, of Great Britain, 37

Column formation: advantages of, 33; complexity problems of, 33; square patterns, 33

Combat, 77–80; aftereffects of, 83–91; many faces of, 80; training v. reality of, 122; veteran's silence about, 78

Comrades, soldier's questions regarding, 80

Congress of Vienna, 21

Conscription, 97–105; alternatives to, 105–11; conscription law (1889), 104; fairness of, 103; and France, 102; and French Revolution, 99; and Germany, 104; and Great Britain, 105–10; intrusiveness of, 103–4; Marxist opposition to, 101; and middle-class dominance, 101; nationalism component of, 99; nobility and, 99; objections to, 100–101; Prussia's model of, 100; and Russia, 100; Socialist's view of, 101; socialization aspect of, 99; threats associated with, 102; and Twenty Negro Law, 111; undesirables filtered by, 117; U.S./Canada and, 110–11

Crimean War (1854–1856), 23, 86; military system weakness exposed by, 97

Davout, Louis Nicolas, 19, 21

De Gaulle, Charles, 186

Death, surrendering v., 88

Desertion: hunger/thirst as reasons for, 58; by soldiers, 42, 80

Discipline: and punishment, 136–41; of soldiers, 40–43

Dix, Dorothea, 87

Doctors (military), lack of knowledge of, 84

Dreyfus Affair, 41

Dreyse, Johann Nicholas von, 55

Drilling (of soldiers): importance of, 32–36; moral/psychological justification for, 34; nonmilitary purpose of, 34; panic prevention through, 35; physical fitness component of, 36

Duke of Brunswick: and Battle of Valmy, 3; retreating army of, 4

Duke of Wellington. *See* Wellesley, Arthur

Dumouriez, Charles, 3, 40

Dunant, Jean Henri, 86–87

Durand, Peter, 62

Education, 37–43; music and training component, 38–40; political/discipline component, 40–43

Egalitarianism, of French Third Republic, 102

Enemies: tactics against, 35; winning cheap victory over, 34–35
Enlightenment thinkers, 12
Ethnic minorities, and uniforms, 66
Europe: Catholicism of, 128; Civil War (U.S.) as understood by, 98; conscription's importance in, 99, 101; deadliness of combat in, 79; primogeniture system of, 9; war's constancy in, 7
Expeditionary Forces (U.S.), 126

The Face of Battle (Keegan), 77
"False consciousness" of nations notion (Marx), 30
Fayolle, Marie Emile, 131
Ferdinand, Franz, 113
"Fighting friar." *See* Castelnau, Edouard Noël de
First Battle of Marne, 170
First Coalition of France, 16
First Punic War (265–241 B.C.E.), 57
Fitzgerald, F. Scott, 178
Flamethrowers, 149–50
Flanders, Hapsburg-held province of, 6
Food: containers for, 62; and desertion, 58; and drink, 164–67; hardtack biscuits as, 62; living off land for, 58–59; marching and need for, 57–64; preservation of, 61; Russian soldiers destruction of, 60–61; sutlers supplying of, 62; technological advances in providing, 61–64; War of 1812 authorized, 63
France: Allies defeated by, 4; anti-German ideology of, 103; anti-Semitism of, 127; call to arms by government of, 14; conscription and, 102; dismal border fortresses of, 6; First Coalition of, 16; *franc-tireurs* (free shooters) of, 79–80; Germany's occupation of, 127; guns of, 151; Hotchkiss machine guns of, 148; "La Marseillaise" (national anthem) of, 39–40; *Levée en Masse* of, 14–15, 102; National Guard of, 12–13, 45; professional v. volunteer army of, 12; Royal Roussillon Regiment of, 13, 67; social stratification of, 4–5
Franco-Prussian War, 57, 68; death's by infection of, 88; end of, 91
Franc-tireurs (free shooters), of France, 79–80
Frederick the Great (of Prussia), 11, 50
Frederick William (King of Prussia), 5, 19–20
French and Indian Wars (1756–1763), 53, 54
French Revolution (1789), 3, 4; Bastille (Paris) beginnings of, 4; conscription and, 99; nationalism and, 126; protection of, 5; soldier's belief in, 15; values represented by, 7
French Royal Army, 40
French Third Republic: conscription equitability of, 104; emerging egalitarianism of, 102
Frontiers, Battle of, 133, 148

Gatling Gun, 57
Generals, weapon concerns of, 51
Genevoix, Maurice, 121
George III (King of England), 3
German Empire (1871), creation of, 100
German Unification Wars, 31; and nationalization, 126–27; Prussian dynamism during, 97–98
Germany, 184–89; anti-Semitism of, 127; antipathy towards, 112; Catholicism of, 129; and conscription, 104; France occupied by, 127; guns of, 151; *Kesselschlacht* tactics of, 184; land mine use by, 158; *Landwehr* units of, 111; *Lusitania* sunk by, 125; machine gun use of, 147; poison gas used by, 155–56; Reichstag of, 138; *Schlachtstaffen* aircraft of, 158; spiked helmets of, 161; volunteerism of, 113
Gettysburg, Battle of, 46, 76; and Little Round Top, 79; soldier's information gap regarding, 79
Goethe, Johann Wolfgang, Battle of Valmy observed by, 3, 4
Grande Armée: of Napoleon, 60, 61, 63, 80; retreat of, 89
Grant, Ulysses S., 169
Great Britain: Act of Union (1707) of, 17; army advantages of, 108; Boers of, 109; Cardwell's military reforms of, 107–8, 109; Coldstream Guards of, 37; and conscription, 105–10; Hessian soldiers hired by, 10; Imperial Defense Committee of, 110; Irish recruitment by, 108; Kitchener armies of, 116; military recruitment difficulties of, 108; new armies of, 116; nonpartisan ethos of, 41; Officer's Training Corps of, 106; Pals Battalions of, 116; Pardons movement of, 136; poison gas manufactured by, 156; Prisoners of War Directorate of, 185; Reservists of, 109; Royal Field Artillery of, 114; Royal Flying Corps of, 158; Royal Horse Artillery of, 152; social/political indifference of, 107; soldier loyalty of, 31; Special Reserve of, 114; Victorian ideology of, 106; Volunteer Aid Department of, 187; volunteerism of, 113, 114; War Office of, 110
Great Terror (of France), 16
Gregory, Adrian, 113
Grognards (grumblers), soldiers of France as, 73
Guibert, Jacques Antoine, 11–12
Gunners, "hurricane" barrage techniques of, 153
Gun(s): of France, 151; Gatling Gun, 57, 146; of Germany, 151; machine, 147–49; Maxim gun, 146–47; needle, 55; siege, 153; Tommy gun, 149

Haig, Douglas, 134
Hand grenades, 149–50

Hangings, as punishment, 140
Hardtack biscuits, 62
Her Privates We (Manning), 121, 126
Heraty, A. J., 114
Herbert, Sidney, 86
Hessian soldiers, Britain's hiring of, 10
Hindenburg Line, 129
Homesickness, of soldiers, 42
Horne, Alistair, 77
Hospitals, military, 84, 86–88; horrors of, 86; Napoleon's network of, 85
Hotchkiss machine guns, 148
Hugo, Victor, 23

Imperial Defense Committee, of Great Britain, 110
Imperial Guard, of Napoleon, 36, 76
India: Sepoy Rebellion of, 105; volunteerism of, 114
Industrialization: and artillery innovation, 57; of warfare, 99; weapons cost reductions from, 54; and weapons technology, 49–56
Initiation/in-group rituals, of soldiers, 35–36
International Red Cross, 87; prisoner of war camp inspections by, 89
Ireland, Great Britain's recruitment from, 108

Jacobins: military medicine nationalized by, 85; propaganda of, 72; soldier's rewarded by, 91
Jäger battalions (of Germany), 54
Japrisot, Sébastien, 139–40
Jemappes (Belgium), French victory at, 7
Justice. *See* Military justice

Keegan, John, 77
Kesselschlacht tactics, of Germany, 184
Kitchener armies, 116
Knapsack kits, 67–68
Krupp, Frederich, 51
Krupp-manufactured rifle, 57
Kubrick, Stanley, 138
Kulturkampf anti-Catholic movement, 129

"La Marseillaise" (French national anthem), 39–40
Land mines, 158–59
Landwehr units, of Germany, 111
Leadership, 80–82; Lee's inspiring, 81; levels of, 132–36; Napoleon's inspiring, 81; officers and, 131–36; Sherman's inspiring, 81; soldier's questions regarding, 80; Wellington's inspiring, 81
Leave, of soldiers, 173
Lee, Robert E., 46
Leopold (Emperor of Austria), 5

Les Misérables (Hugo), 23
Levée en Masse (French call to arms), 14–15, 102
Line tactics: complexity problems of, 33; discipline required for, 32
Lister, Joseph, surgical advances of, 87–88
Little Round Top, 79
Livens, William H., 150, 155
Loos, Battle of, 156
Louis XIV (King of France), weapons used by, 50
Louis XVI (King of France), 5; execution of, 7; wars of, 8
Louis XVIII (King of France), 21
Lusitania, Germany's sinking of, 125

Machine guns, 147–49
Machines, of war, 145–59
Manning, Frederic, 121, 126, 135, 139
Marching: and equipment's weight, 68; and feeding of armies, 57–64; and knapsack kits, 67–68; railroad's combined with, 76
Marie Antoinette (Queen of France), 5
Marne, First Battle of, 170
Marx, Karl, 30
Marxism, conscription and, 101
Maxim, Hiram, 146
Maxim gun, 146–47
McClellan, George, 75
McNeill, William (historian), 39
McPherson, James, 72
Medicine, military: Jacobin's nationalization of, 85; 19th century limitations, 84; Prussia's advances in, 87; and treatment of wounded, 84–88
Memory of Solferino (Dunant), 86–87
The Men of 1914, See *Ceux de 14*
Mercenaries, 10
Metternich, Clemens von (Austrian Prince), 8
Mexican War, 63
MG machine gun, 149
Middle-class dominance, conscription and, 101
Military justice, 42, 136–38, 137
Military medicine: Jacobin's nationalization of, 85; 19th century limitations, 84; Prussia's advances in, 87; and treatment of wounded, 84–88
Military recruitment: after Napoleon, 20–24; during World War I, 111–18
Military training: complications of, 29–30; religion/morality changed by, 29; reshaping worldview of soldiers, 30
Miners Battalion (Great Britain), 116
Minié rifles, 54, 55
Missions, dangerous, as punishment, 139–41
Mitrailleuse rapid-fire weapon, 57

Mobilization: complexities of, 74; defined, 73; of soldiers, 73–77
Moltke, Helmut von, 75
Monarchical absolutism, 72
Moroccan crises (1905,1911), 104
Motivation: loss of, 130; nationalism as, 126–31; and religion, 128; of soldiers, 72–73
Mottos: "Every citizen a soldier, every soldier a citizen," 6–7; "Second to none," 37; "Wait until you see the whites of their eyes," 44
Mukden, Battle of, 178
Music: on battlefields, 38; as cohesive force, 39; education/politicization component of, 38; as soldier's entertainment, 38–39
Muskets: to rifles, 52–56; smoothbore, 43–44

Napoleon, 7, 13, 58; chicanery by, 15; expansionist ideas of, 18; *Grande Armée* of, 60; Imperial Guard of, 37, 76; inspiring leadership of, 81; military hospital network of, 85; military recruitment after, 20–24; Prussia's attempts at engaging, 19
Napoleonic Wars, 28, 31, 71
National Defense Act (U.S./1916), 126
National Guard, of France, 12–13, 45
Nationalism: and conscription, 99; and French Revolution, 126; and German Unification Wars, 126–27; as motivator, 127–28
Nationhood, definitions of, 31
Nations, Battle of, 79, 178
Nature, artillery's destruction of, 154
Needle guns, 55
New Armies, 116–18
New York City, anti-draft protests of, 111
New Zealand, volunteerism of, 115
Newfoundland, volunteerism of, 115
Nightingale, Florence, 86
No Man's Land, of trench zone, 170, 179, 181
Nobility: conscription's popularity among, 99; military service desired by, 8–9
Nursing, during Civil War, 87

Officers: care required by, 37; and leadership, 131–36; line, 133; punishment meted out by, 137–38; WW I expansion of, 135

Pals Battalions, 116, 125
Panic, preventing of, 35
Pardons movement, of Great Britain, 136
Pasteur, Louis, 87
Paths of Glory (Kubrick), 138
Patriotism: of soldiers, 11, 72; and volunteerism, 113
Paved roads, Roman Empire's creation of, 75

Peasants: assets hidden by, 60; as suppliers of food, 59
Pellissier, Robert, 130, 131
Peninsular Campaign (1809–1814), 79
Pershing, John J., 126, 128
Pétain, Henri Philippe, 131
Plumer, Herbert, 131
Poincaré, Raymond, 131
Poison gas, 154–57
Political preferences, of aristocrats, 41
Preparation, for war, 121–26
Primogeniture system, of Europe, 9
Prisoners of war, 88–91, 185–86; advantages of, 88; caring for, 184–89; interrogation of, 179; leniency shown to, 89; Russian, 184; wounding of, 83–91
Prisoners of War Directorate, 185
Productivity, conscription's influence on, 101, 106
Prussia: conscription model of, 100; dynamism of, 97–98; military medicine advances of, 87; and Napoleon, 19
Punishment: capital, 138–39; dangerous missions as, 139–41; and discipline, 136–41; hangings as, 140. *See also* British Field Punishment No, 1

Raids, of war, 177
Railroad(s): and Civil War (U.S.), 74–75; soldier's use of, 74–75
Rawlinson, Henry, 116
Red Cross. *See* International Red Cross
Regiments: as largest unit of soldier's identification, 27; noncommissioned officers as heart of, 27–28; personal freedom lost in, 41; subunits of, 28
Reichstag, of Germany, 138
Religion, as motivator/deterrent/guidance, 128–29
Remarque, Erich Maria, 121
Reserve soldiers, 115–16
Rifles, 146–47; flintlock, 52–53; *Jäger* battalions use of, 54; Kentucky Rifle, 53; Krupp-manufactured, 57; Minié rifles, 54, 55; to muskets, 52–56; smoothbore muskets, 43–44
Roberts, Frederick Sleigh ("Bobs"), 105
Robertson, William, 106, 108
Rochambeau, Jean Baptiste, 9
Roger de Lisle, Claude-Joseph, 39
Roman Empire, 102; paved roads created by, 75
Roosevelt, Theodore, 111, 117, 125
Rough Riders (of Theodore Roosevelt), 111
Rousseau, Jean-Jacques, 11
Royal Field Artillery (Great Britain), 114
Royal Flying Corps, 158
Royal Horse Artillery, 152

Royal Roussillon Regiment (54th Infantry Regiment), 13, 67
Royal Sussex Regiment (Great Britain), 66–67
Russell, William Howard, 86
Russia: anti-Semitism of, 127; and conscription, 100; Crimean War defeat of, 23; prisoners of war of, 184
Russian Revolution (1917), 130
Russo-Japanese War (1904–1905): and Maxim gun, 147; trench warfare of, 170

Sassoon, Siegfried, 134
Saturday Afternoon soldiers, of Great Britain, 114
SBR. *See* Small box respirator
Secondat, Charles-Louis de. *See* Baron de Montesquieu
Ségur Ordinance (1781), 4–5
Sepoy Rebellion (India), 105
Serbia: Austro-Hungarian ultimatum to, 112, 113; sympathizing with, 112
Seven Years' War (1756–1763), 3, 8, 75
Sherman, William Tecumsah, 81
Shrapnel, Henry, 56
Siege guns, 153
Small box respirator (SBR), 156
Socialists, conscription and, 101
Society, soldier's relationship to, 8
Soldiers: alcohol commonality of, 64; chance as greatest role of, 83; crimes committed by, 42; daily life/education of, 37–43; desertion by, 42, 80; discipline of, 40–43; drilling's dominance in lives of, 32–36; equipment of, 162–64; under fire, 177–84; "fire discipline" practice by, 5, 6; homesickness of, 42; initiation/in-group rituals of, 35–36; intuition of, 180; leave of, 173; licentiousness of, 29; living off land by, 58–59; loss of personal freedom of, 41; loyalty to home of, 29; mobilization of, 73–77; motivation of, 72–73; offensive of, 179–84; patriotic motivations of, 11, 72; as reformers, 11–20; replacability of, 28; reserve, 115–16; tactical training difficulties, 34; trench life of, 171–73; war writing of, 173–76; worldview reshaping of, 30
Soldiers, of Civil War (U.S.), 77
Soldiers, of France: amateurish tactics of, 5, 6; belief in French Revolution by, 15; as citizen soldiers, 6; Dumouriez's leadership of, 3; as *grognards* (grumblers), 73; illiteracy of, 78; indiscipline/crude tactics of, 7; Jemappes, Belgium, victory of, 7; knapsack kits of, 67–68; messianic idealism of, 72; nobility's dominance of, 8; professional status of, 13; uniforms of, 160; Voltaire's denigration of, 6; volunteer composition of, 6

Soldiers, of Prussia: needle guns used by, 55; uniform issues of, 67
Somme, Battle of, 116, 153, 157–58, 178
South Africa, and Boer War, 109
Spanish-American War (1899), 111
Spanish Flu, 189
Special Reserve (Great Britain), 114
Specialization: artillery, 45; bayonets, 44, 46; light infantry units, 44–45; small arms, 44; of soldiers, 43–46
Spiked helmets, 161
Square formations, complexity problems of, 33
Surrendering: death v., 88; voluntary, 89
Sutlers (camp followers): advance knowledge supplied by, 76; food/alcohol supplied by, 62; sanctioning of, 63

Tanks, 159
Tannenberg, Battle of, 184
Technology: advances in weapons, 49–57; Europe's advantage of, 79; food and, 61–64
Tender Is the Night (Fitzgerald), 178
10th Service Battalion of the Royal Fusiliers, 116
Thompson, J. T., 149
Tolstoy, Leo, 35
Tommy gun, 149
Training: amateurism in, 123; improvisations of, 124; limited people resources for, 122; for war, 121–26
Treaty of Tilsit, 19
Trench(es): life in, 171–73; warfare, 169–84
Truces, of war, 176
12th Kings Own Yorkshire Light Infantry. *See* Miners Battalion
Twenty Negro Law, 111

Ultimatum, of Austro-Hungary, 112
Uniforms, 159–61; and boots, 162; bright v. earth tone colors, 66; difficulties supplying, 65; and ethnic minorities, 66; of France, 160; and head gear, 161–62; lack of, 124; purpose of military, 65, 66
United States: and conscription, 110–11; internal security of, 110; military medical services of, 85; National Defense Act of, 126; National Guard of, 135; Reserve Officer Training Corps of, 126; veteran soldiers treatment in, 91; westward expansion by, 17

VAD. *See* Volunteer Aid Department
Valmy, Battle of: and Duke of Brunswick, 3, 19; Guibert's foreshadowing of, 12; as new era for soldiers, 4; and "new era" in world's history, 3–8
Verdun, Battle of, 77, 154

A Very Long Engagement (Japrisot), 139–40
Veteran soldiers: information sifting by, 76; pensions of, 90–91; readjustment difficulties of, 90; silence maintained by, 78; training conducted by, 122; of U.S., 91; war's aftereffects on, 83–91
Victor Emmanuel II (King of Italy), 131
Voltaire, French soldiers denigrated by, 6
Volunteer Aid Department (VAD), 187
Volunteers/volunteerism, 113–15; of Australia, 114–15; of France, 6; of Germany, 113; of India, 114; of New Zealand, 115; of Newfoundland, 115; and patriotism, 113; reserve soldiers v., 115; self-discipline of, 17; skills lacking in, 115; of World War I, 111–12

Walter, Jakob, 74, 76, 84
War: aftereffects of, 184–89; elemental appeal of, 80; machines of, 145–59; memoirs of, 121; raids of, 177; training/preparation for, 121–26; truces of, 176; underground, 169–84; writings about, 173–76
War for Independence (America), 54
War of 1812, 17, 63
War of the First Coalition, 4
Warfare: changes in, 98–99; industrialization of, 99; mobile, 159; trench, 169–84; types of, 124
Warfare of, 170
Washington, George, Hessians raided by, 10
Water, need for supplying, 64
Waterloo, Battle of, 9, 79, 177
Weapons: artillery development, 56–57; Civil War inexperience with, 50; Eli Whitney and, 50; funding for, 51–52; General's concerns regarding, 51; grenades/flamethrowers, 149–50; hand grenades, 149–50; land mines, 158–59; learning curve with, 50; machine guns, 147–49; mass production of, 50–51; 19th century designs of, 49; poison gas, 154–57; rifles/guns, 146–47; smoothbore muskets, 43–44; tanks, 159. *See also* Guns; *Mitrailleuse* rapid-fire weapon; Rifles
Weapons manufacturers: mass production by, 50–51; profits made by, 51
Weapons technology, change/industrialization of, 49–57
Weapons training: on bayonet, 44; on small arms, 44; of soldiers, 43–46
Weber, Eugene, 103
Wellesley, Arthur, 9, 18
Whitman, Walt, 84
Whitney, Eli, 50
William II (King of Prussia), 3
Wilson, Woodrow, 117, 125; hangings approved by, 140; World War I idealism of, 129
Wood, Leonard, 125
World War I: and aircraft, 157–58; artillery of, 150; military recruitment during, 111–18; outdated formations of, 123; oversized armies of, 134; rifles of, 146; as war of machines, 159
World War II, 127
Wounded soldiers: caring for, 184–89; medicine and treatment of, 84–88; transporting of, 85; treatment of, 186–89
Writings, about war, 173–76

About the Author

MICHAEL S. NEIBERG is Professor of History and Co-Chair of the Center for the Study of the War and Society at the University of Southern Mississippi and was formerly Professor of History at the U.S. Air Force Academy. He is the author of *Never Such Innocence Again: A History of the First World War* (2005), *Warfare and Society in Europe, 1898 to the Present* (2004), and many other titles.